THE
INVISIBLES

*A Tale
of the Eunuchs of India*

ZIA JAFFREY

VINTAGE DEPARTURES

Vintage Books

A Division of Random House, Inc.   New York

 FIRST VINTAGE DEPARTURES EDITION, FEBRUARY 1998

The Library of Congress has catalogued the Pantheon edition as follows:

Jaffrey, Zia.
The invisibles : a tale of the eunuchs of India /
Zia Jaffrey.
p. cm.
Includes bibliographical references.
ISBN 0-679-41577-7
1. Eunuchs—India. I. Title.
HQ449.J35   1996
305.9′066—dc20

Vintage ISBN: 0-679-74228-X

www.randomhouse.com

Printed in the United States of America
First Edition

2 4 6 8 9 7 5 3 1

ZIA JAFFREY

THE INVISIBLES

Zia Jaffrey writes fiction and nonfiction.
She spent part of her childhood in India
and lives in New York City.

For
Louis-Jean Broman,
in memory

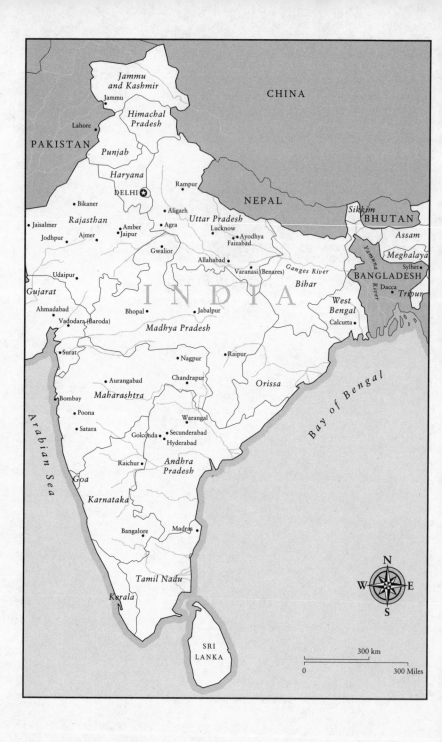

THE INVISIBLES

ONE

THERE WAS ONCE A GIRL, by the name of Angali,
born to the upper-upper-middle-class family of R. K.
Dayal, vice president and chief supervisor of I.C.P. Indus-
tries, Ltd. Mathurs of the Kayasth* clan, the Dayals had
served bravely under the Mughuls, rising through the ranks
as Persian-speaking clerks, and similarly, under the British,
acquiring a vast piece of land in what is now called Old
Delhi, when they hid a certain Englishman, pursued by the
rebels during the Mutiny of 1857, in the servants' quarters.

When the letter came, Mrs. Dayal was overjoyed and
just a bit relieved. She dialed Mr. Dayal at the office, and
arranged for the car. An extra place was set. They sat in the
air-conditioned dining-room as she told him the news,
wringing her plump hands in excitement, wiping the per-
spiration from the folds of her neck with her sari palla—
quite unable to eat. Was this not the match that they'd
hoped for? Millionaires, with one son a movie star, in all
the Bombay papers? And relatives in the same fair caste?
With green eyes like her own, or so she had heard, and ties
to the West, for the boy was studying to be a chartered accountant in London.

Mr. Dayal stroked his head where the hair was gone.

* scribes

3

His hands fell neatly into a ball when the plate was taken. Hadn't Mrs. Dayal prayed and prayed; and hadn't the image of Sai Baba, which hung above their bed, just a week ago dripped a strange honeyish liquid? Mr. Dayal himself had had to concede that he'd received a shock when he'd walked past the picture, and so had taken to avoiding the spot. O, there was so much to do, so many invitations to be sent, said Mrs. Dayal, her eyes fixed upon her husband, for Mr. Narayan had written that he was not a well man, and it was now his sincerest wish to see his youngest son married. They would have to act quickly; the young Ganesh from London was due in three weeks; and the marriage had to take place within the month, Mr. Narayan's doctors had advised. "Let's see," said Mr. Dayal, dipping his fingers into a bowl of lukewarm water. "Ravi," said Mrs. Dayal, "you must tell her." But in Mrs. Dayal's mind, the issue was settled. It was too good a family to pass up.

Quite deftly, Mrs. Dayal had shifted the burden onto her husband, assumed by all concerned to be so weak that he couldn't possibly protest the inevitable blood on his hands. The house therefore braced itself for a terrorist attack: Angali barricaded herself in her room, with her *Mills & Boons*, dressed as usual in white; refused to eat even the gravy and roti left draped over with a napkin outside her door, claiming a host of illnesses, which culminated in shrieks and sounds hitherto unheard of in the animal kingdom. Suffice it to say: the long form of her answer consisted of moaning, thudding, and weeping. The short form was "no."

Let me add that the raging beauty was ill disposed to say "yes" under any circumstances. Her very presence— the mute, tight smile, the frozen posture with hands held together at all public occasions, the private shredding of sketches done by her hand, the inability to commit to anything but a ferocious posture of will-lessness (which, by its very negation, did indeed suggest an extremely powerful will), the asthmatic rings below the eyes—all came in the form of a paradox: for the opposite of Angali's "no" was yet another "no," and any attempt to circumvent this paradox resulted in terrified withdrawal.

Now, one would think that any parent, when confronted with such a revolt, would soften. Certainly it seemed to leave the Dayals with only one option. But, reasoned Mrs. Dayal, such opportunities were few and far in a lifetime. And hadn't she already agreed to the meeting with the Narayans? The daughter had to be produced. Or, shall we say, a daughter had to be produced. It was in the course of such thinking that Mrs. Dayal stumbled into the arena of the last resort, by the name of Sita, calmly studying away beneath the palms of Bombay. The younger, the more practical, the more dark-skinned one: daughter number two.

It was a brilliant plan, conceived and executed by Mrs. Dayal herself, to summon Sita from her pre-exam status, allowing her to believe that she would be heading straight from the airport to meet her elder sister's future in-laws, and, well, omit the fact of Angali's resistance. Indeed, it was only Sita who wondered why her sister was "late" for the meeting, which concluded in the child's being anointed with ghee and garlanded by the frail hands of Mrs. Narayan, with the words, "She will do."

What really happened, we will never know, but this, at any rate, is the way stories are told in the lanes of Old Delhi, with a little bit here given from one house, and a little bit there, given from another, then add the information of one servant traveling from Number 16 to Number 17, and subtract the observations made by the cigarette walla, and filter it through the local gossip, who will take it to the garden party, and from there it may reach the ears of the businessman off to Hong Kong, and then go on to New York via the diplomat's wife, by now reaching mythic proportions; and perhaps, through the aforementioned's son, who has arrived in Delhi for his semester break, it now appears on the stage of life as a fact. Give it another week, and a fact becomes the fact, and from there it goes on to legend.

This, then, was the subject of the great debate of cousins, which I entered upon my arrival in Delhi, inadvertently on the occasion of Sita's wedding. Typically, the youngers of the clan had called several emergency meetings under the guise of listening to the latest "Amrikan" L.P.'s. They landed up in droves—on their scooters and in Fiats—armed with all kinds of ideologies. There were the memsa'ab feminists, who bulldozed their way through considered opinion with slogans against the institution of arranged marriage, flinging their newly waxed arms and gold bangles into the air. The moderates, for their part, fell into kurta-and-jhola-style factions from which ensued a long debate on predisposition—"Was it in the nature of the child to contradict the will of her elders?"—and those polyester-clad conservatives who argued, "What's done is done: best to prepare her for the future, to safeguard against the failure of women to pursue their educations after landing a man." And then there were those manly young men, swaggering under an imaginary strobe light and smelling of airport cologne, who purported to be personally insulted by the groom in question—"Londonite, yaar, must be having lots of girl friends," and those who objected purely on aesthetic grounds, because the groom, like his namesake, Ganesh, was rotund—and finally—the greatest insult—"nondescript." Here it seemed that on personality alone, the fellow was a poor loser to Sita, who at least had been "a passionate, tree-climbing girl" in her youth. Somehow, amid the clamor and the pakora eating, all agendas were left to be negotiated by me, the only "Yank" in the room—a status which bestowed on me both immediate, if undeserved, radicalism, as well as a form of contemptuous respect. As a *firangi*, or foreign-born, it was claimed, I could exert the influence of the world in my arguments. To Angali, then, I was dispatched with Rilke's *Letters to a Young Poet*, to encourage the budding artist within, to give the mute, hazel-eyed nay-sayer a voice. And as for Sita, all conceded that it was probably too late, but possibly I could encourage the eighteen-year-old to continue her studies, as "What was it all for, the coming first in her class each year?" Greater eligibility? Male, kshatriya caste, foreign educated, wheat-ish complexion, seeks homely female, caste no bar, educa-tion a plus?

Then came that final point of Hindu departure, that paradoxical twist of the hand, that gesture that embraces and releases all that has come to pass: it has many vari-eties—from the fingers-tightly-gripping-a-light-bulb style, to tips held open as if to allow an imaginary bird to land, to the chapati thrown up in the air—in short, it is that closure of discussion through the hand's motion that seems to signify the opening of even greater mysteries. "We neither accept, nor do we reject," the hand seems to say: rather than a solution, it is a riddle.

I was born with that gesture in my brain, that spiritual wishy-washiness, that "after you" to the next world. I was neither Indian, nor American, and upon all my other-ness was exerted the burden of a paradoxical truth; not knowing the Dayals, nor even their children, liberated me to convince them of another path; but it was one they were unlikely to choose because I did not belong to their land.

And how could I be prepared for the events that followed? For the words of Sita, whom I, with the gang, perchanced to see for an ice cream, later that week? She stood in a bright orange sari, licking a vanilla cone. It was the second time she and Ganesh had met. There was no eye contact between them. Last seen, he was fondling a Bon Bon, then retrieving the lost chocolate from the back seat of his scooter. Impressed on me was the urgent need to speak to Sita on the subject of her impending marriage, but she was happy and mild, at once herself, unlike many women I knew in New York, who changed themselves so completely in front of men as to become unrecognizable in their discomfort. I admired and pitied her, and could not bring myself to mention her forthcoming exams, only a month away, which she would be unable to attend, because she had to fly to London with the groom. "Sita," I said, when we were alone, "do you want to get married?" A look of terror, then a hesitant smile, as though she sensed my impotence as a firangi, my lack of consequence: it freed her to tell me the truth. "Eventually, I would have. . . . This is just sooner rather than later." "And . . . you like him?" "I don't know. . . . He's okay."

O Limca-land, with your posters for Lipton tea! For what was the education, the St. Xavier's, the Tiny Tots school of a thousand nations, the rewritten Marxist books? But now, I, too, was swept up in the rules of tradition, the hundred Mathur eyes that looked upon my jeans with disdain, the creeping, seeping looks as I walked the lanes, lost in the thought of what-to-do's in a situation like this. Suddenly I was summoned by the elders of the clan, rushed to waxers and haircutters, to the banks with their safe-deposit boxes of handed-down jewels, to the tailors with their lechy looks and the smell of sweat and cotton, to be fitted and pushed into brassieres and blouses, as the censorious tailors cut the necklines to suit not you but their definitions of propriety, always with the bosoms so pointy, yaar, that it defied all purpose. Push and prod as you may, it's not for no reason that the sari must be draped across the chest, hiding the obscene thoughts of the tailor.

But I'm an American, I kept proclaiming, I've come here to study the culture, not to become one of its victims. Few listened, as I was dipped in wax and plucked and bleached, fitted with bangles, bunned and all. It was pointed out, in my protest, that not to dress as such would call more attention to itself: to blend in, one had to dress to the utmost. A skirt and a blouse, say, would mean all eyes were upon me. And these silent, staring old women of the lanes never missed a thing: their glances began bizarrely with the forehead, dropped rapaciously to the feet, then rose slowly to assess every nook and cranny of the creature before them, seizing upon the lone hair of the brow not plucked, correcting the neckline, sniffing out the crude cut of amethyst in the ring—thus you were chopped into bits by the eyes, and each part graded; and if you were a "darkie," so much more compensation for an unfortunate birth was required. No matter what you did, the judgment, at its best, was "she was looking very good, in spite of herself."

And my own attempts at study had come to a halt, what with all the pandemonium. I had come to India to pursue ancient philosophy, I had come as an American; I wished to travel invisibly, to see the country, to come to know it, objectively, anonymously, without reliance on family, caste, or color; instead I, too, like Sita, found myself immersed in two thousand years of history, swept up in traditions that seemed to have no finite point of origin, could not be explained, and persisted without inquiry. Futilely I had tried, between the tailors and teatime, to enter St. Stephen's college, to be interviewed by the dean himself, who explained why it would be impossible to pursue a course at his college. Said the Oxford-educated bureaucrat, "In your country, it may be possible to 'sit in' on a class, but here, I am afraid it is not possible. At this 'estage,' I would have to ask, what have you done for me?"

And try as you might with the vice dean: "Vhy didn't you come to me in the fust place? Last veek, I could have assisted you. But, you know, this veek there is the Vorld Cup. So vhy don't you come back in two-three veeks' time?"

"But, sir, it's already ten days into the semester."

"Ha-aa, doesn't matter. I can fix it up . . . But are you sure you vant to study, er, Indian philosophy? Vhy not Bertrand Russell?"

"Beta, my feet are aching so, could you just press them?" said my aunt, Sarojini, with whom I was staying. "Oof fo, all day, walking, walking, wedding this, wedding that," she said, dislodging a foot from her chappal and placing it in my lap. "You know, beta, when I first saw that boy, I couldn't believe it. He was such a . . . such a nothing. No energy. And for Sita, who's so spirited? His eyes look, but they don't see. Who does he think he is, na? Some sort of maharaja, is it? Too young. Not on the outside. On the outside he looks like a middle-aged. But on the inside. He may have traveled abroad, but so? These Indians, they stick to themselves in every country, I know, I have seen it with my own two eyes. Then they come back with airs. What is she going to do all alone in London? I think it's a mistake, and hard for me to believe that R. K. would do this. Doesn't he remember his own marriage? He cried and cried. Nobody can forget it. She was such a runty thing when she got off the train. With two thin braids. And now look. Same thing all over again. And he's letting it happen. This tradition, tradition, it makes the women overbearing, and the men impotent. If you ask me, a son should go out into the world and make his own decisions. Not stay at home. The whole thing is wrong. In the West they say 'family, family' because they've lost it, those values, but there is such a thing as too much. I tell my son, go. Just go. Don't carry on with your grandfather's business. But they don't, they think of everybody else first, they never think of themselves. And the daughter is all the time trying to please in-laws."

Meanwhile, Rilke's *Letters* did little to alleviate Angali's suffering. She chose the back veranda for our interview—the light streamed in and gave her a ghostly look. She had to whisper, she said, for she'd recently lost her voice. Water came to her eyes as I stressed the importance of going forward, listening not to what people say; and then I asked her, what with all those Monets and Manets she had repainted, hadn't she thought of putting the talent to her own work? "For what?" she replied, with a crooked, pained look. "What use is it? I have nothing to say." When I pressed about a career, she said, "Sometimes I think I'd like to be an air hostess."

The servants had adjusted to Angali's moods as if to a kind of weather; ordered about loudly by Mrs. Dayal to boil and filter water, thrash out carpets and chop the heads of living chickens, in preparation for the wedding, they were nevertheless protective of Angali, stopped to ask if there was anything she wanted, shut the blinds if the sun seemed too direct, supplied the unasked-for lemonade; she, in turn, spoke to them softly, by instinct, as equals.

And I had noticed: Urdu has a pronoun, *aap*, like the French *vous*, for those one greets formally. Hindi uses *tu* both for those very intimate *and* for servants, for those one disrespects. Now, how a great memsa'ab of the house could entertain visitors with chaats and sweets, ladoos and tea, using the polite form, *aap*, and in the same breath, and in your very presence, reserve for the servant at hand a tone so rude, so sniping, so malicious, and still be thought of as a human being was beyond me. It was like witnessing a form of schizophrenia; the imperative, with the diminutive of the pronoun, issued from the lips reflexively: "Miss, you must be soo thirsty, do have another lemonade, no, no, it's no bother, please . . . You! Go and get it, and don't put too much salt! I'm always telling him not to put so much salt, but does he listen? No, sometimes I think he wants to poison us all with the amount of salt he puts." Remarkably, the abuser felt no shame doing it in public, as though it were a genetic right, the authority of higher caste, as though not to do it, that is, to allow for simple human decency, were itself indecent. This memsa'ab-speaking-to-servant-self did not exist in relation to propriety; it believed itself to be invisible, just as the servant was invisible; he and his class existed merely as shadows, were neither here nor not here; in him an error, or possibly theft, constituted the only validation of having ever been present.

Meanwhile, as guests appeared from around the world, minor crises threatened to undermine the chart of events; Kishan Singh, the gardener, picked up along Ring Road by political thugs, had hurled himself from the truck and arrived at the gate with a gash in his head; hours had to be spent convincing him to go to the hospital—O, such ignorant people, cried Mrs. Dayal; when they'd finally succeeded, and left him waiting for Dr. Bose, the chap had disappeared, and now the roses had an untamed look. And on the day of the dowry viewing, Ram Das, the cook, had wanted to return to the hills, as he had just learned that his eldest daughter, recently married off by arrangement, had run away from her husband's family. Said Ram Das, "Memsa'ab, I know her, she's a good child, if she had run away, the only place she would have run is home." Nobody wanted to say what everyone suspected. Mr. Dayal promised an investigation into the matter, but he himself privately conceded that there was probably no hope—the local police had most likely been paid off.

Such goings-on coexisted with the fact that Sita was herself immersed in a tradition which destroyed whole families, but that sense of self which in the West was naturally extended to others—grief, pain, loss—was somehow not extended to those of other classes in India. It was assumed that they had different goals and aspirations—and everyone remembered the absurdity of Western diplomats who had come to the country and tried to treat their servants as equals, even asking them to sit at the same dinner table. This was rationalized thus: Think how ludicrous, not only for the family, but mostly for the servants. They like to know their place, they are proud of their uniforms, these Americans, so naive, everything has an order, exists for a reason. Just try to get the cook and the sweeper to drink from the same cup!

Go on.

No, really, bapre, I'm telling you the truth.

And go on it did.

TWO

Outside the gate, the drivers lean on cars or gossip, crouching in small groups. Through the lanes of Old Delhi, the groom approaches on a white horse, clasped from behind by a small child. An endless wave follows, some on foot, others slowly driving their gray and white and black Ambassadors. Inside the gate, men in suits wait near where women huddle in silk saris, with gold borders.

Now the men dressed as women appear, past the drivers, through the "other" gate. They huddle in tattered saris, and belt out one dissonant note after another, one on tambourine, another on drum. They are old, as old as stones, and not pretty. They jeer at the men in suits, and flatter the floating women, screeching obscenities in husky voices, voices that have a cadence in them, an unmistakable rhythm through repetition. Their hands mirror their obscene words: the hand becomes a swollen belly, over and over the contour of the baby, the contour of lust and of labor. Some laugh, others ignore. The outsider turns to the elegant man, sipping a scotch on the green.

Who are they?

With a turn of the hand, he says, Oh, the eunuchs. They always come.

The eunuchs?

The hijras.

Who invited them?

Nobody invites them. They just come.

How do they know?

They just know—like that. The hand in the air.

Why do they come?

Like that. For good luck. I don't know why they're supposed to be good luck.

But they don't sing in tune.

Haa. They create a ruckus, you pay them, and they leave.

The turn of the hand. The archaic rhythm of it. The drum. The priest uttering vaguely Sanskrit words no one understands. The walk around the fire. Around and around the eighteen-year-old girl and her chartered accountant from London. The paradoxical hand that accepts and rejects.

THREE

FIRSTLY, I WISH TO EXPLAIN that it was only because I didn't belong to India proper that I could have entertained such an idea; nextly, let me say that I could not help but be fascinated. But there was also this: When you are like a blind man, and you wish to know the society around you, are you going to just go about relying on those with sight, waiting for something of import to happen? Especially when this society goes on very politely without ever noting that 85 percent of the population does not belong to it: the servants, the jewelers, the chappal sellers, the sweepers—ha-aa, one needs services, so one goes or has him come, but ultimately, these worlds do not meet, do not need to know anything about the other. Curiosity itself was foreign when it came to the lower classes.

Let me give you a for-example. In the above-mentioned case, the gentleman at the party, dressed as he was in a wery Vestern suit, said that the eunuchs "just come," na, "like that": he doesn't know how, some sort of perverse miracle, isn't it? But, after all, he is a logical sort of man, runs a very successful travel business, surely sensitive to such matters as how to get from point A to point B, done rather well for his community, one daughter married and living in the U.S. of A., and all college reminiscences consist of high praise for the fellow who was head of the debate team—and this same doesn't know? Doesn't know, doesn't really want to know, doesn't even think to know. So how does a fairly intelligent man manage it? It's what I call permanent affliction to that part of the brain responsible for curiosity, due to the effects of prolonged exposure to castism, or conversely, a sort of gentleness of the meninges—a spiritual wishy-washiness, as I have mentioned before—an "all things have a purpose, an origin, but it doesn't concern me—as long as it abides in peace." So you roll up the window when the lepered hand approaches, and for now, the driver feels like more of a driver, call it driverness, even—an immanence, a dharma—the memsa'ab, more memsa'ab—the sa'ab, most sa'ab—a true calling.

But the point is this: eunuchs in the twentieth century? Did the man really say eunuchs? No, he said "yunucks," a combination of "you" and "nakoo," the Hindi word signifying, of all things, mucus of the nose. That is, with an inherent sense of disdain—beneath us—jhuta, ghunda—unclean, untouchable, contaminant, snot.

"You know, beta," said Sarojini Mausi, "some things are better kept quiet, na. Why don't you study something useful, like our urban development planning—so many houses are just coming up. Or the gypsies, they're very interesting, very interesting, Lal Bhai can help, because he has some dealings with those people from way back. But this eunuch thing, it's a dirty business. Those people, they like to lift up their saris for no rhyme or reason, just like that, so everybody can see where it's cut off. To shock. You know, just last week they went to Tinku's house and kept badgering and badgering, to give money, and they reached in through her window and scratched her arm. Yah, really. They're horrible people. Filthy people. Can you imagine—all alone in the house with a newborn—so frightening. There's a reason nobody talks about them. If you're going to write about India, why don't you choose a subject that shows our good side? Not the eunuchs. Nobody wants to know. It's like all those snake charmers and yogis and whatnot the West is always making a big deal about. All the exotics—it's not the real India. We're a very advanced country now, and in only forty years. Think how long it took America? Our middle class is expanding every day. That's what you should write about."

But I was drawn to them as an outsider, looking in. With their whimsy and genderless faces, they reminded me of Shakespearean fools. They were like the shadows and the critics of society. Everything about them suggested paradox; they were not men, nor were they women; they were not invited to perform, but neither were they uninvited; they carried the instruments of song, but made no pretense of being able to sing; they blessed the bride and groom, but through a stream of insults; they were considered a nuisance, even extortionists, and yet they were deemed lucky; they were paid not to perform, but to leave everyone in peace; they partook of the rites of passage that they themselves were incapable of—marriage and birth. They were clearly outcasts, yet were able, through a comedy of manners, to transcend the barriers of rank, caste, and class, and reduce everyone to ridiculous equals—subject to the same desires of lust, greed, and envy. In their buffoonery, they could tell all, and lose nothing.

So: from what century did these fools come to play the chorus in a restoration play? Now, as far as I knew, that era was over, noted by scholars in books from Turkey, China, Egypt, and Persia.

I wanted to travel backwards in time to understand the strange confluence of law, "tradition," religion, and sociology which could accommodate this disturbing institution. Had Islam brought with it eunuchs, who continued to thrive today? Or did Hinduism have its own strain, predating Islam? Was this essentially a slave tradition that had become a voluntary one? Or did elements of slavery today coexist with choice? Was the word *eunuch* even vaguely appropriate for these cross-dressers? Who became a eunuch, and why? And how, finally, could this anachronism persist?

The answer to one question, at least—"How do the eunuchs know?"—came in the form of a little newspaper clipping. In said clipping, the writer, William Claiborne of the *Washington Post*, described the very thing that seemed to elude the great people of the subcontinent— namely, the so-called "miracle." Perhaps he actually talked to some of the other great people of the subcontinent, known as the "local inhabitants." And so he was able to establish that the eunuchs find out about weddings by—and by now you may have guessed it—word of mouth. Who, after all, does not know that there is going to be a wedding, what with all the pandemonium? He went on to say that the eunuchs mark the sites where the weddings will occur with a date and sign peculiar to each "house" of eunuchs—invisible to the untrained eye, but discernible to other eunuchs. Each group had its own sign and assignation of "territory"—land boundaries registered with the local police. And they also frequented maternity wards. Has a child been born? When? Of which house? And lo and behold, they "miraculously" appeared to bless the child shortly after it was born.

The end of the article went on to describe some trouble, and this bit eluded me too. The unionizer of eunuchs of Delhi, a Mr. Bhola, a mechanic, had recently claimed that there were eunuch "impostors" in India, men dress-

ing as women to make a living—known as "zenanas"—
and that they had transgressed into the eunuchs' territory.
The article concluded with one so-called fact—and we
shall probe its veracity later—that there were 50,000 eunuchs in India today.

Another foreigner, Jonathan Broder, of the *Chicago
Tribune*, put that number between 50,000 and 1.25 million. "The wide discrepancy," he wrote, "underscores the
mystery that surrounds the eunuchs and their shadowy
half-world of superstition and crime." Broder cited an Indian ministry report, and one by a U.N. commission,
which alleged that "up to half a million children" in India
and Pakistan had been abducted and castrated against
their wills. A well-documented case had appeared in *India
Today* in 1982. Broder had interviewed a eunuch named
Gita in Old Delhi, who had "dismissed the case as rumor."

"No way, yaar," said Sanjay. "It's not safe to go. They
live in the old quarter, where there are goats' heads and
Muslim riots."

"Hijra means 'neither male nor female,' " said Ravi.
"Sometimes used in colloquial speech to connote an ambiguous position in an argument."

"Just what that little speech makes you, hiji," laughed
Seena.

"You know," said Mira, "I was reading in *Illustrated
Weekly* that, in Gujarat, they kidnap boys and make
them into eunuchs. Small boys, only six or seven."

"Because, otherwise," said Sanjay, "who would join?"

"They've taken to parading on Curzon Road," said
Mira.

"Haa, prostitutes," said Ravi.

"But, you know," said Mira, "if they kidnap boys and
cut it off when they're so young, they should be able to
sing. But their voices are painful, yaar."

I had been able to glean only a few bits, but in this taboo subject resided every manner of contradiction; no, no, we don't want to hear about it, but can't you just hear the chairs scraping to come closer to the teller? Indeed, I often had to cut the evening short because my voice tired before their ears gave way: not one caste or class was exonerated from this most uncomfortable, and indeed, grotesque, fascination with the subject; oh, and the abuse that leapt from the lips of the gentle old ladies of the lanes, without whom there would be no tea, no petite bourgeoisie, no sense of the clan, no green eyes to marry off to green eyes. And then there were the friendly-advice types; and the uncle who said, "Why not study tribals?"; and the aunt who refused tea. What with such a disagreeable subject, almost everyone had a word or two; and sometimes the listener's enchantment betrayed, well, a thing or two.

And now, everybody was laughing and clapping around the dinner table—that motion in one's face being the known gesture of the eunuchs, a sort of wide-handed upward clap, compounded by the exaggerated nasal voice the hijras used in speech. Remember the one about Nehru? When India was gaining independence? Everyone wanted to do their part for the new nation, and so did the hijras. So they went to Parliament House and asked Nehru what they could do; so he thought a bit, and appointed them all traffic directors—you know, with all the ambassadors coming through Delhi then, to see them standing on those podiums, directing traffic! Swaggering men in the most macho of uniforms, guiding traffic with their effeminate gestures—"My Lord, take a left at the next corner"—"Oh my Life, take a right when you reach the main road . . ."

"They can be very polite," said my uncle. "Their Urdu is *just so.*"

"In my father's day," said Yogesh mama, "they used to call them 'bhands.' They wore trousers, so you couldn't tell . . ."

"They were such gentle people," said Ishrat Khan of Pakistan. "One called them, you know, a whole army would come, to peel garlic—or to crush red pepper—and they would sit there for hours, tears streaming down their faces. They were so trusted, they were even midwives."

So there we were on Curzon Road, too many people to be invisible in the car, with Sanjay at the wheel, around and around in wide circles, and the smell of night lilies—I don't know how she talked me into this, I never thought I'd be looking for eunuchs. Yank comes, causes chaos, dangerous to be out, yaar, until Mira shouted, "There's one!" "My God, I never thought I'd be happy to see one," said Sanjay, after we'd been driving around for half an hour. Desperately we tried to make the sound of the motor disappear, which amounted to a *putt putt putt*—to be able to slink up upon the tall hijra, who, sensing us, disappeared, shawl and all, behind a hedge. "Mar gaya"—"we're dead"—exclaimed Sanjay, as we lost the fellow to the shadows; and so we drove around and around, hoping to catch the eunuch as he reappeared, until we stumbled upon not one, but six silk sari–clad eunuchs, buns and all, who appeared like stallions in the dark of night, and piled into a waiting taxi. Upon spotting us, the driver sped off madly; we followed it madly, and watched the car turn up a hill, and into the driveway of the Oberoi Hotel, no less.

Let us now pass on to talk of another province, whose name is Bengal. This also lies towards the south on the confines of India. In the year 1290, when I, Marco Polo, was at the court of the Great Khan, it had not yet been conquered; but the Khan's armies were already there and engaged in the conquest. This province has a king and language of its own. The people are grossly idolatrous. The province contains many eunuchs and supplies them to the nobles and lords of the surrounding territories. . . . The Indians come here and buy the eunuchs . . . who are very plentiful here because any prisoners that are taken are immediately castrated and afterwards sold as slaves. So merchants buy many eunuchs in this province and also many slave girls and then export them for sale in many other countries.

Marco Polo
The Travels of Marco Polo
1271–91

FOUR

To get to lal bhola's shop, Ravi and I drove deep into the hectic, dust-blown suburb of Trilokpur. The air smelled of crude petroleum, and the broad street looked like a gigantic auto-parts shop, with an engine here, a hub-cap there, scattered for miles along the oil-wet earth. With a few sharp turns, we located the narrow open cubicle called a "shop."

Bhola was not in view, but soon a boy emerged and pointed to the half-eclipsed figure who lay under a car: There, tending to various auto parts, amid a zoo of engine sounds, was the unionizer of eunuchs. Bhola gestured, with a black oil-covered hand, that we should take a seat inside the shop.

Eventually, Bhola came in, a small man in a dhoti, with a round, bald head. He namaskared us, in a slightly obse-quious way, and pulled up a stool. The small boy was dis-patched to get us tea. As Ravi explained the hope that Bhola might lead us to the eunuchs of Delhi, Bhola ap-peared to be on intimate terms with him. Not once did he meet my eyes. He spoke in Hindi, but soon resorted to Pun-jabi, in an effort to convince Ravi, who knew the language, of his true and egoless interest in the plight of the eu-nuchs—"You understand, Ravi"—all the while dictating to another fellow, who lay beneath the car outside the shop, as to how to fix the bottom of the vehicle. So every now and then, our conversation was punctuated with a *putt putt putt*, as Bhola yelled out, "I said the *large* wrench over there, you idiot, not the small one!" then returned with a softer voice, "Forgive me, what was I saying . . ."

The hijras, said Bhola, rhapsodizing, were like his own children. He was doing God's work by helping them. Recently they'd been maligned by the Indian press and accused of kidnapping. He felt that he had to get involved when they asked him. It was a calling. He was like their lawyer, he said, and they did nothing without his say-so. Nothing. He had gained their trust. When he died, who would scatter his ashes in the Yamuna river? He had nine children of his own, but it would be the eunuchs who would send his soul to the next world. He was doing Gandhiji's work, he said, he had been a Congresswalla all his life—and these were *harijans*—untouchables; they thought of him as their father, their Bapuji.

"How did you first get involved?" Ravi asked.

"You see," said Bhola, "there was a dispute among the shopkeepers, and they came to me to resolve it, because I am a big man here, I am head of the mechanics' guild. Afterward, the hijras asked me to represent them, and I sent letters to Congress demanding respect for these people. I got them ration cards too."

"What dispute?" I asked.

"They were coming here to beg," said Bhola. "And the shopkeepers said it was taking away from their business. But I said, 'Why don't you let them beg? They have nobody, nothing.' They are God's children, madam. They are harijans. Gandhiji was on their side. That's what he would have wanted me to do."

"So you argued in favor of the hijras?"

"Yes," said Bhola. "So gradually I got to know them—their ways—and they began to trust me. And I suggested that they unionize."

But now Bhola swerved into Punjabi again, and got into a long struggle with Ravi.

"Just between you and me," said Bhola, "this is an American lady and she must be having money. So the way I see it, she can afford to pay for the information. You understand, it goes right to the fund for hijras, with a small cut to me, very small, because I can tell her all about their mythology, their ways. I can also set up a meeting with the eunuch elders. One full hour with the bigwigs of Delhi."

"She doesn't have that kind of money, bhai," said Ravi.

"Look, she's from America, brother, she has it."

"She's just doing research," said Ravi. "Besides, there's a moral issue here, she's going to help your cause, so why make her pay?"

"I have to make all the arrangements," said Bhola. "It takes time, brother, and they won't talk without me. I have to be there."

"How much does he want?" I asked.

"Two thousand dollars," said Ravi.

"Dollars? Not rupees?"

"Dollars," said Ravi. "Look, he's trying to swindle you, but I'm trying to find a way out of this . . . Have some tea, otherwise he'll get offended."

"What's she saying?" asked Bhola.

"She says she doesn't have that kind of money," said Ravi.

"Then no-can-do," said Bhola, in absurd and unexpected English.

"Listen," said Ravi, "I'll personally pay you for your time . . . Two hundred rupees is the best I can do."

"Then no meeting with the eunuchs," said Bhola. "Five hundred rupees is the absolute minimum. For one half hour of my time."

Ludicrously now, Bhola tried to persuade us of his genuine motive in protecting the eunuchs from exploiters. From somewhere within his dhoti, he removed a dozen soft cards—"so *many* people have come . . . from around the world"—just to ask *him* questions about the hijras: and he had set up no such meetings for them. In fact, he'd told the eunuch community not to speak to them. The BBC . . . *Der Spiegel* . . . the *Chicago Tribune* . . . the *Washington Post* . . . French TV . . . Channel Four . . . Australian TV . . . the BBC came twice, he said. But without his say-so, the hijras would not speak.

I parted with the money in frustration, reasoning that Bhola could answer the basic questions, even if they were laced with "half-truths." There was the question of religion. The prophet Mohammad had himself disavowed castration, saying in the *Hadiths* that "the one who castrates himself does not belong to my religion. In Islam, chastity takes the place of castration." Because of this interdiction, in Persia, Turkey, and Egypt, the rulers did not allow castration on the premises of their courts, but instead, bought already castrated youths in slavery, or emasculated prisoners who did not belong to the "realm" of Islam. Preference was given to "outsiders"—to the alien, to the one deemed "ugly," and to those lacking dynastic ambition. The crime of the queen in the *Arabian Nights*, for example, for which she lost her head, was sexual dalliance with a black slave, his race being the transgression. As a rule, castration of the "other" did not always work: slaves revolted, overthrew regimes, and formed their own monarchies.

Had eunuchs come to India with cultural Islam? First, there were the Arabs, in the eighth century, then the sultans, and finally the Mughuls. The word for court eunuch in India came from Persian—*kwaja sara* (*kwaja*: honorific, meaning "real master"; *sera*, to decorate), thus male members of the royal household who "decorated" the "real master." The word used for the Indian eunuch today was *hijra* ("neither male nor female"), said to be of Urdu origin, the language the soldiers used in the Mughul bazaars, a combination of Hindi, Persian, and Arabic.

"There is no connection, madam," said Bhola. "The hijras have descended from Hinduism, from olden times, right from the *Ramayana*."

The *Ramayana* was one of India's most famous epics, religious poems, composed in Sanskrit between 200 B.C. and A.D. 200. In it, the god Ram must endure a period of exile, and the abduction of his wife, before he can return to the city of Ayodhya to claim his kingship.

"When Ram was in the forest," explained Bhola, "about to cross the river and go into exile, all the people of the city wanted to follow him. He said, 'Men and women, turn back.' So the hijras didn't know what to do, because they were 'neither men nor women.' When Ram returned to Ayodhya after fourteen years, they were still there, on the outskirts of the city. So Ram blessed them. Even he recognized their right to exist."

"Arjun also was a hijra," said Bhola, invoking the hero of the Sanskrit epic, the *Mahabharata*.

I quietly wondered at these claims. To place the eunuchs within Islam would be to place them in a minority tradition—which would certainly be controversial in India today. But it would also be to admit to their anachronism, because the days of sequestered harems were over. Castration, it seemed to me, was not a particularly Hindu idea. There was, in the pantheon of Hindu gods, every form of sexuality, most notably Lord Shiva's, whose manifestations moved from dancer to hermaphrodite to bisexual to ascetic to the phallus itself, but nowhere could I summon the idea of a castrated deity.

"How are the hijras organized in Delhi?" I asked, changing the subject.

What issued from Bhola's lips now was a long list of numbers and percentages, like a bad poem: there were nine "localities" of eunuchs, he said—in Old Delhi, New Delhi, in the new settlements, in Number 7 Railway Station. There were two kinds —75 percent went to weddings and to bless newborns, 25 percent stayed at home. Among those who stayed at home, 5 percent were the best off; they were known as the "gurus." Ninety-five percent of all hijras were "chelas" or disciples of this 5 percent elite. There were, among hijras, "respectable" and "not respectable" families. Good houses, bad houses. The elite of the Delhi hijras lived in Old Delhi; they were called "Wazirwallas" and "Badshahwallas." There were seven "houses" or "lineages" of hijras—jats—nationally. The known all-India count of eunuchs was 50,000, but the true number was closer to 1 million. After all, how to categorize them, na, as male or female? The Indian census had no third-gender category. They were born as males and usually registered as such. They voted with their born names. There were hijras in Pakistan, in the Mideast, Burma, Singapore, Malaysia, Thailand . . .

I suggested that the names—Wazirwallas and Badshahwallas—implied a connection to Islam. *Wazir* meant "minister," and *Badshah*, "emperor," in Urdu. (*Wallah* meant "man.") Could these families of eunuchs have once been attached to the households of the medieval sultans or to the later Mughul courts?

"No," said Bhola. "This is strictly Hindu, madam."

"Why, today," I asked, "does one become a eunuch?"

"Because," said Bhola, "they think of themselves as women. They grow up wearing women's clothes. They are transsexuals . . . There are transsexuals all over the world, and India is no exception."

"They want to be castrated?"

"They volunteer to be castrated," said Bhola.

"At what age?"

"Fifteen, sixteen," said Bhola.

"Volunteer, or are kidnapped?"

Bhola took great offense at the suggestion. He repeated his cry that the hijras were helpless people, victims of the press, God bless their hearts. But he did not say no; he waffled, he avoided, he denounced the "zenanas" or would-be eunuchs who imitated the hijras—cutting in on their trade—though I hadn't asked. Beyond this, Bhola would not speak; his half-hour was up; chalo; we'd have to pay him for more information which, he said, the eunuch community would never grant us. They had an injunction of silence against any member of the community who revealed its secrets. The penalty for such divulgence was harsh, and resulted in excommunication. So it would be useless, he said, to seek them out on my own.

Surely the eunuch community was not that organized, nor one man so powerful that he could convince them all not to speak. Bribery was a very useful tool, at the very least; I also hoped that if I could reach the community in time, they'd never have to know that I'd consulted this small-time hustler of a local politician.

In the car back to Old Delhi, to Civil Lines, I asked Ravi about the claim that Arjun, the hero of the *Mahabharata*, was a eunuch. To my surprise, he did not disagree.

"You know," said Ravi, "that the epic's about the five Pandava brothers who were destined to wage war against their own family? Arjun was the leader of the Pandavas. All

of them, in exile, went to seek employment in the court of
King Virat. Arjun taught Virat's daughter how to dance:
and the story of how he learned this art is very interesting . . . He learned it from a year spent in the god Indra's
court, where one of the *apsaras*—the minor deities—had
fallen in love with him. But Arjun had looked toward her
as a mother, and he had said, 'I can't go to bed with you.'
So she had cursed him and said, 'You will be neither a man
nor a woman for the rest of your life.' So Arjun went to Indra and begged, 'Father, this is the curse I've been given—
what shall I do?' Indra then persuaded the *apsara* to reduce
the sentence, and she said, 'For *one* year, you will be neither a man nor a woman.' Therefore he used that year to
hide in the garb of a dance teacher."

At home, I headed toward the locked-up books in the
living room, and brought down A. L. Basham's *The Wonder That Was India*. My eye fell on this passage:

"The erotic life of ancient India was generally hetero-
sexual. Homosexualism of both sexes was not wholly
unknown; it is condemned briefly in the law books, and
the *Kama Sutra* treats it, but cursorily, and with little en-
thusiasm. Literature ignores it. In this respect ancient India
was far healthier than most ancient cultures. Another un-
pleasant feature of ancient civilizations, the eunuch, was
also rare, though not completely unknown. Castration,
whether of men or of animals, was disapproved of, and
harems were generally guarded by elderly men and armed
women."

On the other hand, there was some evidence to suggest
that the eunuch tradition had derived from Hinduism. Unlike the court eunuchs, the Indian hijras were dancers, and
today, at least, wore female, not male, clothes.

I pulled down the *Kama Sutra*; and just what everybody
thought I was doing, leafing through illustrations of coital

positions, including animals, I will never know. Nobody here spoke about sex. I avoided the headlong glances, as conversation buzzed on around me about "her man Bhola," "ghunda, yaar," "avoidable," and "could be dangerous." By now, my obsession had taken over the room.

"Indian family, foreign-born, educated," chided my uncle. "Prem's family has asked after you."

"But precisely because I am all those things," I replied, "I can never do it."

"Ah, that is a paradox," said my uncle.

"Prem's family," I said, "they're not Mathurs, even."

"These days," said my uncle, "Banias, Muslims—anything goes."

"But you just must let go of this eunuch thing," warned my aunt, "or no man will want you."

Which is precisely why the subject appealed to me: because it was, in the last and final analysis, the only way to be left alone in India—what with all the where-are-you-goings, and why-don't-you-bathe-more-frequentlies?

The author of the *Kama Sutra*, Vatsayana, had devoted a whole chapter to "eunuch" courtesans. These pages were bizarre, mainly because they were so free of judgment. Advice was given on how to make love to a eunuch, or rather, how to receive pleasure from a eunuch. Two kinds were discussed: those who assumed "a bust," were "without body hair," and appeared "like women," and those who took a male form, and "imitated men's beards." But Vatsayana seemed to imply not eunuchs precisely—castrati, or the fully emasculated—but impotent beings, unable to bear children, perhaps hermaphrodites, or those born with unusual gender characteristics, who had little choice but to become courtesans. His word for them was *pota*.

I turned to *The Ocean of Story*, a Buddhist tale of the eleventh century A.D., in which an English scholar, Norman Penzer, had catalogued the incidence of eunuchs in the ancient Sanskrit books—the *Vedas, Dharma Shastras, Upanishads*, and *Laws of Manu*. But again, the words for eunuch were ambiguous—*kliba, vadhri*, and *sandha*—and could mean either "eunuch" or "impotent."

The eunuch, or "long-haired man," wrote Penzer, was not allowed to inherit property, and was to be maintained by the king, who could take his inheritance as though it were his own. He was excluded from the sacrifice to honor ancestors, because he was "deemed unworthy." He could not pour oil or wine on the ground or on a sacrificial victim to worship a deity. No one could accept alms proffered by a eunuch or consume food prepared by him. Since eunuchs were considered "incapable of keeping a secret," they could not serve as witnesses, nor could they be struck in battle, "in contempt for their effeminacy." A "special penalty" was imposed for killing them. Because they were sterile and therefore "ill-omened, the very sight of them was defiling." A eunuch could not be converted or ordained, and was not allowed near the king during consultations. They were permitted to marry women. In human sacrifices of one of the Vedic periods, a eunuch was the victim offered to Misfortune.

And here, apparently, was Bhola's claim: according to the *Mahabharata*, there was a subset of dancers, "of low caste in India," who "were castrated."

Every man of sense and understanding knows that the best way of worshipping God, consists in allaying the distress of the times, and in improving the condition of man. This depends, however, on the advancement of agriculture, on the order kept in the king's household, on the readiness of the champions of the empire, and the discipline of the army . . .

It was from such views . . . that his Majesty entrusted his innermost secrets to the Khwaja-sara I'timad Khan[1], a name which his Majesty had bestowed upon him as a fitting title.

> Abu' l-Faz'l Allami
> *"The Imperial Treasuries,"* The A'in-i Akbari
> 1590

[1] "I'timad means trustworthiness. Khwaja-sara is the title of the chief eunuch. His real name was Phul Malik. After serving Salim Shah (1545 to 1553), who bestowed upon him the title of Muhammad Atgah Khan, he entered Akbar's service. Akbar, after the death of Shams ud-Din Muhammad Agah Khan, his foster father, commenced to look into matters of finance and finding the Revenue Department a den of thieves, he appointed I'timad Khan to remodel the finances, making him a commander of One Thousand . . . and conferring upon him the title of I'timad Khan. He appears to have performed his duties to Akbar's satisfaction. In 1565, he conveyed the daughter of Miran Mubarak, king of Khandesh . . . to Akbar's harem, took afterward a part in the conquest of Bengal, where he distinguished himself, and was, in 1576, appointed governor of Bhakkar."

FIVE

One thing was clear. This journey was not going to be a linear one, and sorting through fact and fiction would prove difficult indeed. To investigate the allegation of kidnapping, I arranged to meet one of the journalists who had written about it for *India Today*, the magazine that looked and behaved just like America's *Time*, down to the detail of the cover's red border. Below a photograph of three fierce-looking hijras, the headline read:

FEAR IS THEIR KEY—to survival. Robbed of their traditional heritage as guardians of royal harems, India's estimated 50,000 eunuchs inhabit a twilight world born out of superstition and fear of the unknown . . . Apart from their sexual deformity, and their uncanny appearances at weddings and births, very little is known about the tribe and their tightly controlled existence.

Mohammed Hanif Vora is believed to be the first person to have broken out of the half-world of eunuchs with a first-person account of their lives, their brutal tribal rites and the hierarchical system under which they ply their bizarre trade. Vora's story offers a major clue as to how the eunuchs maintain their numbers, despite the fact that they are doomed to remain childless. A minor family quarrel forced Vora to run away from his family in Chotta Udepur and he arrived in Baroda, in search of a job. He found employment carting around a water trolley in the streets but had no friends till a couple of eunuchs started conversing with the boy regularly and eventually gained his confidence. After about a month, they made their move. One night, last April, he was grabbed by the two eunuchs, pushed into an auto-rickshaw and taken to a suburban area where he was locked up in a room.

For an entire week, he was kept locked up and beaten regularly to instill a fear complex to prevent him from attempting to escape. After satisfying themselves that Vora was suitably terrified of retribution, he was given feminine garments and started accompanying the eunuchs on their rounds. For three months, he was part of the group and taught to behave like them, the seductive walk, the obscene gestures and the ritualistic hand-clapping peculiar to the tribe.

Vora was jealously guarded in the initial days though treated like a prize possession with each eunuch vying for his attention. Often jealous quarrels would break out between them for him. The group that Vora was with travelled from village to village and made good money by their presence at weddings and births. The simple-minded villagers actually considered them a sign of good fortune and paid them handsomely for their presence.

The group, which consisted of a dozen members, earned an incredible 40,000 rupees in just one month of touring the rural areas . . . Throughout the three months of wandering, the eunuchs gave Vora no chance for escape and he was never left on his own. Finally satisfied with his performance, they decided that he was ripe for initiation and the real nightmare began. One night, he was taken by three members of the group in a taxi to Kalol, 140 km. away, on the pretext that they were going to visit relatives. There he was lodged in the house of an old woman who obviously knew the eunuchs well.

According to Vora's later statement, he was roughly woken up next morning by four eunuchs who stripped off his clothes and held him down on the bed . . . A man and an old woman then entered the room, the latter bearing a wicked looking dagger . . . The initiation rite was mercifully brief. In one stroke, the old woman sliced off the boy's sexual organs and he passed out . . .

Dilip Bobb belonged to that Western breed of reporter, casual, in jeans. He offered me a Coke. If I wanted to find the historical links, and understand the tradition, "you might be wasting your time in Delhi. You might be able to find the rare old-timer, but the average class of hijra—you can meet them all over here—Connaught Place is full of them."

"Were they always so despised?" I asked.

"They've come down to that level now," said Bobb, "but Jaipur and Hyderabad are places that still have a strong tradition and strong royal-family background."

"Is prostitution a big part of this life?" I asked.

"I don't really believe that," said Bobb. "For one thing prostitution doesn't really pay them all that much money. Because the kind of people who would use them for sex is a very low class of people. The way they get their money by their traditional methods now is much easier."

"Where do they live?"

"They all live in one area," said Bobb, "in the older part of Delhi. Actually, they're all over the place . . . They operate in colonies: it's like any kind of extortion gang anywhere. They have an incredible intelligence system that tells them immediately when there's a wedding . . . because of the fear that they generate, they don't have a problem getting the information. They've reached the stage where they can just walk into a house and demand the money.

Ninety-nine percent of the people just pay them to get rid of them."

"And the kidnapping case," I asked. "How frequent would you say something like that is?"

"It's frequent enough, I would imagine," said Bobb, "because . . . I don't know who has figures on the hijra population, but it's . . ."

"Well, fifty thousand," I said, "is quoted as the figure from you."

"Yah, right," said Bobb. "That's the approximate figure. There's no—"

"I mean, I've had others," I said. "I've had one million, I've had one and a quarter million . . ."

"There's no census," said Bobb. "There's nobody who's done any research on hijras in India, so there's no real figure, there's just an approximation—fifty thousand would be pretty accurate. They have an annual gathering near Baroda—that's the only time you can figure out how many there are, because they all come there. And there are about forty-five thousand. But the figure hasn't really come down drastically, which means that the only way they can increase their numbers is by kidnapping young people, because they can't really reproduce on their own."

"You think there are not enough people who want to join of their own volition?"

"I don't think so," said Bobb. "I don't think *any*one would join of his own 'violation.' It's not the kind of thing a normal kid would want to get into. In an area dominated by hijras, possibly, because he doesn't know any different, but that would be the only reason."

"But what," I asked, "separates this from homosexuality and a child who has some problem, and seeks out a community like any other?"

"Well, I'll tell you," said Bobb. "If they take a child into their community, it's at a very early age, usually six or seven, and at that age, I don't think any child knows . . ."

"I agree with you," I said, "but I have heard that they come voluntarily, and they don't really join until about fifteen."

"That used to be the case," said Bobb. "Because in those days, the eunuchs were the keepers of the king's harem. So it was a pretty sought-after job. But right now, no kid of fifteen, even if he's a homosexual, is gonna join. Because it's a very painful thing. It's like a very crude form of castration."

"Do they have to undergo it?"

"Well," said Bobb, "if you're taken in at a very early age, then they have ways to restrict the growth of your organs. But if you're fifteen or sixteen, they have to. They do perform an operation. It's very crude and barbaric. It's done by force. I mean, if you read that story we ran . . ."

"What kind of people," I asked, "are susceptible to kidnapping—you think it goes on quite frequently?"

"Well, this one case," said Bobb, "is possibly the only case that received the kind of publicity it did. Usually, either it's ignored, or the police don't really make an effort—because once a kid is kidnapped and gets into the hijra network, there's no way in the world you can really trace him, because they're all over the place. And it's a very tightly knit community. And there's going to be no one telling you what happened to that kid, or where it's gone. It's like a mafia."

"So it's like," I suggested, "when people are kidnapped into a terrorist organization, and then they themselves become terrorists? They are kidnapped into the hijra organization, then become 'reformed' into its way of thinking, so that they don't want to tell the police?"

"Well, yah," said Bobb. "Once they've got into it, it's

very difficult to get out. They are kept there by fear. The first four or five years, they're very, very tightly guarded. And they're threatened. And they're only there because of fear of what will happen if they do try and escape or go to the police. In this case, this kid did manage to escape and did manage to go to the police—which is how we got to know about it. But in nine-tenths of the cases, they're just too young—too young and too scared. Plus there's the social shame of going back into normal life after four–five years of . . ."

"Castration," I said. "Yes, he's sort of unfit . . . But I've heard that the hijras grow up wearing women's clothes, that they feel homosexual, and that this is a community that would accept them. I wonder if these are just cover stories, made up later?"

"I would tend to think so," said Bobb. "At least the recent cases. But, in India, at least in the cities, it's really no longer that great a sin to be homosexual. It's changed a lot in the last few years. There are a lot of gay people around who flaunt it quite openly."

"It's not even gay-ness, exactly," I said. "It's a desire to be a woman. Which—a counterpart in the West would probably be a transsexual."

"Well, okay," said Bobb. "But even then, it would depend really on what kind of background you came from: Because the hijras are from a very, very low class background. If you're from that background, and you're homosexual, or you're a man with very strong female characteristics, I guess the only way that you could display it openly would be to join the hijras. Sure. But any level above that, certainly not. I don't think that you would do it willingly. Because the hijras are about the lowest of the low, in terms of social acceptance, which counts a lot in this country. So I don't think there are too many people joining it willingly."

"So, it's an old institution that has outlived its use?"

"Totally."

"Well then, why would it persist?"

"It persists," said Bobb, "because, for one, these people don't have any other way of earning a living."

"So, poverty."

"Poverty, yah," said Bobb. "It's one very major factor. The second is that it's a community that takes care of its own. If you're a hijra, you're not going to starve. There's gonna be someone taking care of you. They all live in one part of whatever city they're in. So you've got a house, you've got a bed to sleep on, you've got food to eat. Which counts for a lot in India."

"When you covered this Gujarati case," I asked, "did you actually speak to the hijras, or did you just speak to the boy, Vora?"

"No, we did speak to the hijras," said Bobb.

"And what was their story?"

"Well, obviously," said Bobb, "their story was that the guy had come willingly, which is almost impossible to believe, because he gave his own story to the police, which is what we quoted from. I mean, if they kidnap somebody, they don't keep him in that one place, they take him away, about a hundred miles away—then he's kept there for another year."

"So it's doubtful," I said, "the hijras' story . . . But why do you think they chose this boy to kidnap?"

"Well," said Bobb, "one reason is: he was living in that locality where they dominate. So there's very little chance of them getting caught doing it. Secondly, the kind of people they do kidnap are usually the types who wouldn't go to the

police and make a big noise about it, or have the influence
or the money to chase it up. You would never find a rich kid
being kidnapped by a hijra, because it's too much of a risk."

"According to this," I said, "in the hijra community,
there must be young boys . . ."

"I don't know if you'll find them," said Bobb. "The ones
you see on the roads are not young. They never take kids
out with them when they're going to a house and trying to
extort money . . . There's another angle to this which is not
well known. There's a guy in Delhi who lived in America
for twenty years—and he came back here just last year.
And he'd bought a house and moved into it, and a bunch
of hijras came in—just walked into the house—and sat
down. He didn't have the same kind of attitude that other
people have toward hijras. He refused to pay. And they
made a big racket, and finally he opened the door, and
started dragging them out. And one of them grabbed his
shirt and pulled it, and then scratched him across his stomach. And twenty days later, his whole side was full of rash.
He went to the doctor and was told he had herpes! I mean,
it's pretty obvious that it would happen to them, because
it's obviously a homosexual—"

"It's not homosexual," I said.

"Yah, well, okay," said Bobb. "Because the kind of life
they lead is pretty sordid."

In Hindustan, especially in the province of Sylhet, which is a part of Bengal, some inhabitants emasculate their sons and hand them over to the province governor in lieu of payment in nature for their taxes. This custom has spread to other provinces. Every year, innocent children are thus mutilated for life and rendered incapable to procreate. This practice has become common. I have proclaimed an edict so that, from today on, this abominable practice be abolished and the trade of young eunuchs cease. Islam Khan and the other governors of Bengal have received very strict orders to severely punish those persons guilty of such crimes. I hope that, by the grace of God, this custom will cease completely and that no one will dare undertake such an odious and unprofitable practice.

Emperor Jahangir
Tazak-i-Jahangiri
1607–27

SIX

No man would let me go there on my own, so they were all coming with me. The eunuchs that Jonathan Broder had interviewed lived in the old quarter of Delhi, where the Emperor Shah Jahan had built the Red Fort in the seventeenth century, a high red brick wall whose color became the city at dawn, mingling with the scent of coal and dung burning in the air—an indescribable smokiness that hung over the land, where women washed the cloth they dyed in the shouting colors of worship. It was a warm red that stretched on for miles, like the red of the betel nut, which was chewed and spit, and left stains all over the streets of India. But gazing at the wall, one couldn't help but be reminded of blood, and the many hands that had fought for the city. Timur-ul-lang, or Tamerlaine, had conquered it in the late fourteenth century; a hundred years later, his descendant Babur floated along the river writing poetry, after his army secured the city again, wresting it from the sultans. Monkeys once roamed freely here, their tails hanging, warning children of the dangers to come in rackets of sudden noise, till one day, as though overnight, they all disappeared, the victims of medical research.

To the east, the wall faced the Yamuna river and the Hindu cremation grounds; to the west, it gave on to the old city, alive with sound and memory, and living in many centuries at once. Daily the Jama Masjid called Muslims to prayer from the hundreds of small buildings and bazaars that were wedged into crooked streets.

When one speaks of third-world poverty, the tendency of most travelers is to think of it as abject, cruel, miserable—half-clad people running barefoot in winter, their lives the casual coincidence of brutal blows struck by fate. But that parody—though it did exist—failed to convey the truth about the majority who were simply poor. And it was an ordinary day for the neighbors of the hijras. A rickshaw walla lazed against his bicycle, softly singing a tune from a film, forgetting the words in mid-stride. Women shook their pans looking for stones in rice. Men lounged on beds of rope chatting in the midday sun. Children's hair was parted and braided with grease, with the smell of coconut. There was the sound of hammers, the motion of saws. Goats' heads appeared here and there, as roosters strutted along the streets.

So, when we asked the rickshaw walla where to find the house of the hijras, he looked up and smiled: "Take a left, then a right, then another left. Then ask. Everybody will know," and with that, returned to his singing. And here, with our Levi's and sneakers and cameras, we were truly the foreign ones. We spoke to an elderly gentleman, in his dhoti. "Oh, the hijras," he said calmly. "It's that house down on the left." He looked at his watch. "But they're probably not home. They've probably gone to the market."

The order of things. Like the order left behind: the high walls of Civil Lines, enclosing gracious gardens and the homes of the Indian *sahibs*, knowable from the silent rhythm of the sweeper as she moved along the square pattern of stones beneath the fan; knowable from the steps of the ironing woman who daily took her bus from one of the new suburbs, having been relocated during the Emergency, as Sanjay Gandhi swept the roads, "cleaning" them up— wrapped in a thin white shawl, the mother of two, whose eldest son had become a government janitor, she said. The order of things, knowable from the architecture of fear the night watchman carved with his wooden stick as he made the rounds, and with each turn there was always a waiting; for the beat of the stick, its slow and knowable sound; and the sleeper, not yet asleep, wondering, if on this night he had finally met with an ill fate. A river of lives running into each other, and yet not meeting.

Given Bobb's portrait of fear, one would expect the house of the eunuchs to be a squalid shanty, an uneasy quilt of tin, burlap, and clay, slipped in between concrete buildings. But it was the big white house down the lane, an elegant structure that rose above the shacks, newly painted, shuttered, and well maintained; a house that had on it a large bolt—in India, a friendly presence, a sign that someone will be back with keys, hung from the waist of a petticoat. The house of the eunuchs bespoke a kind of wealth and status, stood like a monastery in a small Spanish town, below which the city kept pace with its motions.

We knocked. No answer.

While debating whether to wait or return, one in our crowd spotted a hijra. He or she was dressed in a sari, and wore a tattered Kashmiri shawl around the shoulders. Unmistakable with her bun, she seemed to have bypassed the house and was wending her way along, with a large green plastic basket, empty, on her arm. Ravi ran up and gently touched her elbow. As we caught up, she turned, and smiling, took in the breadth of the spectacle before her: an ironic look. Ravi explained that I had come "all the way from a foreign country just to talk to her." She laughed: "Me? But I'm just a small fry. There are much bigger fish.

Why don't you go and catch one?" With that, she turned, and tousling the hair of two children as they ran past, went on her merry way.

How can I explain it? There is a much bigger India, too, that you cannot find in the books, on which the "grand" India, the India of the "imagination," was built. And these people, on the boundaries of things, somehow point the way to what is missing. They are defiant, paradoxical, and made of words; but what they give is laughter, at the moments when laughter seemed most necessary. I was having no luck at all; and yet I felt that, in this indirect way, I would stumble upon the truth—not just of these people, but of the spectators, us, without whom the spectacle could not exist.

A man sitting on the pavement, smoking a cigarette, had noticed our vacillations. He rose, as though on unseen command, and introduced himself as Shamir. The eunuchs, he said, had gone to their annual *puja* or convention; all the "big fry" were in Ajmer, and the "small fry" weren't authorized to talk without their permission. This Gita—Broder's interviewee—was not in Delhi. But, he said, there was a smaller house of eunuchs around the corner, and a little boss—not one of the major "gurus," but someone named Gulzar—was probably at home; why didn't we try there? He didn't mind leading us to it.

Shamir took us to the second house, about three lanes away. Large and also white, it had a tired look, though it stood three stories high, and towered over the adjoining buildings. Shamir left, and loitered nearby. We knocked. After a few minutes, a young hijra answered, of mild temperament, with a cotton-sari-rumpled-hair-just-at-home look. We explained that we wished to interview Gulzar. She asked us to take a seat in their house, on a low wooden platform, a *taqat*, replete with pillows. Inside, it was strikingly clean. There was a refrigerator, a radio.

The young hijra said, "Just a minute, I'll go and call her," and kept her eyes lowered in the manner of a new bride. Then the one whose name was Gulzar came down, accompanied by much tinkling of bangles and anklebells. But she merely glanced at us, a spectral figure in a bright blue chiffon sari, then disappeared upstairs again.

The young hijra said, "Gulzar told me to offer you tea or soda, to look after you. Because you have come with respect, we will treat you with respect. She will meet you. But there will be no interview." She explained to us that Gulzar was her "guru," she was Gulzar's *chela*, or disciple. Clearly, though, she was reluctant to speak. Through much giggling, we ascertained that her name was Kamla.

Gulzar eventually came down in quite a perspiring, disgruntled mood: he or she had a plump, extremely light-skinned, verging-on-pink face, of which one might say Afghani or Kashmiri. She wore heavy gold earrings, and a big gold watch. The chela made a great fuss over her, a great fuss to arrange the cushions for her to sit on. She was uncomfortable, she was comfortable, she needed a glass of water, she was flushed, she was in a great hurry, she said, she had just been performing, but mainly she was silent. Among themselves, I noticed, they referred to each other as "he." We sat there without speaking. Gulzar seemed to be deliberating.

When she spoke, it was slowly, and with great gravity. "Why," she asked, "have you come to us?"

Ravi explained: "To learn the truth about your people."

Gulzar paused. "The truth?" she said. "The truth? Let me tell you about the truth . . . First the BBC came. Then the *Washington Post*. Then Australian TV. And now, you."

She looked down, in mock sadness. "They've taken their photos," she said, holding an imaginary camera in the air. "They've shot their film," she said, slowly rotating a hand by her ear, as though filming. "They've written their articles," she said, making the gesture of a river-like pen. "And do you know what they've said?"

Silence.

"They've said that we don't respect Mataji," bellowed Gulzar, her bangles shaking in anger. "That we don't respect our country. That we're thieves and prostitutes. That we kidnap children." Then she lowered her voice till it was almost faint: "It is all untrue . . . all untrue . . . We are simply fakirs . . . We are ascetics . . . We have given ourselves to God . . ."

We listened. Ravi complimented Gulzar on "her" language—she spoke in such an ornate, old-fashioned way, he said. She had referred to Indira Gandhi as "Mataji"—Mother—and to India as a "kingdom." And he did not mean any offense, he said, but wouldn't Gulzar submit to an interview? I, he argued, meant to discover who the hijras really were.

"I'm just a beggar," said Gulzar. "That's all you need to know."

She had spoken like a film star; but hers were prideful words. And when Ravi tried to offer her money for the time she'd given us, Gulzar refused.

And the news was all over town by the end of the day: what, the hijras, had refused money? Arre yar, unbelievable. And they had offered tea? Unbelievable. And they had refused to speak? Refused. Refused.

~

The French traveler François Bernier wrote, in *Travels in the Mogul Empire, 1656–68*, that the eunuchs were the most trusted servants of the Mughul rulers. Because of their uniqueness of gender, they were allowed to travel freely between the mardana (the men's side) and the zenana (the women's side). They guarded the prized women of the harem, attended them as loyal servants, and cared for their children. Their utter physical and emotional dependence on the ruler often reached the point of devotion. There is story after story: It was the eunuch Chah Abas, the servant of one of Shah Jahan's sons, to whom was entrusted the task of taking the fort at Soorut, and who repeatedly warned the young prince of the perfidious intentions of his brother Aurangzeb. Or: the beloved daughter of Mumtaz Mahal, the favorite wife of Shah Jahan, for whom he built the Taj Mahal, was so protected by her father that he did not ever seek a husband for her; and so she took lovers, each one disposed of by the eunuchs loyal to Shah Jahan. Of the opposing brothers, each fighting for the kingdom: Aurangzeb murdered not only his brother, but also Chah Abas, fearing his loyalty. And of another, deserted by his army, fleeing for his life in what is now Afghanistan, only his beloved eunuch servant followed him, and in the end, bandaged the head of the prince who died in the eunuch's lap.

The beloved eunuchs of Agra had lavished upon them huge rewards of money with this irony: because they were not allowed to leave the domain of the king, they could establish life nowhere but with the king, and so spent their money on elaborate and bejewelled tombs. As intimate servants, they were entrusted with the letters that passed between the king and his sons, and the rule of the palace in the king's absence. In the Indian miniatures of the Mughul period, the eunuchs are depicted as present at the birth of kings in the zenana. And, according to some, they were the lovers of those kings and princes who couldn't possibly "satisfy" all the women of the harem.

This is part of the invisible history of the eunuch; observed in the journals of the Mughul period, but whose origins and mythologies are strangely absent, as is the history of the entire subcaste, the all-present, invisible Indian subject: the domestic, the slave.

SEVEN

Now what was i to do? I considered traveling to another city—Bombay, Lucknow, Calcutta. Yet strange things were happening around me: once, when I was not home, a group of eunuchs landed up outside the house and told the gardener, "We heard that there was a Lady here looking for us." The gardener had taken it upon himself to defend the family's honor: "Oh, yes, that Lady was here, but now she's gone off to Kashmir, and won't be back for months!" Alas. Who were these hijras and how had they found me? A rival faction? Transvestites, not eunuchs, who defied Lord Bhola's grasp?

And word of mouth had another effect: It so happened that a certain cousin went to a certain party on Curzon Road, and mentioned to a certain movie star that a certain relative was studying the hijras, where a certain retired deputy police commissioner happened to overhear him— the conversation having arisen because of the traffic of eunuchs outside the window; and he had said, "Tell her to come to me. Because I have actually seen it—the initiation ceremony." Thus word reached me that I should contact a Mr. Shahpur Chenoy of Hyderabad, now residing in Delhi. And though I had sought to defy the way in which India worked—a labyrinth of names and connections—I found myself inevitably moving through that tide.

Meanwhile, I was able to locate a few secondary accounts. Serena Nanda, an American anthropologist, had studied the hijras of a southern city she named Bastipore to protect her informants. She sent me some of her research, which later became a book, *Neither Man Nor Woman*. All the hijras she interviewed told Nanda that they had joined the community voluntarily. Though her work was mainly ahistorical and ethnographic, Nanda cited references to the Sanskrit epics—Ram, Arjun, etc.—and drew the conclusion that the hijra tradition had descended from Hinduism, although she noted that the phenomenon was found mainly in north Indian cities—and to my mind, at least, suggested a more than casual link to Islamic culture. Nanda saw Islam's influence as mainly one of prestige.

The hijras underwent the "operation," as she put it, "ideally" at the hands of a hijra midwife or "dai ma." This person had "no special training." The operation, called "nirvan," connoting transcendence, was done in secret because castration was illegal according to the Indian Penal Code, wrote Nanda. It took place in the early morning, "between 3 A.M. and 4 A.M.," in a room in which only the midwife and her assistant were present, she wrote, and she stressed the religious connection between "castration" and "rebirth," emphasizing a transsexual aspect. But I quietly wondered about the more pragmatic link between the hijras' arriving at the homes of newborns, and having access to women and harems, and thus, perhaps, to midwives. Midwives were also illegal abortionists in India, and could be linked to death.

The hijras worshipped Besraji Mata, wrote Nanda, or *Bahuchara Mata*, the "Mother Goddess." Shaivite in sect, the main temple of Bahuchara was outside Ahmadabad in Gujarat, as Bobb had confirmed. This goddess was associated with impotence, sexual abstinence, and mutilation.

Childless women frequented the temple to pray for a son. By legend, Bahuchara was an attractive woman who was attacked by thieves on the road; to prevent rape, she cut off one of her breasts and offered it to the thieves in exchange for her virtue. She died, and was later enshrined.

The hijras had told Nanda the story of a king who prayed to Bahuchara for a son; this he was given, but the child, Jetho, was impotent. In a dream, Bahuchara appeared to the impotent son and asked him to serve her by cutting off his genitals and wearing female clothes. He did so, and the hijras got "a call from the goddess in their dreams to be emasculated"; refusing the call resulted in "seven incarnations of impotence."

Nanda was entranced by the "third sex," but I was not yet prepared to endorse it. If India was indeed so tolerant of an alternate sex, then why castration? Why the pressure of this definition, and not another? In the West, a transsexual was defined as one who felt himself or herself to be born into the wrong body—was therefore not a member of a "third sex." Castration, it seemed to me, renounced, not embraced, sexual ambiguity.

The second document was an Indian Ministry Report of Social Welfare, written by S. N. Ranade. Ranade had also had no luck interviewing the eunuchs of Delhi, and so had resorted to the "excommunicated" set—those who had left or been ostracized from the main houses, were living on their own, and could therefore speak more freely. Of the hundred Ranade interviewed, 76 were castrated, 13 were hermaphrodites or "pseudo"-hermaphrodites, and 11 were transvestites—"zenanas." Of those, 51 said they were male, 49 said female, but none said they were "neither male nor female."

What was a pseudo-hermaphrodite?

A medical distinction defining a male type who had

testes and some aspects of female genitalia, but no ovaries, and a female type, who had some aspects of male genitalia and ovaries, but no testes. The "true hermaphrodite"— those born with one testis and one ovary—was statistically quite rare.

"The majority of Hijras are castrated males," wrote Ranade. The transvestites were a "minority," and "the hermaphrodites constitute a very small proportion of the population of the community . . . This group [has] a prestigious place in the eunuch community . . . In the case of hermaphrodites, the parents hand over the children to eunuchs or such children are handed over to institutions who in turn hand them over to eunuchs." The hermaphrodite, Ranade argued, had always existed in Hindu mythology, and was referred to as a "third sex."

"It is mainly," wrote Ranade, "after the Arab invasion [eighth century] that the practice of castration and use of eunuchs became more widespread." Ranade corroborated Bhola's claim about the hierarchy of eunuchs: "There appear to be no known sects amongst eunuchs in Delhi. However, it appears that long ago they were divided into two main groups on the basis of residence." Those in Parhargang and Najafgarh, and in central Delhi, were called "Badshahwallas," and those near Delhi Gate and Sabzi Mandi in Old Delhi were called "Wazirwallas." "The names," Ranade wrote, "seem to indicate that one group claimed proximity to Royal households, and the other to ministerial households." Ranade concluded that because harems were entrusted to eunuchs alone, they, "under those circumstances, were assured a place in society since they were seen as performing an important function. Circumstances have now changed and the eunuchs are looked upon with disdain, if not horror."

At the back, Ranade had attached several disturbing case histories:

> At the age of 10, I realized I was born physically defective . . . and found it difficult to pass urine. My parents did not show any understanding or affection . . . I knew I would never be able to marry. I was depressed and frustrated. I consulted some eunuchs and on their advice got myself castrated at the age of 10 . . . This way was the only alternative.

> At the age of 6, I ran away from home after quarreling with my elder brother and came to Punjab from Bihar. Here I started working with a family as a domestic servant. My master ill-treated me. Some eunuchs stayed nearby and I became friendly with them. They lured me to Delhi and sold me to my present *guru*. Gradually I picked up eunuch habits and mannerisms, and ultimately due to continued coaxing I got castrated. Now I am a part of the community. I also changed my religion and now I am a Muslim.

> I was born physically defective . . . my male organ did not develop with age. My aunt spread the news when I was just a child and the eunuchs forcibly took me away. My parents complained to the police and the case was fought in court and my parents won the case. But the news regarding my physical defect spread so widely that it became difficult for me to continue in normal society. As a result, one day I ran away from home and joined the eunuch community by getting myself castrated by an older eunuch at the age of 13.

The purpose of Ranade's report was to "develop policies and programs for 'the protection of children' and the 'rehabilitation' of the eunuchs." Ranade's bias was the opposite of Nanda's—it deified no one. "Normal children," wrote Ranade, "who are castrated generally come from poor families . . . They are courted and seduced by eunuchs who persuade them to undergo the operation. It is also possible that sometimes the children are kidnapped or purchased from parents during times of acute distress caused by flood and droughts. Living, as they do, in crowded locales, the eunuchs are able to observe and establish contact with children who are unhappy, insecure, and disturbed."

Finally, there was Harriet Lynton and Mohini Rajan's *The Days of the Beloved*, a book about the sixth and most famous ruler of Hyderabad, Nizam Mahboob Ali Pasha, who had reigned from 1861 to 1911. In it was a chapter called "The Unworldly Ones," told from the point of view of one hijra—though actually a composite of four voices, from four different eunuch households in Hyderabad. Those the authors had interviewed all had male, not female, names—Abul, Vijay, Nirmal, and Rahman Baksh.

"Listen to my words," the narrative began. "This has come down from the ages. We have heard from the mouths of our elders that there have always been Hijras. It is written in our people's fate that we must eat of the charity of the worldly ones." The voice depicted here was so stylized as to seem facile, and yet, as the authors noted, could be taken as an allegory.

Accordingly, the hijras only sang and danced for a living. They abjured all sexuality, willingly underwent castration, and lived as proper women might in a conservative household. Of his childhood, he said, "I used to play among the girls, borrow my sister's sari and play with dolls, stay at home doing woman's work." For this, he explains, "my uncle . . . used to beat me. They used to put ground chile in my eyes. For two days at a time, they did not give me food. Enough, I realized, my life is not with you."

So he left home and joined the "zenanas" or transvestites. They lived an unchaste life, and there he was "spoiled" by a "rough fellow." He spoke to a few hijras, whose door, he said, closed promptly at nine. "It must be good there," he thought to himself. When he arrived at the eunuch household, they said, "Well, son, you have come here wanting to join the hijras, but first you must sit on the Lal Gundaiji (*kootah*, an instrument of torture)." What he meant was a phallic instrument, which may or may not have once been used as an "instrument of torture," but this the authors did not explain. He did not refuse, but the hijras said, "We only said that to frighten you," meaning, if he had run away at the very thought, they would have surmised that he did not really want to become a hijra.

He lived amongst them. He learned their trade. He dressed in a sari. One day he took a walk to a village with an old man and was taunted by somebody there who refused to give him alms, claiming that he was not a "real" hijra. At the age of fifteen, he then "went into the jungle" and "cut" his "organ at the root." The next day he "took a bath and put on an old bandage." He "invoked the name of the goddess, Besraji Mata, soaked the bandage in the oil of her lamp, and applied it." He returned to the village and proved to the "smart aleck" that he was indeed a true hijra. Then the "old man" took care of him for two weeks.

One could read the story this way: a boy feels alienated in his childhood. He leaves his family, takes a wrong turn, a test, which makes him realize what he must do. He seeks out his true society. There he must endure yet another test of his beliefs. He passes, but still feels like an impostor, because he has not undergone the initiation ritual—a rite of passage. He leaves the society, and without witnesses, except in the eyes of God, he takes matters into his own hands "in a jungle," outside the bounds of civilization. He returns anew, a celibate, a member of an old order, a priesthood. This pattern can also be likened to the evolution of the *sanyasi*, the Hindu ascetic or religious beggar, the *sadhu*.

But: Did he actually castrate himself? Who was the "old man," his companion? What jungle is he alluding to near Hyderabad? What of all this business of *not* sitting on a wooden phallus? Has he not covered his bases, making sure that he implicates no one in his castration? It's a very clean story of transformation, and its fable goes unchallenged by the writers.

~

In the late 1600s, a young Venetian man named Niccolo Manucci stowed away in a ship travelling east from Italy and arrived in India. There he joined the forces fighting against the son of Emperor Shah Jahan. Eventually those forces lost to Aurangzeb, and Manucci had no interest in working for the new emperor, who had murdered his brothers and imprisoned his father; but in order to travel freely, he often had to consult the court of Aurangzeb, which continued to implore him to work for them, as foreigners were much in demand. The man he encountered most often in Agra was the eunuch I'tibar Khan, a "grandee" or nobleman, appointed governor of Agra, and proxy of the emperor in times of absence or illness. Manucci had nothing but loathing for I'tibar Khan, whom he refers to as a "baboon," and his contempt caused him to include in his three-volume travelogue a brief history of the eunuchs of India at that time:

"It is easy," wrote Manucci, *"to understand the nature of this eunuch from what he did to his parents. They came from the country of Bengal as far as Agrah, having heard that their son was governor of the fortress. They anticipated the receipt of something to help them in their old age and poverty. On reaching the gate, they stayed there several days, the door-keepers not consenting to permit their*

entrance, until they swore they were the parents of the governor. Thereupon came a door-keeper at the time of full audience (I was there myself), and reported to the eunuch that an old man and an old woman had been at the door for several days. As they had been refused entrance, the old people swore they were the parents of his excellency.

"For a little while I'tibar Khan sat silent, like one to whom something has happened that he does not like, then said under his breath, 'Are the wretches still alive?' He ordered them to be brought into the audience-hall. On their appearing, he inquired angrily who they were, what their names were, where they came from, what was their village. To all this they replied in such a manner that by this time I'tibar Khan could have no doubt that they were his parents. Recognizing that most certainly they were such, he said publicly to them: 'How have ye the timerity to come into my presence after you have consumed the price of my body, and having been the cause, by emasculating me, of depriving me of the greatest pleasures attainable in this world? Of what use are riches to me, having no sons to whom I could leave them? Since you were so cruel as to sell your own blood, let not my auditors think it strange if I betray anger against you.'

"He therefore ordered each to receive fifty stripes. Through the courage that inspired me, I took up my parable and told him the story of Joseph and his rise to the greatest place in Egypt, and how God made use of the cruelty of his brothers to raise the patriarch to the highest dignity. Then I made the application to his case, so that, quieting down, he forgave them, and ordered one hundred rupees to be given them, enjoining them never to appear again, for if they did, he would without fail take their lives.

"Let not the reader be astonished at the eunuch ordering into his presence his miserable, poverty-stricken parents, *for it is against our nature to have arrived at high rank and yet not be annoyed at having to disclose the misery from which we started, and allowing it to be found out that our progenitors were of lowly origin; but it is notorious that all eunuchs, grandees as they may be, have no other than poor and miserable progenitors, who out of absolute hunger have sold their sons. Nor do they themselves hold it out as otherwise, deriving hence occasion to vaunt themselves of their own high abilities and great deeds, through which they have risen to such rank.*

"It was very revolting, the strange manner by which this eunuch treated his own parents, and angered thereby I resolved to leave Agrah. This eunuch was such a close-fisted fellow that it soon came to his selling the dung of his elephants and horses, thereby he made ten thousand rupees. With this money he bought an elephant, which one day escaping broke one of its legs, and the populace, who in Hindustan are very free of speech, began to shout as a joke that it was no wonder the elephant broke its leg, for it was an elephant made of dung. In spite of all this avarice, he built for a memorial during his government an outer wall . . . round the whole of Agrah Fort, which cost him a great deal of money, it being good work and decorative.

"Before setting out, since I'tibar Khan has given me occasion to speak of the race of eunuchs, I give here a short account of that sort of brute. It may be that everyone doesn't know what is meant by a eunuch, and may imagine they are like the eunuchs of Europe who are employed as singers . . . If they are rich they do not fail to have in their houses chosen women, with whom they have converse. If they cannot do this, owing to deficient income, they go in search of them in all directions, seeing that no doors are shut to them, nor do women hide from them.

"Among the other qualities of this sort of animal, one is

their extreme covetousness in collecting gold, silver, dia-
monds, and pearls, and they are immeasurably avaricious.
They are afraid to spend money even when it is necessary;
fond of receiving, niggard in giving. Still, they are anxious
to appear well dressed, and when they are astride a fine
horse, they are as elated as if they were the greatest men in
the world. Well may they hold themselves in such estima-
tion, for they are the favourites of princesses, who are very
liberal to them, in order to win them, and from time to time
get permission to enjoy that of which I cannot speak. They
are useful for the introduction secretly of men into the
harem, and through them a husband's favour may be obtained. For the houses of the great are ordinarily under the
direction of these persons.

"Another of their qualities is to be friendly to women
and inimical to men, which may be from envy, knowing
what they have been deprived of. The tongue and hand of
these baboons act together, being most licentious in examining everything, both goods and women, coming into the
palace; they are foul in speech, and fond of silly stories.
Among all the Mohamedans they are ordinarily the
strictest observers of the faith, although I knew some who
did not fail to drink their little drop, and were fond of
wine. These men are the spies for everything that goes on
in secret, whereby they are always listening among the
kings, princes, queens, and princesses. Fida'e Khan, aware
of the character of these monsters, did not allow such to be
employed in his house . . . he was indifferent to the fact
that this sort of people are kept in the houses of princes and
great men."

> Niccolo Manucci
> Storia do Mogor; or Mogul India,
> 1653—1708

EIGHT

MR. CHENOY AND HIS WIFE had the feeling about them, rare in India, of a couple in love. As he welcomed me into the living room, I sensed the officer he had once been: in full command, yet with a curiosity that suggested another life as a scholar. Prem, a bit younger and in jeans, moved about the space organizing breakfast. What's all this, na? she seemed to be thinking. I didn't know Shahpur knew anything about the hijras . . . Chenoy made no judgment about them; in his eyes, all forms of life were equal. He began in the middle of his thinking . . .

"The Sixth Nizam," said Chenoy, "Mahboob Ali Pasha, had a household of these eunuchs. They were 'old-style' hijras—people in whom he had a great deal of confidence."

"What year?"

"This will be . . . 1880," said Chenoy. "The hijras really became very powerful in the household of the Nizam—and because the ruler had a number of them in his employ, all the noblemen followed suit. They also thought it would be a good idea to employ these people . . .There were three categories of hijras. One was: the confidante and advisor. The second was: the supervisor in the house; he used to look after the children, take them to schools, and if the women—the zenana—had to go anywhere, like to a marriage, or to a public function, these people would also go.

69

The third was: the menial domestic. They were excellent cooks, they did the work of ayahs—taking care of the children, the washing of clothes."

All the big houses in those days, Chenoy explained, were self-contained units. They had their own poultry farms, herds of goats, vegetable gardens . . . all but the cereals, which one purchased in the market, and the hijras, he said, would go and do the shopping.

"The proportion," said Chenoy, "used to be—maybe—seventy to thirty. If you had a hundred servants, seventy would be hijras—in all these categories."

"Really?"

"I'm talking of Hyderabad," said Chenoy. "I'm not talking of any other place . . . Now, what had happened was that the heir apparent, Osman Ali Khan, sent for the hijras because a son was born to him. This was 1908, if I'm not mistaken. And from another Lady—a son was also born to the reigning Nizam, Mahboob Ali Pasha, his father. So Osman Ali sent for the hijras to come and sing and dance and bless the child, because it's considered very lucky, going back to the time of the *Ramayana*, evidently. Now, when the hijras learned that a son had been born to Mahboob Ali Pasha—he was the actual Nizam extant at the time—they all descended on Mahboob Ali's to sing and dance, hoping for larger rewards. And Osman, more or less, then took a vow that when he came on the throne, he was going to break the power of these people."

"Why?"

"Because of the affront," said Chenoy. "The insult. He had sent for them: halfway to his house, they turn around and go to his father's house. So when he came on the throne, he scattered them—he literally broke up their community . . . Otherwise they were a solid block in one part of the city. They had their own customs, their own judicial system, they were never produced in court; if they did anything wrong within their society, it was the 'Council of Sardars'—as they are called—who decided if they were fined, or made to do extra work; they were a township within a city. They had their *own* system . . . So Osman scattered them. And for a number of years—for maybe as many as twenty years—they were in the wilderness. You see, the trend was set by the ruler. Once a ruler sets a trend, then the citizenry follows. Then, the hijras went and apologized—I mean, they literally prostrated themselves before the Nizam and begged forgiveness. And then, he issued a farman, a decree, an order, that, all right, you can come back. But he made it very clear: 'whatever is given to you, you will accept. You will not pressurize any person and *demand*.' "

"He's turning them into beggars?"

"No, not beggars," said Chenoy. "They can go and sing and dance. But they can't demand *more* than what is given to them. That was the penalty that was imposed. Then Osman loosened the shackles in the late 1930s, early 1940s, and they started reviving again . . . Now, their system, as far as I could make out, was that since they were also domestic help, and they were part-time workers—they would find out about a boy in the neighborhood who was physically weak—who had underdeveloped sexual organs—and if he had these signs, they would *induct* that child—take him away and induct him into their society. Otherwise their society would die out."

"How did they come into it before?"

"This is exactly it," said Chenoy. "This was the system. For years. For centuries."

"The villagers, the citizenry," I asked, "would understand that the hijras had a natural right to the child, and there was no dispute over that fact?"

"The child," said Chenoy, "would go and *join* them because he had no place in society. You see, he was reviled if he went to school. They used to make fun of him. They would push him and prod him and tease him. And so he found a place in a society of like people. Now, only once have I attended an initiation ceremony . . ."

I reached for a cigarette.

"Mind if I join you?" asked Chenoy. "I'll tell you why it came about . . . There is a place in Hyderabad—Hijron ka Allawah—which means, 'where they stay.' It is also called Sher ki Maut, the 'hunt tiger.' In the area in which they stay today, you will find on all the walls a tiger, painted in yellow. It will be a vivid yellow—it is *their* color: the color of the Nizams of Hyderabad was yellow, and so, they have also kept that color. In their houses, you'll also find that the walls are a very pale ocher, coming on to yellow: they consider it good luck. Now, what had happened was that I was in the police, and those hijras had a certain problem in their locality."

"They're still all contained?"

"Not really," said Chenoy. "Not in that one area. But they do have one central location—and then, they have other localities also—as in all major cities of India. But this is the most amazing feature of the hijras: they have a central fund, and they will, without fail, pay 20 percent of their earnings to this fund, because this fund, should they fall ill, will take care of their hospitalization and their medical bills—nobody starves in that community! When he becomes old, he goes and stays with the sardar."

" 'Sardar' meaning 'guru'?"

" 'Sardar' meaning 'chief.' The 'head.' "

Prem now called out to us from the dining room.

"Breakfast?" Chenoy shouted. "All right," he said, resigned. Then a smile. "Oh, we're still smoking, Prem, can we have ten minutes?"

This response brought Prem into the living room. "I see you're smoking," said Prem, ironically. "But eggs are getting cold. So you'll have cold eggs then."

Chenoy ignored her. Prem sat down with us.

"Now," continued Chenoy, "these people have a lot of freehold property—the hijras. A lot of their property was deeded to them by the—"

"Nizams?" I asked.

"Not the Nizams," said Chenoy, "but by the noblemen under whom they had served. And what they did was, they gave what is called a makhta. A makhta is a piece of land which is attached, maybe, to their own land holding—it's in perpetuity. Now, that land started becoming valuable— naturally, with this tremendous growth of the city. So the hijras were being pressurized. So the sardar approached me, saying, 'Please do something.' "

Now the cook arrived, announcing breakfast. Again Prem implored us to move.

"Come," she said, warmly. "Finish your cigarettes there."

But nobody moved.

"So I sent my inspector," said Chenoy, "to inquire into the matter. And he came back, reported to me, saying, yes, that certain prominent politicians were interested. And since his level was very low to deal with, I said, All right, I'll deal with it myself. Well, the usual thing that happens in this country is that when a local politician is interested in acquiring land that doesn't belong to him, he starts putting pressure on that chap: the tax collector will go, and the municipal inspector will go, and the sanitary inspector will go, and say, this is not done, you're at fault for this, you have to appear before this tribunal—so the man eventually gets fed up and says, let me get rid of this headache; and he'll sell off that land at a tenth of its value, or 30 percent of its value—whatever. So having known the local politicians who were involved, I sent for them, and said: This is not on. They're defenseless. First, society doesn't accept them, the community doesn't accept them, they have no religion of their own, they can't appeal to any religious body for any help . . . And if you continue to do this, they have no defense whatsoever. I'm their only defense. And I must say, out of respect for me, they said, All right, we won't. Then the head of the society—let me put it down as 'society,' because that's all it is—he approached me, and said, 'Sir, we're holding an initiation ceremony, would you like to attend?' So I said, 'Yes, certainly.' Now, I couldn't use my car; I had to go to a certain place, and then I had to get out of my car and walk. And they took me through such alleys and little byways that I would never have been able to find my way there again. That is *their* defense against the rest of society who want to crash into their ceremonies. And the first thing, after we'd sat down and drinks were served—they don't normally drink, but good liquor was served to me—there were *marriage* ceremonies that took place. They pair them off! They make them into couples: one looks after the house, the other goes and earns."

"So," I said, "the ones we see on the streets are the males?"

"There's no male and female there," said Chenoy. "They're all passives, as far as I can tell, or have been given to understand. Now, in the last three to four years, what I have come to know is that there are some healthy males who take the guise of a hijra because it's easy money for him. He'll go and kick up a shindig at a marriage, or if a child is born in your house, he'll come barging in, take the money from you. He'll clap, like the hijras do—he'll most probably jiggle his bottom for you. Hire a couple of musicians, one with a tabla, one with cymbals, and come and take some money. This has prevailed in all the cities. The healthy male goes on his own. He doesn't join. Now you take a city like Delhi, with a population of what, six and a half million? And there are about what, two thousand hij-ras?"*

"I don't have a figure for Delhi," I said.

"There is a hierarchy," said Chenoy, "amongst the hijras. There's a Council—that's the supreme body that governs them. After that, there are the drones, the workers. The ones who have become too old to work, to fend for themselves—they're the elder statesman. They counsel the younger ones. They show them the ways and means of earning. They meet once a fortnight, or maybe once a month. And instructions are issued to them, as to their behavior. In Hyderabad, they make a conscious effort not to antagonize anybody. Which is not true of the hijras in Delhi. They just don't care a damn."

"In other words," I said, "they show up at a wedding, they are expected to dance and perform—"

"Nobody wants them to dance and perform," said Chenoy. "They just come."

"They come," I said. "They're given the money. They leave."

"No, they want more," said Chenoy.

"In Hyderabad?"

"In Delhi," said Chenoy.

"And in Hyderabad?"

"They come," said Chenoy, "they dance, they sing,

* 15,000 in 1994, quoted in *India Today*

they're given food at the weddings, they eat it, and whatever is paid to them, they take it. If it's meager, they ask for more, but they ask in a *good* way. They don't wheedle, they don't beg. They just say, '*Bhaisa'ab*, you've given just one rupee, it's not worth our effort,' sort of thing."

"No harassment, no violent harassment—"

"No, not violent," said Chenoy. "They might come out with something humorous like, 'This is not sufficient, even for our tea . . . ,' in a nice way. They make you feel a bit small, I've seen this happen, until something more is given, and then, quite satisfied, they leave. Now one other thing I've noticed in Hyderabad was that, if they traveled in buses, the conductor never issued a ticket or asked them for money."

"Why was that?" asked Prem.

"This was a tradition since time immemorial," said Chenoy.

"Like bards they were," said Prem.

"They were low strata," said Chenoy, "of musicians and dancers. So . . . they held marriage ceremonies. There were a number of couples who were married. They were told what their duties were . . . with respect to each other, and how they were expected to behave; what their duties were toward the rest of the society; what their behavior and attitude had to be toward this Council of Ministers, as I would like to put it, and to their chief."

"What does a hijra 'marriage' consist of?" I asked. "Is it a sexual relationship?"

"Nothing of the kind," said Chenoy. "This couple was brought out to the dais on which the sardar was seated, and two of these retired hijras—the elder statesmen—were brought down and introduced to the sardar, who got down and put garlands around them. Then one of these chaps stood up and read out what their duties were going to be. And then they were told they were man and wife."

"And from then on," I asked, "they were addressed as 'he' and 'she'?"

"No 'he' and 'she,' " said Chenoy. "They were just married."

"But how do they address one another?"

" 'Aap,' that's all," said Chenoy. " 'You.' I am using the words *man and wife* because that's the only thing that strikes me for a couple. But: 'You' and 'you' are married. 'He' and 'she' were not mentioned by the sardar. 'You have married you.' "

"What kind of duties," I asked, "did they have toward each other?"

"Toward each other is," said Chenoy, "that the person who earns must be well looked after by the person who does the domestic help. That to treat that person with respect because that person is the earner. That in times of difficulties, that person will be looked after by the other one. And I was told later that their roles were interchangeable. Maybe for three months, one person would be the domestic help, and one the earner, and after three months, the other one would be. And fairly harmonious. You know, they don't have many fights amongst them."

"What kinds of jobs do they do," I asked, "except for their coming to weddings and births?"

"Well," said Chenoy. "They come to your house during parties, they're good cooks. Quite a few of these hijras work in houses as domestic servants."

"What about prostitution?"

"It is there," said Chenoy. "Traditionally—they do go out and—they are pederasts. After all, their sexual enjoyment is that. They're passive recipients."

"But are they doing it for money?" I asked.

"They will do it for money also," said Chenoy. "Mainly for money. They'll hang around on streetcorners. There are amongst, let me say, healthy males, a proclivity towards taking a hijra to bed. So there it is. And especially with this Arab influx in Bombay."

"They must be doing famously," said Prem.

"Oh yes," said Chenoy. "As a matter of fact, I was told by a dear friend of mine that, in a very posh hotel, this Arab and this man . . . He said, 'Look, it's got nothing to do with you. He's my guest. Or she's my guest. Or whatever.' And that was it. So that prostituting themselves is part of it all. It always was. It's traditional . . . But coming back to this: After that, a young boy—must have been about fifteen or so—he was wrapped in a sarong*, and he had a silk kurta put on him, and he was brought, and he was asked whether he wanted to be initiated, and he said, 'Yes.' "

"He was a boy?" I asked.

"A boy," said Chenoy, "but with very weak sexual organs."

"Not really born as a neutral gender," said Prem.

"He was taken around the hall," said Chenoy. "Every hijra present viewed him . . . And he was brought back. Then the people present were asked whether they approved of his being brought into the society. Then they said, Yes— or the approval was given—whether it was unanimous or not, I couldn't gauge, because there was a sizeable crowd there. And then the sardar said, All right, he should be initiated. There was an open space, and they'd brought a wooden platform, on which was fixed a wooden phallus— like a big penis—very thickly oiled. And then the drums started beating, and this boy was taken by two strong

* lungi

hijras, and he was made to sit on this thing, and the tempo of the drums increased, and he was pressed *down* on it, and the boy fainted, and the barber came and just removed his testicles! With one sweep of the razor, they were removed. And then that area was cauterized."

"And they *all* go through it?" I asked.

"I don't know whether they all go through it," Chenoy said. "This is the one and only time I have seen it."

"They *asked* you to come? Is it very open?"

"Yes," said Chenoy. "I mean, it's *not* very open. I suppose I was privileged, let me put it that way. They accorded me a privileged viewing of an initiation ceremony—which they don't do. And this was it. And afterwards, food was served, and everything was normal! But then, my curiosity got the better of me, and after about a month, I said I wanted to meet the sardar. They said, Certainly. And I asked him, 'What happened to that boy?' He said, 'Which boy?' So I said, 'You know, the one who was initiated.' He said, 'He's not a boy anymore. He's a hijra. He's become a member of the society.' And they said, 'He's one of the best earners for the society! He's one of the best dancers! He's got a lovely voice! He sings! He's in great demand! And he's perfectly all right.' "

"Now tell me one thing, Shahpur," said Prem. "Would he, after the removal of his testicles, start having his female glands overtake?"

"I'm afraid I can't answer that," said Chenoy.

"They do get flesh around the hips," I said.

"Yes, they do," said Chenoy. "And on the chest, they become like small female breasts . . . naturally, because there's no testosterone being manufactured. There'll be less growth of body hair . . . and more hair coming on their heads . . . For instance, if I start taking female hormones, I'll start growing my hair too."

"Surely," said Prem, "if that was the way . . . a lot of baldies would do it."

"I'm telling you," said Chenoy, "it's a fact. And then, I asked whether I would be able to meet him. The sardar said, 'Yes, I will send him over to your house.' And I saw this boy. Very happy. He told me that he's fitted in very nicely in the society. He's taken care of. He's amongst his own people. He has no regrets. And that was it . . . And one other thing I want to make a point of: They have no burial ground of their own, the hijras."

"What about Hindu hijras?" asked Prem.

"There is no Hindu and Muslim hijra!" said Chenoy. "They're all buried! There is no religion amongst the hijras. No Muslim goes to a mosque, and no Hindu to a temple."

"But they must," said Prem, "be born to families that are . . ."

"Sure," said Chenoy, "but, after that, there are no religious ties. Their only religion is the society of hijras. They're cast out by their families, they're not accepted. They're outcasts in schools—so they have to band together. So what they do is, they find out if anybody has died, and then, in the early hours of the morning—between one and four—they dig up that grave, and they dump the body there."

"They put it on top of the coffin?" asked Prem.

"Where's the coffin?" said Chenoy. "Is anybody buried in a coffin in India? They just wrap a cloth around them."

"No coffin?" insisted Prem.

"Oh come on, for god's sake," cried Chenoy. "Why do we say *cuffun ka kapra*?"

"I don't know," said Prem. "I only know that the Hindus burn their—"

"Oh come on, Hindus get buried also," said Chenoy.

"No Hindu—" insisted Prem.

"There are sects," said Chenoy, "amongst the Hindus that are buried. As a matter of fact, many years ago, in the police department, we had what was called an 'Inspector for Hijras,' who used to look after their welfare, and see that they were not troubled. And he said that after their death, there's no carrying of the body, there's no bier as such—they walk them, drag them—like a three-legged race—and actually, they have their own methods of secrecy so that it just doesn't matter. The death of a hijra is never known at large . . . And with his death comes the death of my story."

Over eggs and toast, Prem suggested that I go to Hyderabad. Delhi, she said, has become a "soulless" place. Chenoy gave me the name of his younger brother, Naozar, who would be able to take me to the hijra community, he said, because he knew the "old city" very well. There was also a detective, Dherni Dhar Prasad—an "old coot"— who knew these people "through and through." And I should look up his dear friend, Mr. Pavitran, the commissioner of police, who would be able to put me in touch with the detective.

And, dear reader, I'm afraid to admit that I had listened to Chenoy's tale with an Indian mind. It did not occur to me to say, for example, What? You were a police officer, and you didn't make any arrests? A minor involved without consent of his parents? And castration, illegal? All because Chenoy had spoken of a "tradition." And this was why, perhaps, in India, regardless of whether one imposed laws against it, fourteen-year-olds were arranged in marriage, dowries were procured, children worked as indentured laborers in factories and did not attend school.

That evening, I called him: "Why didn't you make any arrests?"

"Why?" asked Chenoy. "There was no complaint, there was consent."

"But he was underage."

"Still, someone has to challenge it, which no one did."

"How would one prosecute, then?" I asked.

"Forcible mutilation," said Chenoy, "would be one way, which falls under aggravated assault—'doing bodily harm with a deadly weapon'—section 326 of the Indian Penal Code."

"Isn't castration illegal?"

"Of course," said Chenoy, "it is a punishable offense. But the authorities don't usually take cognizance of it. And especially where the hijra community is concerned."

"When did this happen?"

"1975."

"Who was the chief guru, or sardar, at the time?"

"I believe his name was . . . Rahman," said Chenoy.

Rahman. The Rahman who had spoken to Harriet Lynton, who had helped paint a fable in which the hijras claimed to castrate themselves, and who had invited Chenoy to an initiation ceremony.

Among the principal eunuchs, there is always one set above the rest who directs and looks after everything that goes on in the mahal. The man holding this office is largely esteemed by the king. He has a large allowance, has charge of the treasury, is master of the wardrobes . . . in short, it is he who has charge of all expenditures . . . The nazir generally has under him other eunuchs, young and old, of which some have access to the mahal, either to carry bulletins or other messages, as the service of the person employing them requires. There are others who are posted at the doors to see who comes in and out of the mahal. They search everything with great care to stop the entry of bhang, wine, ophiom, nutmegs (noix muscades), or other drugs which could intoxicate, for all the women in the mahals love much such beverages. Nor do they permit the entry into the place of radishes, cucumbers, or similar vegetables that I cannot name. When any women come to pay a visit or otherwise, if they are not known they are searched, no respect being paid either to the position or rank of the person. What forces the eunuchs to such strict measures is the continual fear in which they exist that some young man in disguise might enter in female dress. When masons or carpenters, or other workmen are wanted to carry out any job, their names are registered at each gate *they pass through; the descriptive marks on their faces and so forth, are taken down. A paper showing all this is delivered to other eunuchs, who are required to conduct them out in the same way, and to take care that they are the same persons with the same personal marks.*

When the princes . . . have reached the age of five, they are taught to read and write the paternal tongue, which is the Turtan, or the ancient speech of the Turks. After this they are made over to learned men and courteous eunuchs, who bring them up with great strictness, and teach them the liberal and military arts . . . Usually to amuse them they have acted before them many comedies, or their teachers conduct before them legal argumentations, actions of law, or some imbroglio, after which judgments are pronounced. They show them combats and fights . . . The whole with a view to their having, should they ever obtain rank, some knowledge of the world's business.

Niccolo Manucci
Storia do Mogor; or Mogul India,
1653–1708

NINE

Let me say that this is a hybrid book, with a hybrid subject, in a hybrid form, written by a hybrid herself, as indebted to say, John Locke, as to Dimple Kapadia. Now I couldn't just walk into the country, like an arrogant American, and say this was wrong; nor could I say this was right. It existed, and I was a giant ear into the culture, using whatever method I could, wearing whatever dress I wanted, moving through any tense I so desired. Like a chameleon I went, cross-dressing and cross-bordering in time and place.

Now: Chenoy had said that the tradition of eunuchs went back to the *Ramayana*, evidently. So I went back to the *Ramayana*, to the most scholarly translation I could find, but nowhere was there any mention of a eunuch or eunuchs waiting for Ram outside the fabled city of Ayodhya. Instead, Ram was greeted by a warrior and his disciples. So: had the hijras written themselves into this history?

Then there was the *Mahabharata*. The well-regarded van Buitenen translation described Arjun this way, through the eyes of King Virat: "A handsome man, completely endowed / A swarthy youth like an elephant leader/ Who is wearing bright conches set into gold/ And sporting a braid and a pair of earrings." This depiction of his hair and earrings, but not his dress, makes Arjun appear effeminate.

"No man of your stature resembles a eunuch," says King Virat, "in any which way, it seems to me!" Arjun replies: "I sing and dance and make fine music/ I am good at the dance and a master of song . . . / The reason I have this form—what profit/ Is there in recounting it but great pain?/ Brhannadā, sire, is my name, deserted by mother and father as son and daughter." The king has him examined and finds him "not a man." But the name Brhannadā, writes van Buitenen, is a feminine word meaning "having a large reed;" thus it is a joke—Arjun being "well endowed," though seeming effeminate.

The Indian scholar Pratap Chandra Roy, however, translated Arjun's state this way: The women of the court examined him and found that "his impotency was of a permanent nature." The word for "eunuch" used in this context is the Sanskrit "prakrti," apparently meaning a "neuter," "bereft of either a masculine or feminine nature." The two authors suggest, therefore, that Arjun was not a castrated being, but came in the guise of a natural-born eunuch.

The *Laws of Manu*, of the second-century B.C., provided this hint: castration, wrote Manu, was specifically a punishment for adultery, and for the upper castes, an optional one at that: "A man who has violated his guru's marriage bed should declare his error and sleep on a heated iron bed or embrace a red-hot metal cylinder, and by his death he is cleaned. Or he himself may cut off his penis and testicles, hold them in his two cupped hands, and set out towards the southwest region of Ruin. Or, to dispel the crime he should restrain his sensory powers and carry out the 'moon-course' vow for three months, eating food fit for an oblation, or barley-broth." Which one would you choose? Alas, the lower castes had no such choice. There is only one other instance of castration in Manu, involving a lower caste urinating on a member of a higher caste.

But Manu had quite a bit to say about "impotent" men, whom he likened to thieves and atheists, and who were deemed "unworthy of the offerings to the gods and ancestors." And his list of what "impotent" beings were excluded from corresponded exactly to Norman Penzer's citations of "castrated" men in the ancient texts. So: Had the British scholar mistranslated the word, perhaps seeing around him numerous examples of castrated men in late nineteenth-century India?

Interestingly, while Manu had only contempt for the impotent being, he himself descended from a hermaphrodite: the male half of the original Manu mated with the female half, and gave birth to the world of human beings. But just what kind of world were they plunged into? "To protect this whole creation, the lustrous one made separate innate activities for those born of the mouth, arms, thighs, and feet. For the priest [mouth], he ordained teaching and learning . . . For the ruler [arms], protecting his subjects . . . and studying. For the commoner [thighs], protecting his livestock . . . and studying . . . The Lord assigned only one activity to a servant [the feet]: serving the other classes without resentment."

And woe to the one who tried to transcend his caste! Seven incarnations of this and that hell awaited him. Because the caste system functioned in precisely this way: a common humaneness could not be found; one belonged to such and such a caste, of such and such a subcaste, of such and such a trade, of such and such a village. Castism, therefore, exploited difference: you are not of us; we are not of you. In this concept of exclusion lay the paradox of "identity." The hijras, then, had managed to form a "caste" of their own, the caste of "the excluded," and therefore "an identity," though equivalent to the untouchable. Theirs was an anti-caste caste—both an embodiment and criticism of castism itself. But I came from the land of "separate but equal," and though it was only an abstract allegiance in America, it became my citizenship as I traveled through India.

I flew to Bombay and from there took an overnight train to Hyderabad. At Victoria Station, the ticket seller suggested that I choose a "first-class, private, air-conditioned" compartment. When instead I asked for a "second-class, semi-private, non-air-conditioned" compartment, he looked disgruntled. "Then bolt the door, Madam," he said, "and keep your possessions away from the window. People just reach in and take things."

And perhaps it was the result of the nameless official, but my compartment, with four berths, remained empty throughout the ride. A woman traveling alone was a strange thing in India. One veered between the extremes of male protection and lechery. One was jostled, stared at, grinned at, tweaked, called names of movie stars— "Hello Julie!" "Hello Bobbi!" Songs erupted from nowhere, then trailed off into the air. The scooter-walla kept one eye on the road, and one eye on the female, sometimes turning to gaze for whole stretches. In buses, the seats reserved for women were usually where one found the men. Just below the surface, one sensed violence, not sensuality: in a minute, a bus could be burned, a theater razed, a school shut down.

But at last, I was free. I had traveled as a 'we' till now, and even in my mind, as a child, a 'we' as I ran through the land among buffalo and cows, seeking the sweet, forbidden taste of maize, as the woman roasted it on coals, then pressed lemons and spices into it. A 'we' as I ran through the sudden monsoon, delirious and naked on a rooftop. A 'we' as I listened to the crows on the telephone line, connecting the child to all sounds and the senses that are India: the singing woman, with the basket of vegetables on her head; the vendor of used magazines from abroad, as he cycled to each house with his library of outdated treasures; the heavy iron weights that were dropped on a scale in a doorstep, with its pyramids of flour; the wild, wet pigs, as they flooded the gullies, led from behind by a man with a stick. Solitude was unnatural here, and taken in the presence of others. Doors to bedrooms were left open, personal eccentricities tolerated, even indulged; and so, when I had tried to book myself into a hotel in Hyderbad, my uncle had objected, and insisted on calling his friends, Shivi and Rajesh, to put me up there. But hadn't I chosen the hijras in an effort to be free? Here was the paradox, yaar: the 'I' didn't exist.

The train was old-fashioned and coal-driven. I opened the windows to its 100-degree blasts of air. Twelve bottles of bislerie water, warm and tasting of plastic, dozed in the sun. We wound our way through the verdant land, and everywhere was the sight of human labor. Men in light cotton moved with the grace of dancers where buffalo and cows ploughed the earth and drank from ponds of greenish-brown water. I saw the village women moving through the quilted land, in brisk, crooked lines, with trays of food on their heads. They were keeping pace with the train, and would be there when it pulled into the first station. Outside the door, I heard the clamor of the women, their trays given and collected. I had been warned not to touch the food—cholera perhaps, or hepatitis. The Indian sense of time and sickness. Upon rising here, the first question of the day was "how's your tummy?" Medicines of all kinds lay tucked into fruit bowls, with their many-colored aluminum wrappers. One sometimes arranged a whole day around the convenience of a rest-room: "Let's meet at the French restaurant at the Oberoi, because in case you have 'the runs,' the bathroom is just down the hall." I watched from the window as the white sun hit metal, and the women wove their way through the distant hills again.

Hyderabad! The last city on the map of the Mughul Empire, on which the sun had set. Like the old American South it was, as stories unfolded beneath fans, beside petit fours and watermelon juice . . . It had come into being in 1590, I was reading, founded by the Kutb Shahi dynasty of sultans, who were of Turkish origin. They had kept their fort in Golconda. In 1687, the emperor Aurangzeb conquered Golconda, and thereby expanded the boundaries of the Mughul Empire to include the south. In 1724, the new emperor sent a viceroy to the Deccan—as this area was known—to manage his affairs there. He became Asaf Jah I, the first Nizam or king of the new line. But Asaf Jah did not want to compete with the Delhi court, and this caveat was written into the Nizam's laws for all successive generations.

India, then, was a place of competing interests between the British East India Company, the French, the Portuguese, the Hindu Rajputs and Marathas, and the Mughuls, who had lost all real power with the death of Bahadur Shah I in 1712, though they retained the myth of empire till 1857. The Nizam's rule was essentially a compromise between French, then British forces.

The British had gained control over the centuries by wresting land from each warring group, in exchange for protection. This, at first, had meant survival for the Indian states, and the power to place troops within them. As the British East India Company grew—originally a group of private merchants interested in trading clothes, saltpeter, silks, pepper, yarn, and indigo—a board of directors was established in Britain, and eventually won parliamentary power; it had become cheaper, in effect, for the British to annex India than to continue its administration through the private mercantile sphere. In the 1600s Britain had gained economic power; in the 1700s, administrative; and by 1850, "moral" authority. Britain stepped in as colonizer in 1858, after the Indian Mutiny. The official written language had been Persian, but it was replaced with English.

There were seven Nizams until 1948, when India marched in to reclaim Hyderabad after Independence. (There had been 562 princely states, all with varying degrees of autonomy.) The main language of the state of Andhra Pradesh (the capital of which was Hyderabad) was Telugu, but the elite had spoken Urdu. The city prided itself on good Hindu-Muslim relations. There had been three categories of nobles: those of the Nizam's dynasty; the second tier, the paigas, who had troops under the Nizam; and the 'umara-nizam'—the premier nobles—those families who ruled Hyderabad, collected revenue, and were also allowed to keep soldiers.

I slept unsurely, in the growing heat, half imagining that someone would grab my feet through the window. In the morning, I saw the village women again approach the train, and this time I could not refuse. I asked the conductor for a plate of whatever smell-less dish had been prepared: south Indian lentils, a *dosa*—or pancake—with potatoes, covered with large pieces of black soot, which I scraped off with a knife.

The train pulled in on time. I made my way through beggars, reunited families, shouting porters, banana sellers, and hands reaching for my bags, wondering how I would recognize Shivi. A small woman near the taxi stand outside looked at me hopefully. She crossed the street and said, laughing, "I told your uncle, how will I find her in all that? But you look just like your mother."

Hyderabad was hot, dusty, mosquito-filled. In the taxi, Shivi said something about not being able to use the car— "Rajesh doesn't even give me money to do things." Along the way, she pointed out the five-star Banjara Hotel: it had once been a palace of the Nizams, one could get excellent kebabs there, and also take a swim.

Shivi and Rajesh lived in the elite, rustic Banjara Hills, a suburb which had been built in the 1930s and was far from the center of town. Reddish boulders were scattered along the roads, and tribal women, the Lambari, with their bright green and orange skirts and blouses, heavy silver jewelry, and long, open hair, could be seen roaming the streets.

The house was a rambling, whitish affair, with a neglected look, on a large, parched lawn. A slightly bullying man, with a round face, in a kurta, came out to greet us: Rajesh. As Shivi told him the story of how she had found me, in an ebullient way, he stared at her as though she were a total stranger.

I called Naozar Chenoy straight away, and said that I had met his brother in Delhi, who suggested that I contact him. Tomorrow was the Parsi New Year, said Naozar, the whole clan was celebrating, why didn't I drop in then?

How I longed for a bath! And only in India was I aware of the luxury of such a thing. Because one could see the origin, the process, of almost everything here; the geyser had to be turned on, and the cold water warmed, and the red light waited for, and then there had to be that staggering between two people's baths, because there was just so much hot water in the tank, and no more; and so one censured even as one bathed, lest one be confronted with a head full of suds, and by now, no more even warm water

left; and so, one weighed all this, and took on the needs of
the household, and its sense of pacing for the day; and
there it was, always a negotiation, even silent, with others—an "extendedness" even in solitude.

The next day, I hailed a scooter and made my way to the
wide, tree-lined streets of Secunderabad, the English cantonment area where the Chenoys lived. The driver felt compelled to dare every oncoming truck; he tweeted wildly
with his little horn for right of way, to the stunned bassoon
of the truck; and turned off the engine at the top of every
hill, so as not to waste the petrol, yaar, as we silently
coasted down.

Many cars were parked outside the estate, where Naozar
was putting someone into a taxi; a thin man, in his forties,
a bit ill at ease. He led me inside to where about twenty-five
strong-boned men in suits and kurtas, and tall women in
white saris, were speaking in educated, anglicized accents.
I was asked how Shahpur was; "Well," I told the elegant
lady who was his mother, white-haired, and as vital as
though she were twenty. You can recognize almost anyone
in India by their bone structure, an Indian architect once
told me: you'll immediately know the whole "clan." Mrs.
Chenoy Senior looked just like her son, Shahpur: as regal,
as direct.

I took a plate of food, and stood apart from everyone,
sensing that I had intruded upon a private ritual. Soon
Mrs. Chenoy returned, followed by Naozar, who hovered
nearby. Turning to Naozar, I said, "I've come to study the
hijras"—as Naozar's eyes flitted here and there—"and your
brother said you could take me to them." Naozar suddenly
focused. The eyes grew wide. He put his plate down, and
now I was being led to the door, with a hand on my elbow.

"You," he said. "Go. Just go. There's a scooter parked out-side. Take it." *Tum jao*, he said, in that rude Hindi.

Now, an elder had just told a junior to go, but I didn't turn around and say something American, because there was that Indian grace to consider, na, that turn the other cheek, rise above it. But gradually it dawned on me why I was being ushered out: Somehow, I had implied that Naozar had inti-mate dealings with the hijra community; and not only did I know this, I had announced it to his *mother*; in fact, it was such common knowledge that even his brother had fla-grantly suggested that he could lead me there!

I headed for the Banjara Hotel, because there I could sit by the pool, eat kebabs, and be anonymous—and not have to care what others were thinking at all. But I didn't have a bathing suit, so I went to a nearby shop to find one. The best I could do was an absurdly assembled one-piece; somehow the bottom half separated from the top at the waist, in the front only, for no reason I could imagine, ex-cept maybe peeping. It was made of terry cloth, and had large pads in the breast area, which could not easily be re-moved. This assembly went from impractical to lamentable in a pool; for upon emerging, the bottom drooped, and one hand had to be kept on the two parts that separated to avoid exposure, while the other had to prop up the cement-like bricks that had fallen from each breast, now, with no hope of readjustment, in the broad light of day. In spite of this, or because of it, the men around the pool, behind newspapers and sunglasses, scraped around in their metal chairs hoping to catch a better view.

I called Shivi and told her I was going to the Salar Jung Museum to bury myself in books. What were my dinner plans, she asked. "Rajesh wants to take you to his lady friend's," she said. I didn't know how to respond. "What are *you* doing tonight?" I asked. Shivi had no idea, she said, because the cook hadn't shown up. So I suggested that we meet up at the Banjara later, and postpone Rajesh's dinner.

I took a scooter to the museum, named for a nobleman who had deeded his library and artwork to the city. After being checked for weapons at the door, I was directed upstairs to the librarian who spoke English. The room he inhabited was vast, surrounded by stall after stall of glass-enclosed books. A small man asked me to sit at his desk, and brought in a cup of tea. Soon he wrote a note in pen to be delivered to the Urdu-speaking librarian, on this question of the hijras' history, the "kwaja saras," as they were known. Meanwhile, what was my good name? Where did I hail from? Never in all his years had he had a request about the eunuchs. Had I read Harriet Lynton's book? Then he placed two calls to the other libraries; please to look under "hijras" and "eunuchs," he said to them. In the evening, he said, he would meet with the society of librarians, and would check with them. Another American lady had come once, he said, and she had given him such a lovely soap. We waited. In the meantime, would I like to look at *Pictorial Hyderabad*? There might be some eunuchs featured in this large photographical tome about the Nizam's dominions.

He took me to an empty room, to a table, where two books, smelling of mothballs, were brought out by a thinly clad helper. "Come back to me in an hour," he said. I leafed through the double-volume set. I could find nothing but a roster of famous Hyderabadi personalities. Salar Jung. Mahboob Ali Pasha. Osman Ali Khan. Maharaj Krishan Prasad. Commissioner Reddy. At five, I found the head librarian again. Nothing on his end, either. The Urdu-speaking librarian had a good memory, but he couldn't remember seeing anything about the *kwaja saras*. He was familiar with the Nizam's private papers too; nothing there. Not to give up, though. Call him tomorrow. Next time, I would remember to bring a soap.

At the Banjara Hotel, I found Shivi in the shade by the pool, sipping a Kingfisher beer. She had been busy since we last spoke, she said. She'd made arrangements for us to have tea with her friend Meraj Pasha, a noble woman, who might know something about the hijras. Then there was a Mathur uncle, thrice-removed, who'd heard from my uncle in Delhi that I was in town.

"Have you heard of a Mr. Pavitran?" I asked.

"Oh yes," said Shivi. "Why?"

"I'm supposed to call him."

"Oh," she laughed, "I don't think you'll be able to meet him about this. Everybody wants to meet him. He's the most sought-after dinner guest. And, these days, he's the talk of the town. He's front-page news, because of the court case."

Pavitran, it seemed, was being investigated for fraud and had been suspended as Police Commissioner. The court case involved Mr. Pavitran's use of allegedly illegal funds to invest in property. But Shivi—with many Hyderabadis—felt sure that it was a "political" case to oust him; besides, Shivi said, he had independent means, why would he allow himself to be bribed? In fact, it was obvious that he was not corrupt; he had stood up to political pressure by opponents, and that was why they now wanted him out. How had Pavitran met this fate? By being instrumental in the changing of the road patterns in Hyderabad, siding with those who had fought for them, so challenging the status quo, the corrupt ministers in government, who were in the pockets of realtors and developers. The man himself was clean, Shivi said, in itself a rarity. So the consensus was that he had been framed.

The daughter of emperor Shah Jahan, wrote Bernier, *"although confined to the seraglio, and guarded like other women, received the visits of a young man of no exalted consequence, but of agreeable person . . . Shah Jahan was apprised of her guilt, and resolved to enter her apartments at an unusual and unexpected hour. The intimation of his approach was too sudden to allow her the choice of more than one place of concealment. The affrighted gallant sought refuge in the capacious cauldron used for the bath. The king's countenance denoted neither surprise nor displeasure; he discoursed with his daughter on ordinary topics, but finished the conversation by observing that the state of her skin indicated a neglect of her customary ablutions, and that it was proper she should bathe. He then commanded the eunuchs to light a fire under the cauldron, and did not retire until they gave him to understand that the wretched victim was no more."*

A generation later, the lovers of Aurangzeb's daughter met a similar fate: *"Rauchenara Begum, after having for several days enjoyed the company of one of these young men, whom she kept hidden, committed him to the care of her female attendants, who promised to conduct their charge out of the seraglio under cover of night. But whether they were detected, or only dreaded a discovery,*

*or whatever else the reason, the women fled, and left the
terrified youth to wander alone about the gardens. Here he
was found and taken before Aurangzeb; who, when he had
interrogated him very closely, without being able to draw
any other confession of guilt from him other than that he
had scaled the walls, decided that he should be compelled
to leave the seraglio in the same manner. But the eunuchs,
it is probable, exceeded their master's instructions, for they
threw the culprit from the top of the wall to the bottom . . .
Aurangzeb determined, however, to inflict a severe and ex-
emplary punishment upon the eunuchs; because it was essential, not only to the honour of his house, but even to his
personal safety, that the entrance into the seraglio should
be vigilantly guarded."* Wrote Bernier of Aurangzeb, *"It
seems . . . to be the general opinion that he cannot long escape the power and the malice of the eunuchs."*

> François Bernier
> Travels in the Mogul Empire
> 1656–68

TEN

I HIRED A DRIVER through Rajesh's company. He came first thing in the morning, in a chocolate-colored Ambassador. His name was Ramzan. He was twenty-three years old and gentle by nature. He read Urdu detective novels in his free time, stayed away from gossip, and listened to classical music on the tape deck he had installed in his car. He owned the car, he said proudly. And he bathed that car with such love, one would have thought it was a newborn. Ramzan was a Shi'a, and always washed his feet before he got into it.

And, for some reason, he knew where everyone lived. So we were finally on our way to the Hijron ka Allawah. We took the inner road through the cantonment area, with its wide streets, where the British resident had lived, crossed the bridge along the Musi River, and entered Hyderabad proper, that part of the city that had been built in the sixteenth century by the Kutb Shahi kings.

With Ramzan's expert hands, we wove through the old Char Minar section, its bulls and carts, mourners on foot, and cyclists, with whole families on the crossbars; around two-wheeled scooters, three-wheeled scooters, and urinators; behind spitters, men calmly washing, and marriage processions; through the heart of the red chile district, where the wind hurt one's eyes; and into the crowded bazaars of gaudy shalwar kameezes and brass lamps, past Char Minar itself, a beautiful structure meaning "Four Minarets," which was built in 1591.

The Hijron ka Allawah—which meant "Mansion of Hijras" or "Hijra Palace"—was a large off-white building in the bustle of things, but on a corner, and set apart. Two steps led to a canvas-colored curtain; the large wooden doors were pushed open, telling a different story from the hijras of Delhi.

We climbed the steps, and pulled the curtain aside. Our eyes met a squatting hijra, drawing water from the center of the courtyard, in a shaft of sudden, soft light. The feeling was pious, orderly, serene. The hijra, young and bunned, and wearing a bright flowered sari, with a hibiscus in her hair, rose to greet us. With a smile, she asked us in. We explained that we wished to speak to her guru. She gently pointed behind her with a wrist that revealed a large, metal, masculine watch. In the distance, two elderly eunuchs sat on a kind of raised area. The courtyard gave on to many rooms. It was very clean, and from this view, reminiscent of a monastery—pillows here, the water jug there, the framed pictures—just so. A few mahogany doors, carved and bolted.

"Come in, come in," the voice of an elder bellowed in the background.

"So nice," said Shivi, referring to the neatness of the place.

The elder eunuch beckoned us toward him. And I use the masculine here, because his voice struck me this way, but as I drew closer, I noticed the white cotton shirt through which one could see the protrusion of small breasts: braless, the hijra sat cross-legged in an off-white petticoat, from which hung keys, around the rim; her hair was gray and pulled back in a braid. She was about seventy years old, smoked a filterless cigarette, and her face was wide and pocked.

Beside her sat another hijra, with bunned silver hair; she had an ancient, lined face, and her gaze was steady and silent. While the first smiled, and asked us to sit down, the other, like a shadow, reflected nothing back. In my mind at that moment, the first was in color, the second, in black and white. And though the large one was speaking, my eye was distracted, kept finding the second. She had a quality of stillness: and that wizened face spoke of an immense sadness without words.

Shivi namaskared them, and we sat down, cross-legged on a red, cardboard mat. Now the water-drawing hijra came and sat below us, on the step that led to the raised platform. A fourth, young and plump, covered her head with her light blue sari, and sat a little apart, cleaning rice in a metal dustpan, slowly, rhythmically, rolling it for stones. A fifth, stony-faced and suspicious, stood in the doorway to the gulley. She was about fifty years old.

All were listening as Shivi explained that I was from America, was "curious" about the hijras, wanted to know how they lived. The speaker laughed. "We're not that interesting, ma," she said. Shivi continued, immediately putting them at ease with her light, equal banter. Shahpur Chenoy had said that I must meet them, did they know him? No, ma, said Elder Number One, but she had heard him spoken of. Where were we staying? Oh, yes, Banjara Hills. We were the guests of the hijras; already they were hosts.

"Who is she?" I asked, indicating the silent one who sat beside the speaker.

"He is my chela," said the elder. "I am his guru."

Now she nodded toward the others, releasing them to speak. The guru was Kamal Baksh. The one who had drawn the water was Rani Baksh. The one cleaning rice, Kiran Baksh. The ancient face, Sayeed Baksh. The one hesitating in the doorway, Munni Baksh. "Baksh," said Kamal, was the "family" name. It had been handed down. "Rani," "Kamal," and "Munni" were feminine—Kamal meant "lotus." "Kiran"—"ray of the sun"—was ambiguous. Sayeed was masculine.

We sat there for some time, all family-family, getting used to one another. Kamal Baksh asked us, would we take sugarcane juice? Tea? Coffee? Coke? Kiran would go and fetch it. I asked for Coke; Shivi and Kamal opted for sugarcane juice. Did Shivi know such and such a family in Banjara Hills? Yes, she did. Wasn't it sad that the estate had passed into the hands of a corrupt lawyer? So sad, said Shivi. So, is this girl married? Kamal Baksh asked about me. No, said Shivi, they do things differently in America. Oh, but surely she could fix it up, said Kamal Baksh. She would try, said Shivi. Yes, dear reader, the eunuchs were actually trying to arrange my marriage—they, to whom progeny would never be possible—and utterly without irony.

And the conversation went on like this, one mother-in-law key-chain-hung-on-hip to another. Shivi and Kamal Baksh had bonded as Indians, chatting mischievously about the American; odd, it seemed to the hijra, that I had come to study them. Odd, indeed, Shivi was agreeing. But in that strange separation—a "we" and a "they"—lay my paradoxical ability to speak openly to them. And so, shall I say, I acted up the American, in the role they had assigned me, though I had come prepared to be quite Indian, and launched immediately into a few questions, like an aggressive foreign journalist. The procedure was that I passed along the question to Shivi in English; she passed it to Kamal Baksh in Hindi; Kamal Baksh answered in that strange Urdu-Hindi dialect of the hijras; and along the way, Shivi chatted about this and that because something caught her fancy, until I insisted on a translation. The method put the hijras at their ease, because I, not they, was the outsider.

"Where are you from?" I asked Kamal Baksh, sensing it wrong not to begin with her.

"I was born here, in Begum Bazaar," said Kamal Baksh, referring to herself as female.

"How many children were in your family?"

"Nine brothers and sisters," said Kamal Baksh. "When I was small, I used to walk and talk like a woman. I used to wear female clothes. So they used to beat me. They said, 'Why do you do this? It is embarrassing to us.' "

"When did you come here?"

"When I was sixteen," said Kamal Baksh. "Twelve, sixteen, that was the age. Since childhood we used to play with boys . . . Then we became big. We hijras used to hold hands and go about . . . Sometimes we got sick. Then where to go, but to these people? They said, 'This is a bad way to live . . . work and live with honor.' They lent me five and twenty-five rupees and made me well. So I stayed on with them."

"You came to this house?"

"I came to this house," said Kamal Baksh. "They spent the money and got a doctor. See, a child can't be made here. Here you can't have babies. No man is allowed here. Only women live here."

"See," explained Shivi, "she used to do prostitution, and then she got what you call V.D. So these people, the hijras, said, 'Don't do that—live beautifully.' They treated her affectionately."

Now, this speech was beginning to sound suspiciously like the allegorical narrative in Lynton and Reddy's book. But what to do, na, this is what she said. And who was I to judge? Perhaps what Kamal Baksh was saying was also true.

"How did your parents feel about this?" I asked, in a truly American way.

"They used to hit me and curse me!" said Kamal Baksh, her voice rising. "Since childhood they used to beat me! My brother also used to beat me! My sister too! They used to call me 'hijra'! But what could I do, since I *was* like that? Now, my real sister comes and goes from here . . . the progeny of one mother and one father! Sometimes she comes and asks for money."

"You help her?"

"I give her eight, ten rupees," said Kamal Baksh, "and two saris."

"Yeah," said Sayeed Baksh, in a Maharashtrian actor's voice, the hijra voice. "The sister's poor and has children."

"The child of my sister," said Kamal Baksh, "is a servant; he's a polisher—he's just got a job. Now, why should she come? Her son has a job!"

"Do you ever see your parents?" asked Shivi.

"Ma, for nine months she carried me!" said Kamal Baksh, now yelling. "But she died. My older brother died. So I went to them under those circumstances. My older brother—the spirit caught him. I didn't know. My sister came and told me. So I went on the train. They all knew where I was. They took it well that I have become like this. But I didn't go to them, it would have been too embarrassing. My mother used to come here. After all, she carried me for nine months."

"And your father?" I asked.

"He died during my childhood," said Kamal Baksh.

"What did your parents do?" Shivi asked.

"My mother," said Kamal Baksh, "used to work as a laborer, cleaning dung and making dung patties. My older brother was a carpenter. They don't eat out of my hand . . . Ma, they treated me well here. I couldn't have been as happy in my own home as I was here. They taught me. It's like this, ma: we ask the subway walla, we ask the children, we ask the police, we ask the sweepers, we ask the scooter wallas, is there a child born? Is there a wedding? Then we go and make a 'nishan.' We mark the house. Then we ask, when shall we come?"

When Kamal Baksh spoke of her relatives not eating of her hand, she was referring to an old Hindu "law" about untouchables, placing her lower in the caste system than even those who handled dung.

"Are you Hindu?" I asked.

"Yes, yes, Hindu," said Kamal Baksh. "My brother's children come, because I never go to their houses. One of my brothers comes and says hello."

"How many hijras," I asked, "were here when you joined?"

"All the old people were here," said Kamal Baksh. "About five or six hundred. Now they're all dead."

"In this house alone?" asked Shivi.

"No," said Kamal Baksh. "In this whole neighborhood. When I joined, there were fifty or sixty people in this house alone. That whole neighborhood used to be ours. You know, where the High Court is?"

She was referring to the princely, domed, government building on Zoo Road, about a quarter of a mile away.

"Those areas where the road is," said Kamal Baksh, "were all hijras houses. Then the government paid the hijras there to leave, because they wanted to build on the land. See—before the High Court was built, this whole neighborhood was ours."

"Where are the other hijras?" asked Shivi.

"A lot have gone to Ajmer," said Kamal Baksh, "to the

festival. In Ajmer, there used to be a *kwaja sa'ab*, a Muslim
saint, and his tomb is there. All of Hindustan's [India's] hijras go there."

"To do what?" asked Shivi.

"It's like this, ma," said Kamal Baksh, her voice rising
again. "To pay homage to the Muslim saint, and for fights:
all good and bad talk, all quarreling, all this is shared and
resolved there. It's this way, ma: In our community, all the
'children' go there. All the family friends that you have, na?
They all surface, they all talk it out over there. Fines are
paid. All the bigwigs go. *All go.* From Hindustan, from
Pakistan, having their passports made . . ."

When Kamal Baksh said "children," she was referring to
the younger generation of hijras, the disciples.

"From the whole of India?" asked Shivi. "Can you say
how many?"

"How can I tell?" said Kamal Baksh. "Many have
sprung up, like worms! . . . More than we ever imagined!
They're all over the place. All the people from Madras have
filled up Bombay!"

Strange, this somewhat contemptuous language to refer
to the "children" of the community, betraying a deep ambivalence.

"But I thought you worshipped a Hindu goddess," I said.

"Yes," explained Kamal Baksh. "We follow the mother
of Murghi Mata . . . Besraji . . . the Hindu goddess . . . the
mother hen. This goddess is from Ahmedabad, in Gujarat.
From Mahemdabad."

"From Sankhalpur," corrected Sayeed Baksh.

"Do we have a portrait, Kiran?" asked Kamal Baksh.
"Eh, Kiran!"

No reply.

But Kiran Baksh was somewhere in the neighborhood
getting drinks. So Sayeed took the keys from Kamal Baksh

and unlocked a door, just off the main audience hall, and brought us a portrait of Besraji—Bahuchara Mata. A woman riding a hen, in a real silver frame.

"She's an incarnation of Saraswati?" asked Shivi.

"Yes, ma," said Kamal Baksh. "We don't distinguish between Hindu and Muslim deities. All castes are represented here. Hindu and Muslims alike."

"What do you celebrate in the house?" I asked.

"We don't," said Kamal Baksh. "There used to be an occasion—Basant Panchami—when the whole family got together. But we don't celebrate it any longer because there's been a split in the family—a bit of a rift. It used to happen one month before Holi. Now, you know the flower of the mango? They make garlands out of those flowers and then people wear them? The pitcher is filled with water, and they put the garland into these pitchers; they cover it with a spice-soaked scarf and then, with ginger and slivers of sugarcane stalk, they make a strand, and they put the 'Mata'—the goddess—on top of it. Having installed it, they tie the cane slivers together, and the hijras sing, and dancing, dancing, come up to the door—the 'gulal' in one hand, the ginger in another. But now, there's been a split, no? Our family used to do it all together. Muslims and Hindus both."

"And you celebrate Holi?" I asked, speaking of the bacchanalian spring rite, the only day in the year in which any member of any caste or class could throw colored water and powder at each other.

"Yes, with dholaks," said Kamal Baksh, referring to the traditional oblong drum the hijras played, "in what is called 'Jena Rung Raja.'"

"You mean the home of Maharajah Kishen Pershad," said Shivi, "the sixth Nizam's prime minister?"

"I mean his sons only," said Kamal Baksh. "Their place is in Banjara Hills, where their lawyer was."

Kiran had arrived with the refreshments. These she placed soundlessly before us. Kamal Baksh sensed my hesitation.

"No, drink up, everybody!" said Kamal Baksh. "Everything here is our own food, and everyone's food that's good food is our food! To us, there's no big or small. Now, there's this 'chowdhry' in our community who lives here, the head of our clan . . . If there's anything wrong, he comes and sits down and resolves the issue. Now, they call me 'chowdhry.' Well, there might be some who would be scared to ask *me* questions! For a fee, I say, 'You are younger, you shouldn't have said that, shouldn't have spoken back to your elders'—I charge them five, ten rupees—to resolve disputes."

"Are there 'good' and 'bad' families among you?" I asked.

"Whatever families there might be," said Kamal Baksh, "if the Badshah's children come, then we'll have to consider them big, big people, and us, small, small people—the Badshah's people, don't they raise their people up on cable chairs? They're *not* raised up on cable chairs, and *we* don't cower in the gullies . . . So to everyone, the same . . . But four put together, whomever they make big . . . See now, the way I'm sitting, whether I sit here or not, in this palatial position, but everyone else assumes that I'm still *the great one*. I'm not even sitting in the sacred area, but everyone else leaves that space alone."

When Kamal Baksh spoke of the Badshah, she was referring to the oldest family or "lineage" of hijras in Delhi, perhaps a part of the emperor's entourage, associated somehow with the courts under Shah Jahan. She was also indicating a sacred "space," to the left of where we sat, a closed door. By "four put together," she meant a system of appointment—whereby she, Kamal Baksh, had been made 'chowdhry,' or juridical head.

"Listen," said Shivi, "she means, are there some in your community who have a bad character?"

"There are some," said Kamal Baksh, "but such people we don't keep."

"What constitutes 'badness'?" I asked.

"Yes," said Kamal Baksh, "we don't keep them. If they obeyed us, they would be close to our hearts. They would listen to us, and we would listen to them. Since they *don't* want to keep our ways, then that's okay."

"Let them do what they want," said Shivi.

"Let them do what they want," said Kamal Baksh.

"They disown them," explained Shivi, "if they don't listen to them."

"What's a 'zenana'?" I asked.

"Who told you about this?" Kamal Baksh laughed. "Listen: zenanas are different; and hijras are different. We are all hijras. Wherever a child is born, we go and sing and dance; if you say 'zenana,' that means 'singing.' If there's a birth, and if it's a girl, then after giving money, they call the zenana to sing. Twenty-five, thirty, forty rupees for zenanas. But where are they now? They're all finished! They're all washed up! There's not even one . . . There used to be quite a few in Hyderabad, there used to be quite a few in Hindustan. Now they're all through. They stay separate from us. They have a different way of doing things. In every neighborhood, they used to have their strongholds . . . So people used to know, and ask them for their services."

Now, one thing about Kamal Baksh: When she spoke, her words took on the peculiar rhythm of the eunuchs, a lilting rise and fall in the pattern of words that issued from her lips. This cadence was oddly mechanical, and in a softer voice, might have seemed like a hypnotic drug; but in Kamal Baksh, whose voice was loud and low, it became an irritating sawing—whole forests of living things were

felled in three sentences—and should you press a little further, for clarity, say, or the truth, the voice became unbear-
able, those same sentences uttered as though screaming to
a half-dead ox: clear the room, you thought, everybody
take cover. Was this the notorious ferocity of the eunuch?
No, it was just pure volume. She bullied, but was not
wily; she bullied, but did not seduce. The voice of Kamal
Baksh—guru, sardar, chief, madam, father, mother—denoted endurance, a stubbornness even, but was without
malice. Meanwhile, it was her oldest chela's eyes which followed, laughed, commented, were suddenly resigned . . .
whose voice, with its low, melodious sadness, told of an
ambivalent life . . . great wryness was there, and subtlety.

"They don't dance?" asked Shivi, trying to understand.

"They also dance," said Kamal Baksh.

"What makes hijras and zenanas different?" I persisted.

"The zenanas are different," repeated Kamal Baksh,
"and we hijras are different."

Silence.

"They have free will!" said Sayeed Baksh, suddenly.

"Tell us!" said Shivi.

"At their place," said Sayeed Baksh, "drinking . . . eating."

"Not at *our* place," said Kamal Baksh.

"She means," said Shivi, "they live like *prostitutes*. They
have all sorts of fun. Here it is not like that. I've been asking ten times, I don't know why you're not saying it."

"If we say it," laughed Kamal Baksh, "then you'll think
badly of us. We usually don't mix. But if we don't have
enough people, then we ask the zenanas to come and sing
with us. We split the money. Their houses are in the market. And they drink liquor. Not in our place."

"That's why we didn't bring a man in here," said Shivi.
"She wants to know this. That's why she dragged me here."

"Yes, yes," said Kamal Baksh, "but since she's come, even *her* ways we don't understand. If you hadn't come, we wouldn't have said. There are many in America, also?"

"Yes," said Shivi. "But their way of doing things is different."

"They stroll in the evening," laughed Kamal Baksh. "They go for a drama . . ."

But just as we were digressing, in came a young woman, followed by a young man. They seemed surprised by us. The woman politely said hello. The man hesitated in the doorway. They were her tenants, Kamal Baksh explained. The woman asked for something. Kamal Baksh rummaged through a pouch around her waist.

"All the property is in my name," said Kamal Baksh. "They made me 'big' because they knew I wouldn't sell it. I advise everyone. They also come here for medicine for jaundice."

When the tenant left, I asked Kamal Baksh if they would object to being photographed. No, she replied, though she didn't allow "the children" to be in films. She called Rani, who was washing her feet by the well, and Kiran, but I encouraged them to remain as they were. Only Munni seemed put out, and shook her head at me through the lens. I managed to get a shot of her standing in the doorway.

Shivi suggested that we leave because they seemed tired. When could we return?

"Day after tomorrow," said Kamal Baksh, "because tomorrow, we have a court case."

I offered to pay them for their time. No, insisted Kamal Baksh. How about a little makeup? No, she did not allow the youngers to wear it.

"Were you once nannies and cooks in some of the big houses of Hyderabad?" I asked.

"This is our only work," said Kamal Baksh. "To sing and dance at weddings, and if a child is born. Only the zenanas go to work in the houses. It's this way: I was born like a son, but we are like women. We behave like women. So we can go anywhere, people trust us."

"It seems the zenanas," said Shivi to me, "are not a very nice clan."

"Yes," I said in English, "but how is it that the zenanas—not the hijras—were hired in the homes?"

"Weren't there many of you," asked Shivi, "in the harems of the Nizam, and royal families?"

"Those weren't hijras," said Kamal Baksh. "They were zenanas. Sometimes, when big ladies were married, they used to call one from our house, to make the ladies laugh."

Yet the zenanas were transvestites—not castrated. So how could they be the ones who were trusted in the harems?

"So the eunuchs of the zenana—" I insisted.

"No, not us," said Kamal Baksh.

"But the zenanas aren't operated on," said Shivi, avoiding the word "castration."

"No, not us," said Kamal Baksh.

"Don't you have an operation?" I asked.

"No," said Kamal Baksh. "We don't operate here."

"You aren't cut?" asked Shivi.

"No," said Kamal Baksh. "But women are safe with us."

Was the Pope Catholic, na? Kamal Baksh was denying castration. The mere mention of the word "operation" sent her into denial. Perhaps this was in keeping with her rightist codes. She was refusing to admit the very fact that gave her a claim to the hijra identity.

"In the period of the Mughul kings," I said, using the lingo, "those men were operated on."

"Those people were zenanas," insisted Kamal Baksh. And her disciple's face offered no dispute.

~

Aurangzeb is very sensible that the cause of the misery which afflicts the empires of Asia, of their misrule, and consequent decay, should be sought, and will be found, in the deficient and pernicious mode of instructing the children of their Kings. Instructed from infancy to the care of women and eunuchs, slaves from Russia, Circassia, Mingrelia, Gurgistan [Georgia], or Ethiopia, whose minds are debased by the very nature of their occupation; servile and mean to superiors, proud and oppressive to dependents;—these Princes, when called to the throne, leave the walls of the Seraglio quite ignorant of the duties imposed upon them by their new situation. They appear on the stage of life, as if they came from another world, or emerged, for the first time, from a subterraneous cavern, astonished, like simpletons, at all around them. Either, like children, they are credulous of everything, and in dread of everything; or, with the obstinacy and heedlessness of folly, they are deaf to every sage counsel, and rash in every stupid enterprise . . . In a word, the Kings of Asia are constantly living in the indulgence of monstrous vices . . . It is indeed a rare exception when the Sovereign is not profoundly ignorant of the political and domestic condition of his empire. The reins of government are often committed to the hands of some Vizier, who, that he may reign lord absolute, with *security and without contradiction, considers it an essential part of his plan to encourage his master in all his low pursuits, and divert him from every avenue of knowledge. If the sceptre be not grasped by the first minister, then the country is governed by the King's mother, originally a wretched slave, and by a set of eunuchs, persons who possess no enlarged and liberal views of policy, and who employ their time in barbarous intrigues; banishing, imprisoning, and strangling each other, and frequently the Grandees and the Vizier Himself. Indeed, under their disgraceful domination, no man of any property is sure of his life for a single day.*

François Bernier
Travels in the Mogul Empire
1656–68

ELEVEN

MERAJ PASHA KHAN LIVED in Banjara Hills. She gave the impression of listlessness, explaining that she may have to sell the house, it was too expensive to keep, to maintain. This was the plight of many aristocrats in Hyderabad. Meraj had married young—yes, it had been arranged, but she was widowed at the age of thirty-five. She had loved her husband, she said, and had never remarried. She had loved her past, and was, in many ways, reluctant to part with it. A gentle spirit, she harbored within her a brooding, nameless injury. It did not prevent her, though, from rising to the occasion of tea, serving exquisite kebabs and petits fours, brought out by a servant on a trolley, and covered with a mosquito net. Perhaps in this way—graciousness—she kept a little of the life she had known. Softly she spoke to her many servants, and softly she greeted us, as though roused from a nap. Meraj pointed to a portrait of her son—"I used to paint, you know, I used to be quite good . . ." and her words trailed off into that once-sure place of her youth. We sat below the fan, set to a slow dial of three.

"You know," said Meraj, "the other day I was reading in a magazine—a man changing into a woman. Ha? Now how is that, I just don't know."

"What do you know about the hijras?" I asked.

"I just don't know much," said Meraj.

"Do you remember them," I asked, "as coming and performing for you?"

"Oh yes," said Meraj. "Even now, they come to your house, singing. They're very fond of music. They have their peculiar way of overdoing everything, exaggerating everything—the women's facial expressions, or gestures."

"Do you have any memories of when they were in the house?"

"Yes," said Meraj. "There was a hijra in our house. He used to cook for my sister-in-law. And he was a very good cook. They are very good, you know; they work very well in the houses. And they are, sort of, 'chowkidars,' watchmen in the house. They can go in the 'mardana' [men's side], and come in the 'zenana' [women's side] as well. He used to go on a bicycle, wearing a sari—on a man's bicycle—with a braid, and a little ribbon 'round it—and it used to blow in the wind, you know—a cycling he used to go! And there was a policeman—he used to ask him to wait: 'There's no signal for you to go.' Then he would abuse the policeman, and say, 'Oh, you always say that— I'm going—I'll do everything—' The policeman used to look at him and laugh, and let him go. Like that, he used to do all the work at home."

"When was this?" I asked.

"That was about fifteen years back," said Meraj.

"Did he live with you, or outside?"

"Yes, he used to live in the house," said Meraj. "But he used to go to this 'Allawah' too—to meet his kind."

"Was he with your family for his whole life?"

"No, no," said Meraj. "He was with us for seven or eight years. Then he left all of a sudden. I just don't know where or why."

"You knew he was a hijra when you hired him?" I asked.

"He was a hijra all his life," said Meraj. "But he did not have any figure or anything. He was using all the falsies, to look like a woman. And then, the way they sing—oh my, that is very comical. I am so scared of them, I just don't know why."

"And yet, he lived with your family?" I asked.

"With my sister-in-law," said Meraj. "When I used to go to her, I said, 'No, let him not come when I am with you.' So she used to laugh."

"What did she say about him?" I asked.

"He's fine," said Meraj, "you know, he works very well. He's *clean*."

"Did he take care of the kids also?" I asked.

"Oh, yes, yes," said Meraj.

"So he was like a nanny?"

"Yes, like a nanny," said Meraj.

"He was there the full day?" I asked.

"Full day; the night and day," said Meraj.

"And do you remember his name?"

"Hussain-bi, we used to call him," Meraj laughed. "Maybe he was Hussain Khan, or Mohammad Hussain, something like that, but because he used to wear a sari, we used to call him Hussain-bi. *Bi* means a woman—a woman servant."

"Traditionally, what was the reason for having them?" I asked.

"When the baby is six days old," said Meraj, "they usually come to the house. And sing, and take some rice. You know, they make all the peculiar sort of gestures—what old women used to do—clapping—and then, they go away, singing and laughing—happy on their own . . ."

"Didn't they also come to weddings?" I asked.

"Sometimes," said Meraj. "But mostly, for newborns. 'Chhati,' it's called. Chhati means six. So the Chhati day is when the child is six days old."

"Would you invite them?" I asked.

"No," said Meraj. "I just don't know how they come to know it!"

"Servants?" I said.

"Achaa . . . maybe," said Meraj.

"What is the reason for coming to births?"

"Perhaps," said Meraj, "they are so obsessed with womenkind that they want to look like a woman, behave like a woman . . . Those who don't have children, they want to behave like perfect women—it's just God's gift that we are deprived of children . . ."

"So, psychologically?"

"Ha-aa, maybe," said Meraj. "You know, whenever I go out, there's a small hijra who comes and says 'Give me money—come on, I'm a hijra, don't you like me?' "

"So you give him money, right?"

Meraj shook her head.

"Go away?"

"He goes away," laughed Meraj. "Sometimes, even when you have the ceremony for when the girl is four years and four months old—bismillah, it's called—they usually call the hijras. And give them a hundred or two hundred rupees, just to dance, and make the girls happy."

"Who calls?"

"Good families," said Miraj. "The homes. Or they invite them to the son's bismillah, when the child learns to read the alphabet. They congratulate you, take the money, and they usually take rice, and they go."

"Is it true," I asked, "that they had a function in the harems that they no longer have? Or are we talking about two different groups—slaves and—?"

"Yes," said Meraj. "They were a sort of a medium be-tween the 'mardana' and 'zenana.' "

"They would guard the women's side?" I asked.

"Yes," said Meraj.

"Do you have any memories of this?" I asked. "I mean, I don't know how you grew up, but I guess it was during the time of women's seclusion?"

"It used to be a tradition," said Meraj, "to have a eu-nuch in the house. But now, you know—among the older generation—like my mother's or my aunt's—they say that it's *not* lucky to keep them at home. But these royal fami-lies used to keep the eunuchs. But now they say it's not lucky."

"Unlucky how?" I asked.

"Maybe just a superstition," said Meraj. "Maybe they think their boys will learn their ways . . ."

Describing one of the entertainers of Old Delhi, a courtier from Hyderabad wrote: *"Taci is the best of the bhagadbaz* [one who puts on various costumes] *and the leader of the bewitchers* [impersonators] *of Hindustan. He is the favorite of the Badshah* [emperor] *and has access to the private apartments of His Majesty. The nobles and the Amirs accord him a courteous welcome and are keen to be invited to his mehfils* [gatherings]. *He possesses weapons and dresses of all kinds, and the traditional objects of every tribe and nation which aid him in mime. . . . The pederasts and the winsome lads can be seen gathered in the bewitcher's house. The pedlars and the young boys contribute their share by attracting people with their tricks and mannerisms . . . He is the leader of the mukhannath* ["short tusks," and therefore eunuchs]. *Castrated ones bow to him, and seek guidance. The others who abound Taci's residence are catamites . . . and effeminates* [sic] *who are proud to be known as his disciples. Thus his coterie* [also] *includes all kind of people as well as pimps."*

Durgah Quli Khan
Muraqqa-i-Delhi

1739

TWELVE

"PAVITRAN SAHIB? He's a very big man!" said Ramzan.

So, on a whim, we were on our way there. Ramzan was saying that if he had the money he would go to college. He wanted to study Urdu literature. I was saying that in America almost anyone could go to college. Usually, he said, he was the chauffeur for foreigners who came to make movies.

We pulled up outside a tall, black iron gate, near Banjara Hills. Two cars were parked there, beside two squatting drivers. I opened the latch, and a servant, hearing the noise, came out. I had taken a chance in not calling—partly because I did not expect Mr. Pavitran to be able to help—and so this amounted to a social call, on behalf of Mr. Chenoy. Yes, said the servant, the sa'ab was in, and he led me through the foyer into the living room.

There was commotion inside: loud tones, two men, in suits, rustling papers that had been spread out on the dining-room table. A tall man in a lungi extended his arm toward me in a gesture of, please come in, I'll just be a minute.

The man himself. I sat down, just outside the circle of voices, and watched, till papers were rolled, briefcases snapped shut, good-byes said. A woman in a sari appeared, who introduced herself as Mrs. Pavitran, and asked me if I'd have anything to drink. Tea, I answered. Come, come, gestured Mr. Pavitran, mightn't we sit in the living room?

"Every day I deal with these lawyers," said Pavitran. "So, how is Shahpur?" he asked, with interest, and a change of mood.

"Well," I said. "He said I must meet you, and an 'old coot,' Dherni Dhar Prasad." I explained that I was trying to trace the history of the hijras.

"Ha, ha," said Mr. Pavitran, "so what have you managed to find out?"

"They really don't talk," I said. "They have an injunction against divulging their secrets. But they've been pleasant enough. Originally, Chenoy suggested that his brother Naozar could introduce me to the hijra community, but when I said this to Naozar, he literally threw me out of the house!"

"That's very paranoid," said Pavitran. "Poor fellow . . ."

What exactly had I been able to find out, insisted Pavitran. They lie, I said. Yes, said Pavitran, but surely I had been able to glean: what village, what caste, what age castrated, family occupation, etcetera. But it's difficult, I said, they're not forthcoming. They even deny that they are castrated. The "guru" does not let the younger ones speak freely. But was I rigorous in my questions? I can barely ask them, I said. There's so much politeness.

There and then, Pavitran organized my thinking.

"At the moment," he said, "I am suspended from the department, so I will not be able to assist you directly. But, first thing in the morning, you will get a call from me telling you where to meet two officers, and you must be ready to go. I will call promptly at eight-thirty. We'll just pick up one of these fellows, and take him along."

"No, no," I said, "no police pressure."

"You see," said Pavitran, smoothing the air with his hands, "it's like this: it's a gentle form of pressure. The fact is, we use them as informants; in times of distress, we help them. It's an old relationship. Therefore they won't object."

"But I don't want to scare them."

"We won't bully them," said Pavitran. "We'll ask them to come. The way you're going, you won't get anywhere. So we'll talk to them, and talk to them, until we get the job done."

The conversation was all of fifteen minutes; Pavitran was sorry he couldn't accompany me, but he had "this court case" on his hands. He wasn't allowed to "set foot" into his office. "But there you are." Also, he said, he would have a retired census officer, a friend, named Mustapha Hussain, contact me. And in this way, Mr. Pavitran took charge of my program in Hyderabad.

If it could be known, Pavitran seemed to say, then it would be. He was a scholar with executive power, an unusual combination of action and instinct. And there was also the question of my being a "guest" in what Pavitran considered to be "his city." So act as host he must.

And it was Ramzan's city too. On the way home, he asked me if he could take the "scenic" route, along the river, because "I don't think you are seeing much of Hyderabad, memsa'ab." His eyes seemed to be laughing. First the hijras, then Pavitran, what next? Something of the repressive class system was just not in him. It was also true that the subject of the hijras was a great equalizer.

THIRTEEN

By shivi's voice, I thought it was a movie star on the phone. "C'mon, c'mon, get up, are you ready to go?" said Pavitran. "It's all arranged." He was sending me off to Mr. Dhar Prasad's house. There I would meet a Mr. Reddy. Yes, he spoke English. "And please don't keep them waiting," he said, as though organizing his own daughter.

Ramzan and I rushed to the crowded Char Minar section. Near the Allawah, Ramzan got out to ask directions. A few neighbors pointed to a small cream-colored building, to a flat on the first floor. The blinds were drawn to conceal it from the heat.

A young woman let me in; she was Mr. Prasad's daughter, she explained. There was an inner courtyard in view, and, to the left, a living room. There sat Mr. Prasad, on a carpet, and Mr. Reddy, on a sofa. Most shocking, though, was the presence of Kamal Baksh and Sayeed Baksh, there on another carpet, beside Mr. Reddy! Had they been dragged here against their wills? While everybody was saying hello, politely, I avoided the eyes of the two hijras who had told me that they were busy today, had a court case to attend!

I hadn't dared to think that Pavitran would be so efficient; that the whole thing would be executed in less than twenty-four hours, and the same hijras, whom I hadn't named, found and brought to the detective's house. Here I was playing up the foreigner, all trusting, trusting, and then suddenly the police department descends on the Hijron ka Allawah? My fears were only slightly allayed when I noticed the congeniality between Mr. Reddy and Kamal Baksh.

But: the commissioner knew that in front of the police, Kamal Baksh might be encouraged to tell the truth. And, in this case, it was arrived at in a very strange way; since it was against their community's rules to give away the secrets of the eunuchs—indeed, there was an injunction of silence, the penalty for which was excommunication—Kamal Baksh was not compelled to actually speak the truth; she merely had to listen to police versions of their history, interrupting if she disagreed, then letting the officer correct the narrative, never having to say the words themselves. Thus there was little coercion, other than that the situation had arisen at all.

Dhar Prasad had been a street policeman, then a detective, and was now retired. His beat had been the area in which the eunuchs lived. He wore a white kurta pajama, Nehru cap, thick glasses, had few teeth, stained with paan, and looked about a hundred years old. He spoke very little English. His gravelly voice, which he raised often, was wily, obscene, astute. He was a man you couldn't put anything over. His lined face, I imagined, reflected the alleys and lanes he had traveled in.

Mr. Reddy was also a detective, who had once, under cover, investigated the activities of the hijras. He was about fifty, and wore dark-framed glasses, Jean-Paul Sartre–like, in the manner of Indian intellectuals. His face was remarkably clear, which I imagined reflected his purity of heart. The source of his information, he said, came partly from his own experience, and partly from "one of our elders," a former police commissioner in the 1930s, Mr. Sayyid Majidullah, who had written a book on the eunuchs of Hyderabad—an official bound tome in the Police Department.

The system of eunuchs' "maintenance," began Reddy, had been inherited from the Mughul kings. When the first Nizam, Asaf Jah, invaded the Deccan, he said, the eunuchs followed the army and the harems, and as they all settled, established a role in Hyderabad. The eunuchs were "part and parcel of domestic life," said Reddy. The kings, in those days, had four legal wives, according to Islam, but "there was no limit to the size of the harem."

Impotent men, whom Reddy also referred to as "eunuchs," were certainly not new to India: there was ample documentation that those who could not beget could be seen right from the Vedic period, even in the prehistoric period, in the older Hindu system. Impotent men were found in all professions, but they were not used to guard harems.

According to the *Mahabharata*, the great warrior, Bhishma, took an oath that if he came across a eunuch, he would lay down his arms. The oath indicated that eunuchs at that time were considered "helpless" people, who could not be fought with. So while Arjun and Bhishma were fighting, the god Krishna suddenly placed a eunuch in front of Bhishma. His name was Sikhandin. So Bhishma was forced to lay down his arms, which allowed Arjun to kill him.

But these eunuchs were not castrated, said Reddy. They were intersexed, or impotent, or deprived naturally of some physical attributes. Hinduism had many myths whereby men became women or were "transformed," metaphorically, into the opposite sex. Arjun, too, in his guise as Brhannadā in the court of King Virat, was like a woman.

"So where," I asked, "did the eunuchs for the kings' harems come from?"

"The eunuchs were mostly Muslim," said Reddy. "Or converts. And since ages past, they have influenced the locals, also. So in the Hindu community, impotence, and the eunuchs, were already there. So they [Hindu eunuchs] came and joined them [Muslim eunuchs]. Because they had a sort of an association, a gathering—and they had the household system, and had been provided with land. In Hyderabad, there are two palaces for them—Bari Haveli [Big Palace] and Chhoti Haveli [Small Palace]."

"We live in Bari Haveli," Kamal Baksh said, referring to the Hijron ka Allawah.

"Mostly," said Reddy, "they are Shi'a. And they observe Moharram. They go for Ramzan [Ramadan] also. And in those days, they were employed by the king's palaces."

"So then," I said, "originally, there were these houses of hijras . . . they didn't live in the harem? Or did they?"

"Before these eunuch houses were constructed," continued Reddy, "they were living in the township—separated. Then they built these houses. They only went for duty purposes to the palaces and nobles' homes. To be guards. It was on a shift-system that they used to go."

"Were they slaves?" I asked.

"They were not slaves," said Reddy. "But they were permanently attached to the rulers. That slave system was not here . . . You weren't called 'ghulams'—slaves—were you?" Reddy asked Kamal Baksh.

"No," replied Kamal Baksh. "Amongst Muslims, they had *kwaja saras*. It's like this: these people, the *kwaja saras*, could go in and out of the zenana [harem] . . . amongst the kings and in big royal families. The hijra could go in and out of the zenana. They [the hijras] weren't slaves. They used to work. They were employed. The slave is somebody who is bought and sold."

"They were not slaves," said Reddy. "They used to *get*

slaves . . . And they used to be employed. They were on monthly salaries. But, before they were employed, they had to undergo a test, to see whether they had potentiality, or were just posing as eunuchs, though they had male power."

"There were three categories," said Kamal Baksh, her voice rising. "Zenanay. Sankay. Hijra. You're talking of the zenanas! We are hijras! In Urdu, *zenanay* is the same as *kwaja sara*."

"Okay," said Reddy, cutting her short. Kamal Baksh was trying to separate the transvestites from the hijras, once again. But Reddy would have none of it.

"There were three categories," continued Reddy. "One was impotence—complete male power—natural born. The second was: the male organ, dissected—the whole thing, including the testicles. And the third category was male prostitution: that is, sodomy—homosexuality. The palaces and big families used to employ those persons who were completely dissected, and those who were impotent. The third category—the prostitute—they did not employ. Preference was given to those who were dissected . . . because, an impotent is likely to get the power in due course, isn't it? And, as we carry testimonials for our job—so the eunuch had to carry the dissected male organ. They presented it in a glass container—with a splint, and all those things . . . And whenever they went for employment, they had to produce that."

"How did they become eunuchs?" I asked. "How did they get into these houses? What about kidnapping?"

"See, since they had their own 'palaces,'" said Reddy, "their own association, and a society—just as brothel houses attract unprotected or helpless girls—they used to attract such helpless boys. And in good olden days, there was a system of kidnapping, also. In those days, they used to kidnap young handsome boys and make them impotent."

"Yes," grumbled Dhar Prasad.

"So there was a form of slavery?" I asked.

"There was a whole system," said Reddy. "Now that system is not there. Now, almost all their functions are defunct."

But Kamal Baksh objected to something Reddy had said.

"Yes, you did," said Dhar Prasad, arguing with Kamal Baksh in Hindi. "In the old days, forty years ago."

"No, no," said Kamal Baksh.

"What is going on?" I asked Reddy.

"See," said Reddy, "they are not admitting about kidnapping people."

Dhar Prasad laughed.

"You know," said Reddy, "if, in our society, a defective calf is born, such calves are donated to a temple. Similarly, if an impotent boy is born, or a disabled type, such boys were donated or given to the eunuch societies."

"So then, it's not kidnapping," I said.

"It's not kidnapping," said Reddy. "Kidnapping was there; such a donation system was also there."

"So perhaps the tradition of coming to the birth of a child," I said, "predates castration. Dancing, singing, is that all Hindu?"

"Why do you dance?" Reddy asked Kamal Baksh.

"If there's happiness in your heart," said Kamal Baksh, "and you call four of us, we come and make you happy."

"Where did dancing come from?" Reddy rephrased the question.

"That's what we learned from our elders," said Kamal Baksh.

"This is coming down from generations," said Reddy.

"We dance and make our money that way," Kamal

Baksh interrupted. "We can't leave this work. This is what we've learned. And we can't give it up. This is what we've got from our elders. And this is what we have to pass on."

"Not only that," said Reddy. "A census department may miss the childbirths—but not the eunuch. The eunuchs maintained calculated figures of new persons. Suppose my wife is pregnant? I might not be knowing, but a eunuch knows my wife is carrying! Because they come and make inquiries. These feudal systems provided livelihood for the helpless . . . This was one of the welfare systems in those days . . . And from the poorest to the richest house, they had access. They dressed according to taste . . . Then, what happened? At the end of the nineteenth century, that is, 1884—under the British, the Indian Penal Code was framed—laws, rules, and regulations. And the Nizam's estate was one of the feudalistic states under colonial rule, so such laws were adopted here. The British framed a law against these eunuchs, in that dressing as females and exhibiting themselves on the open streets, and inciting the people, became an 'offense.' Because they were attracting boys, and engaging them in homosexual offenses, the police used to take action."

"They couldn't wear female clothes?" I asked.

"They used to wear," said Reddy, "but they were not supposed to come in the open bazaar."

"Ha-aa," said Dhar Prasad. "In Lucknow also, such eunuch 'palaces' are there. And Lucknow eunuchs are more delicate than Hyderabadi. More cultured! More handsome!"

"The prostitutes live on one side," said Reddy. "The eunuchs live on the other side. They mostly live in cities, not in villages, not even in the district levels. They live in cities like Hyderabad, Bombay, Calcutta . . ."

"Delhi, Jabalpur," said Kamal Baksh.

"Lucknow, Bhopal," said Dhar Prasad.

"Nagpur, Jaipur," said Kamal Baksh.

"All important cities," said Reddy. "The eunuchs of Bombay are famous for their beauty; of Calcutta, for their modesty; and of Madras, for their God-fearing. And every eunuch society will have their guru. Every guru will have 'chelas,' disciples." He pointed to Kamal Baksh. "He will have selected four disciples. After his death, the prominent chela will take charge as guru, just the way the Pope is elected. Among the four, they decide who will be the guru. Like that, 'generation' comes. And all the eunuchs will have great regard for the guru. And whatever they earn, they will contribute to the guru. Of course, now the system is not there, when they were looked after by the palaces, and the rulers. There was a rule: When the guru dies, who does his property go to? You mean, that is a poor man? The guru will have a lot of property. So who is the rightful owner? The government. The government is the rightful owner, because they are the protectors. They claimed it."

"In those days?" I asked.

"Not now," said Reddy. "The government claimed their land—the kings used to protect them. So the kings were the rightful owners of the property of the gurus."

"So every time there was a dynastic change," I asked, "the eunuchs had to become favored by the new rulers, because they didn't have a system which provided for them?"

"By the new rulers," said Reddy. "Like that, till the end of the nineteenth century, the system of eunuchs' maintenance was there."

"They don't actually own their land?" I asked. "It's owned, or renewed, by the government?"

"Yes, they own the land," said Reddy. "But they had more land in those days. Now there's nothing . . . They're paupers. So at the end of the nineteenth century, the new ruler, Mahboob Ali Pasha, the sixth Nizam, abolished the system of eunuchs' maintenance by the palace . . . And they were replaced by maidservants . . . And another thing: everybody has seen the death of a common man, but nobody has seen the funeral of eunuchs."

"Why?"

"When we take them for a burial," interrupted Kamal Baksh, "only the family knows, but nobody else pays attention. After we bury them, we see the sun."

"They keep it secret," said Reddy. "They do not follow the body. Theirs is a Muslim system—they bury it. But they do not walk along with the dead body. Somebody else carries it. And it will not be known whose body it is."

"The body's covered?"

Reddy spoke to Kamal Baksh to confirm.

"The body's fully covered," nodded Reddy. "They put it on a structure having wheels, like a hospital cart; and two persons, with white masks, or at the most, three, drive the cart like hospital ward boys, unnoticingly. It looks like a body, but nobody knows, nobody asks, and nobody tells. They go and bury it at night. At night, no?"

"No, in the day," said Kamal Baksh.

"They've got a graveyard near Osmania Hospital," said Reddy. "And you may ask: Suppose a Hindu eunuch is there? So, that's why, those who want it, as in Christianity, at the last moment, if there's no one to look after the dead body, they Christianize it, giving some holy water, and prayers, and bury according to the Christian customs. Here also, certain Hindus, who have no relatives, or who wish to be a 'chela,' will convert himself or embrace another religion—he expresses himself beforehand: better to be a Muslim, to be buried; so, at the last moment, a Muslim preacher will be called, and holy water will be given. Thereby he adopts—embraces—Islam. And their rites will be done according to that religion."

"I've heard—could you please ask her—that they walk the body in the middle of the night, and they find a grave that's been freshly dug . . ."

Reddy related this to Kamal Baksh.

"No, no. Many stories are there," said Reddy, "but it's not true."

"It's not true," said Kamal Baksh. But now she launched into all the untrue stories that had plagued the eunuchs. Something in her martyred, we're-such-victims tone, as though they themselves never lied, prompted Reddy to interrupt.

"You know," said Reddy. "Excuse me—to be very frank: the eunuchs have a monthly course. You understand? Periods."

"I'm sure that's not true," I said. "Ask her."

"See, they are very talkative," said Reddy. "If you question them, immediately they oil the answer. It's just a joke—how their name is utilized: A beautiful eunuch was touched by a male in the open bazaar. The eunuch said, 'Don't touch me . . .' 'Why, what is the reason?' 'I'm having my period.' Then that male said, 'Arre, you are a eunuch, how is it that you are having a period?' 'No, no, I'm having loose motions . . .' "

Reddy and the old coot laughed.

"Diarrhea or something," added Dhar Prasad's daughter.

"Because they commit homosexual offenses," continued Reddy. "They used to say that having 'loose motions' is a menses for them."

The old coot snorted. He said in English, "Not right. This is a joke."

"Okay . . . another joke I'll tell," said Reddy, carried away. "Actually, it's not a joke, it's what happened: For homosexual offenses, the police used to prosecute eunuchs. In those days—the 1930s—when Raj Bahadur Venkatarama Reddy was the commissioner of police. He had magisterial powers. Three posts he was holding. So he used to conduct a court in the commissioner's office, in the 'durbar' hall. So, at about ten-thirty, eleven A.M., the police officers used to take a eunuch and produce him before the court, and lay charges, complaining, 'Your Honor, this eunuch, last night, committed a homosexual offense with so and so—and charge him.' "

"Now usually," I asked, "was this true or not?"

"It was true," said Reddy. "So such a case was put up before the commission. So before giving a conviction or a judgment, the judge used to ask the eunuch whether he had committed the offense or not: he said, 'Is it a fact that you did like this?' So the eunuch said, 'Yes, I did it, because I thought it was mine. If I had known it was government property, I would not have done it.' You follow? Because this organ—this anus—is mine, I utilized it. Had I known that the government has rights to my organ, I would not have done it! The commissioner was very pleased with his prompt answer, and said, 'Excused.' "

Dhar Prasad translated the anecdote for Kamal Baksh.

"It's an old story," said Kamal Baksh, laughing. "This incident happened long ago."

"He knows!" said Reddy. "It's a fact!"

"Among the hijras," I asked, "how many are prostitutes?"

"How many charge?" Reddy asked Kamal Baksh.

"Sixty . . . seventy . . . ," she replied. "But now there are very few . . . a few in Chor Bazaar—"

"There are not even a thousand men?" asked Reddy.

"There are fifty, sixty," said Kamal Baksh. "Not more than that."

"About a hundred?" persisted Reddy.

"About a hundred," said Kamal Baksh. "I can't speak about the people who don't live in our house. I can only speak about the people who live in our house."

But Kamal Baksh was now up in arms, arguing with Dhar Prasad. Reddy joined in, then brought the battle to a halt.

"They don't admit it," said Reddy. "But there are. See, according to their account of legalized, or known persons, under this guru, a hundred persons are there. But there are more than that in Hyderabad, who are not under this particular guru. Usually, those who do male prostitution do not admit it, because it is an offense."

"What exactly is a zenana?" I asked.

"One name is 'eunuch,'" said Reddy, "but among the eunuchs, there are different categories."

"Zenanas used to live with the kings," insisted Kamal Baksh.

"*Zenana* means woman," said Reddy, ignoring her.

"Today, they are the cross-dressers?" I asked.

"We go to weddings," interrupted Kamal Baksh, raising her voice. "And we are the ones who sing and dance! What zenanas are left today?"

Reddy now addressed Kamal Baksh in Hindi, and a battle ensued. She categorically refused to be put in the same sentence with the zenanas—the transvestites—and according to her, the ones who were employed by the kings and nobility. She was also distancing herself from this category of impotence, I gleaned, because it implied prostitution. Reddy was unhappy with her explanation.

"See," said Reddy, "I do not know why this particular

society has neglected them [the zenanas] . . . They are also members of our society. The moment their physique is seen, people feel they are strange. God himself has neglected them. In public meetings, we say 'he' and 'she,' but how to address them? Their names are missing. In which category are we to put them? There is a famous story pertaining to them . . ." Reddy turned to Kamal Baksh: "When was Pemamati and Taramati? Can you say?"

"During the Kutb Shahi times," said Kamal Baksh.

And now Kamal Baksh, who had claimed no connection to the court eunuchs, recited that history as part of her own, speaking in her elliptical way, and using the intonation of the hijras.

"A minister was sent," said Kamal Baksh, "to bring Taramati and Pemamati. He was told by the king to bring them. But the minister said, 'Give me forty days, so that I can sit in "chilla," in seclusion, and when I'm healed, I will come to the court, and I'll go and get the girls.' Before he went, he gave 'something precious' to be kept in the treasury of the king. Then he went to bring Pemamati and Taramati. He brought them, but what happened? The other ministers of the court led the king to believe: Look, you've sent him to bring Pemamati and Taramati, but instead, he's fallen in love with them! And they have fallen in love with him! So the king said that the minister should be hanged. But the minister said that a 'darbar,' a court, should be called—'Listen to what I have to say, then punish me accordingly.' The king said, 'Before you're executed, what do you want?' He said, 'I just want to be present in a court—and hear me out.' After that, when the court was in session, the minister said to the king, 'Sir, when I was leaving, I asked you to keep something of value in your treasury house. Have it brought out, and let your servants open it.' So they opened it. And there was his 'wealth.' The king said, 'What is this?' The minister said, 'You haven't recognized it? So now, sir, you are the king, all these people have misled you. I became like this before I left.' So the king said, 'I'm sorry that I misunderstood you,' and forgave him. Then he was set free."

"His name was Khalij Khan," said Reddy. "Pemamati and Taramati were famous singers. Khalij Khan was a powerful prime minister in those days. Local people celebrate. He's considered to be a saint, not a eunuch."

"Do hijra marriages go on?" I asked.

"Do you marry?" Reddy asked Kamal Baksh.

"Ji-nehi, ji-nehi—no sir, no sir," replied Kamal Baksh. She mentioned zenanas again, as opposed to hijras, who, according to her—"may have something"—did marry. She had the tendency to blame all of the controversial parts of the hijra tradition on the transvestites / prostitutes. Chaos erupted—Reddy, Kamal Baksh, and Dhar Prasad, all arguing.

"Yes, yes," said Reddy. "But what they say is not correct. They don't admit it, because it's directly pertaining to them. They may not divulge such things. It's a fact, you know, that males 'marry' these eunuchs. They go and select them . . . And a eunuch's love is more than a female's. Very faithful, very loyal. If they come into contact with a male, they don't see other men. Never. You can mistrust a girl, but not a hijra."

But now, Kamal Baksh, and Sayeed, who had remained quiet throughout, with his sari palla respectfully over his head, wanted to leave. I didn't know whether it was because of the the Muslim call to prayers, heard over the loudspeakers of the city, or the conversation, or their court case. I offered to drop them off by car; no, a scooter was fine. Reddy helped Kamal Baksh to her feet, and took them downstairs.

And, not once, over the several days that I met him, would Reddy accept money for his time. He argued that he was merely helping the cause of humanity, and the cause of history; he would freely give what he knew, that was what the models of Gandhi and Nehru had taught him; that men might think him odd, in this view, and in his lifestyle, but that he had chosen to live in the freedom of poverty, in a state of humility. He therefore refused to be dropped at home by Ramzan, insisting he would take the bus.

Afterward, Mr. Prasad's daughter, who sat through these meetings because, she said, she was "curious," replied that perhaps he was a bit embarrassed by where he lived—"It's not your style, you see, what you are used to." Though he made enough money, she explained, to buy a house, he preferred, literally, to live in a hut.

"When you take the reins of government into your hands," Shuja-'ud-Dawlah was advised by a well-regarded general in 1765, *"do not forget two points: firstly, put no trust in the Moghuls but work with your other subordinates and khwaja-saras [eunuchs]; second, give up living in Faizabad and make Lucknow your seat of government."*

Shuja-'ud-Dawlah greatly improved his army, appointing a handful of chief commanders. *"None of these had less than fifteen hundred men under him,"* wrote Abdul Halim Sharar, in *Lucknow: The Last Phase of an Oriental Culture.* *"In addition, there were khwaja-saras and young novices who were trained under their supervision and had become their disciples and pupils. Khwaja-sara Basant Ali Khan was in command of two divisions, that is, of fourteen thousand regular soldiers, in red uniforms. Another khwaja-sara also named Basant had under his command one thousand regular lancers and one infantry battalion in black uniform. There were five hundred cavalry and four battalions of infantry under the standard of khwaja-sara Mahbub Ali Khan."*

The cuisine from this kingdom was renowned, and great sums were paid to chefs, who sought employment with the kings. It was reported that Shuja-'ud-Dawlah and his first wife, Bahu Begum, had food prepared for them from six separate kitchens. Among the artful disguises cultivated by royal and noble families' kitchens were foods made to look like meat, bread, vegetables, and curries, but made fully of sugar, which sometimes included the bowls, plates, and tablecloths. Another feat was fashioning replicas of fruit, say, a pomegranate, wherein the kernels were made of almonds, the seeds, of pear juice, the tissues between the seeds, and the skin, of sugar.

The queen's kitchen, and the second royal kitchen of the king, were supervised by Bahu Ali Khan, a eunuch, and Anbar Ali Khan, a eunuch, respectively. The superintendent of Bahu Begum's household and estate was kwaja-sara Javahan Ali Khan. "*Every queen,*" wrote the English traveler William Knighton in 1790, "*had her entourage, her own harem, throne, cooks, reception rooms and halls. The Chief Eunuch was the principal attendant of the king's first wife . . . a man of great influence.*"

FOURTEEN

I WAS A TRAVELER, now, in the ocean of story, at the mercy of what the sea turned up. But the rhythm of the sea—which pattern of time shall we speak of? Did it have a Hindu logic, a Muslim, or a British? Or was it just strange—this infinite repetition with variation—this raga that was in my blood though I was not born here. Because day after day, I would sit and listen to the elders, as the search for origin itself became a labyrinth there was no origin in.

And there were many contradictions here. Detective Reddy had said that the first Nizam had settled in Hyderabad with a group of trusted eunuchs. Shahpur Chenoy had said that at least some of their land was given to them by the noblemen under Mahboob Ali Pasha, who had a household of eunuchs in the nineteenth century. Reddy had said that Mahboob Ali Pasha had abolished the system of eunuchs' "maintenance" by the palace. Kamal Baksh had said there were never any eunuchs in the palace or nobles' homes, and that these people were zenanas or transvestites. Meraj Pasha had said there was a hijra in her sister-in-law's house, and that he had gone to the Hijron ka Allawah to "visit his kind." The hierarchy amongst the hijras was such that the eunuchs, not the transvestites, had prominence. Chenoy had seen a boy have his testicles removed, while

Reddy and Nanda had said that the hijras were fully castrated. So: had the dear man turned away, at the critical
moment, or was there nothing there to be removed? And:
Nanda had referred to midwives performing the "operation," while Chenoy had witnessed a "barber."

Reddy had said that the eunuchs were not new to the
ages; he meant impotent men—in the epic Hindu period—
even in the older Vedic era. His example was Sikhandi from
the *Mahabharata*. She was born as Amba, and captured in
war by King Bhishma, though betrothed to another king.
Upon learning this, Bhishma rejected her and sent her
away. Amba, wrote Buitenen, was "totally disgusted with
being a woman," and became an ascetic, vowing revenge
on Bhishma. She was reborn as a man to King Draupada,
who was told, "You shall have a man child who is a
woman," destined to defeat Bhishma in war. Bhishma's
oath was: "I cannot kill a guru in battle, let alone one who
is a Brahmin, let alone one who is steeped in asceticism."
Thus Amba, who renounced her womanhood, was likened
to a man in her pursuit of asceticism—and thus to a "eunuch." Amba, reborn as Sikhandin, trained as a warrior,
and thus took revenge on Bhishma, who lay down his arms
before him/her.

Actual castration, suggested Reddy, came with cultural
Islam. But here one had to be careful, because there was the
tendency of Hindus to blame Muslims, and Muslims to
blame Hindus, for the more controversial aspects of this
tradition. There was also the tendency of Western scholars
to be more interested in the ancient Hindu texts regarding
this phenomenon, while some Indian scholars were half de-
risive of their work, or indifferent, perhaps rightly sensing
"orientalism" or international neglect. Still, the fact remained that there was no tome on the Indian eunuch of the

courts, perhaps because the "tradition" never quite ended. And there was also the tendency to throw up one's hands and roll up all the contradictions into one, and see India as a place in which "all time space," as one writer commented, "was mixed up."

"We are the ones who sing and dance," Kamal Baksh had insisted. "A low strata of musicians and dancers," Chenoy had said.

Some scholars dated the appearance of impotent men who danced and cursed to the later Vedic era (before the seventh century B.C.). Leonard Zwilling, an American, had studied the ancient Sanskrit medical books, and had found no incidence of castration. But there were many references, he said, to the "third sex." In the *Atharva Veda*, the hymns of the seventh to eighth century B.C., there was mention of the *kliba*, a "long-haired man" who "wore women's head ornaments," and who may or may not have dressed as a woman. In verse 6:138, the *klibas* cast a spell to make a man impotent. In hymn 8:6, there was reference to a charm to "protect a pregnant woman from demons," in which the "wild dancing of the long-haired man" was described: "They danced together at the house doing evil by wailing," said Zwilling.

The scholar Wendy Doniger suggested that the most frequent word for "impotent" in Manu was *kliba*. It could mean, depending on the context, "homosexual," "effeminate," born "not male," or within a spectrum of genders— but always with the connotation of "barrenness." There was poetry to this idea—bands of sexual misfits—the "third sex"—for whom society, as Reddy had suggested, had provided "a welfare system."

Synonyms for "third sex" in the Sanskrit literature—*na-pumsika*—"third gender"—were provided by a lexicologist of the Vedic era, and they were *trtya prakrti* (original nature), *sanda* (desiccated testicles), *kliba*, and *panda* (testicles removed).

Castration would not have been unknown to ancient India, said the prominent Indian historian, Romila Thapar, but "there were no harems in Vedic India," and the words in the later *Mahabharata* implied "intersexed."

Where, then, did the word *hijra* come from?

A Nepali lexicon noted that *hijra* derived from the Persian *hiz*. *Hiz* meant one who is "effeminate," "disdains women," a "catamite"—colloquially, today, "lewd," "lascivious."

According to Muzaffar Alam, a foremost Persianist, *hiz* was from old Pahlavi Persian, a sister language of Sanskrit, before the eighth century A.D. It meant "ineffective, incompetent—one who does not have impact" from "a male point of view," said Alam. "He looks like a man, but is not a man." And he did not necessarily wear female clothes, said Alam; in fact "the suggestion is that he did not." This word, then, was not dissimilar from the Sanskrit *kliba*—"not man."

Other Persianists, said Alam, suggest that the origin of *hijra* was *hich*, not *hiz*. It meant "a person who is nowhere—a thing which has no place—no identity or personality of its own," from *hichgah*—"nowhere." The words for court eunuch in medieval India—other than kwaja sara (which meant "to decorate the master")—were the Arabic *khunsa*, *mukhannas*, and *khansa*. Manucci's I'tibar Kahn, the court eunuch, was called *khansa*, or *mukhana*, both meaning "in between," "derogatory terms for a castrated person," said Alam. Epithets of abuse, he added, existed partly because of court jealousy.

But: there was also the religious, as opposed to the lay, question. When did the temple of Bahuchara Mata, whom the hijras today worshipped, come into being? One scholar, V. T. Padmaja Ramachandran, who studied Gujarati legends of the Sultanate Period, suggested that the temple situated outside Baroda in "Mehsana" became a place of pilgrimage in the mid-thirteenth century, and continued to flourish under the Mughuls. The first part of the temple was built in 1152, and the third, in 1791.

The scholar John E. Cort, citing the *Gazeteer of the Bombay Presidency* on Baroda, suggested that the second part was built by a Maratha named Fadnīs, and estimated that this occurred in the mid-eighteenth century. The first temple was constructed by a king Sankhal, after whom the nearby village, Sankhalpur, was named. One legend of the origin of the temple's followers linked them to the Muslim soldiers of Ala-ud-din Khilji, who "conquered" Gujarat in the late-thirteenth to early-fourteenth centuries. His soldiers were said to have desecrated the Hindu temple by eating cocks within; the goddess caused their stomachs to explode, and Ala-ud-din Khilji was asked by her to leave behind the man who had killed the cocks as a temple servant. Though one could not determine when castration became an aspect of devotion, the dates of the temple perhaps provided a framework. It would have been a time in which Islam, Sufism, and the precursors to the Bhakti, or Hindu devotional movement—wherein the devotee took on an aspect of feminization to be closer to god—influenced each other.

The Census Report of Hyderabad in 1981 stated: "According to the sex the eunuchs are generally classified into two groups, i.e., Dheradar and Be-Dheradar . . . Among [the] dheradar group there are two sub-groups, i.e., (i) by birth and (ii) by conversion. The method adopted for conversion is very peculiar and almost inhuman. The eunuchs of both groups dress like females and outsiders can hardly distinguish the difference between a eunuch and a woman." The census report thus made the distinction between those who traditionally attended births and weddings for a living, and those who were employed by kings and nobility.

Somehow all these traditions met. Islam, said Reddy, gave the hijras the household system; the "native" or natural-born impotent being came and joined these Muslim "associations" of eunuchs, because they had been provided with houses or land. And there did seem to be a bias toward Islam within the community—such as burial, not cremation,* their judicial or "court" system, their "forty days of healing" after castration, mentioned by Kamal Baksh in her anecdote about Khalij Khan, their "four" disciples, and the hierarchy among the hijras, involving the "Badshah," ("emperor"), or leading "good" family of hijras in India. Another explanation for the bias toward Islam could be that it gave the hijras a chance to get out of the caste system altogether. Historically, many lower castes converted; Islam took converts, whereas Hinduism did not.

So here was a theory: The impotent being existed from the Vedic era, if not before it. With the advent of Islam, castration allowed access into wealthy homes and palaces. The impotent being adopted this feature to prove that he was harmless. Since the castrated being had prominence, he was given land by local kings; and there was also the link here to male courtesanship. Somehow, today, the original impotent being, the non-castrated being, was placed lower in the pecking order of the hijra community—perhaps because the power, the tradition, was with those who had the land. It might also be suggested that the rise of the

---

* However, some Hindu ascetics were also buried, the idea being that in life, they were already considered "dead."

Indian hijra was a symptom of the decline of the courts (in which the traditional eunuch increasingly became a luxury), the effeminization of the kingship in general—a later development, rather than an earlier one.

But how did the hijras dress? The court eunuchs wore turbans and male clothes. The Hindu impotent being apparently wore male and female clothes, according to the *Kama Sutra*; intersexed beings were divided into two categories. The *kliba* implied effeminate in hair; the *hiz* suggested the outward appearance of a man. And though the hijras today claimed that they dressed as women, it was not clear that the hijras of yore wore only female clothes.

Then, there were the figures: official estimates of hijras were between 50,000 and 1.25 million, but would that include the zenanas or transvestites? And the castrated being is at one time uncastrated, so into which category is he to fall? An American scientist, Anne Fausto-Sterling, wrote that though it was extremely difficult to calculate the incidence of "intersexuality" at birth, the American scientist John Money had suggested that it was very high—perhaps 4 percent of all children born in "first world" countries. Due to medical advancements, most of these "defects" were surgically correctible at or near birth. So: if India's population was 930 million, then a staggering 37 million might fall into this category. But "normal" men also elected to be castrated, according to Ranade; not all were impotent physically, or born with unusual gender characteristics.

I met Mustapha Hussain, Pavitran's friend, and a former assistant police commissioner, at the Secundarabad Club. He was a light-skinned man, in his late sixties, with a soft, wavering voice. His father, he said, had been commissioner

of police during Mahboob Ali Pasha's time. They belonged
to the "premier nobles" of Hyderabad, he said, not by way
of immodesty, but to place me in the cultural history of the
city.

We sat on the lawn and ordered chips and beer.

"You know," said Hussain, "when the Indian census
was being taken, the big problem arose as to whether they
[the hijras] should be classified as men or women. So the
government gave a ruling that they should be classified according to *what they say*. I was a census officer in those
days, doing the work on behalf of the government."

"They used to say 'she'?" I asked.

"No, they used to say 'he,' " laughed Hussain. "Some of
them would say 'she.' But mostly, they would say 'he.' So
we *couldn't discriminate*. But, even that: why did they have
such a prominent position? Number one: Because the king
could trust him in the harem. And he had the double
advantage of being available at both the places—the men's
side, the women's side. That's the main basis for his
popularity. Then, what happened? Gradually, the nobility
started dwindling. But, in all big houses, they were employed. That was the point . . . What was the information
they gave you?"

"They denied it," I said.

"Ha-aa," laughed Hussain.

"Where can I find the 'Small Palace' of eunuchs?"

" 'Round about Char Minar, only," said Hussain. "You
see, the history's like this: they have inhabited themselves
in certain localities. Nothing this side of the Old Bridge.
And, in Hyderabad, it was a privilege for the people to stay
wherever the ruler stayed. You know that big palace of the
Nizam—Purani Haveli? And 'round about that, all these
smaller palaces? The nobility had their palaces in that area.
So the moment the Nizam moved, the nobility shifted with

him. And these hijras had access to every nook and corner . . . Then what happened? They were so expensive,
as household personnel . . . to be maintained, that nobody
wanted to maintain them permanently in their houses!
After the nobility had gone, everything disintegrated! And
some of them are the *best* cooks, mind you . . . There was
a chap who was working with us—he was a very good
cook, and he was a hijra."

"What happened to him?"

"See," said Hussain, "mostly I used to go out to the districts, and the fellow didn't like coming out. He preferred
to stay only in Hyderabad."

"He came from one of these houses?"

"One of those houses," said Hussain. "Poor man—has
gone a little old now—his hand shakes, and this and that—
but he's a typical fellow from that area. He was one of the
best cooks I had!"

"He came for the day," I asked, "and went back to the
Allawah?"

"Normally," said Hussain, "he stayed with us. Because,
you see, my wife and children used to look after him very
well. Especially my wife. She used to give him all the facil-
ities he wanted."

"I've heard they were nannies."

"They did perform that function," said Hussain, "but
they didn't *relish* the idea. Unless they had a little patron-
ization from the head of the family, wherein their wishes
could be fulfilled. Otherwise, they were *very* uneasy. Very,
very uneasy. Even this man who used to cook for us—one
day or two, he would stick on, and on the third day, he'd
like to go for some cures and come back."

"And he wouldn't say why or where?"

"No. Nothing," said Hussain. "He wouldn't say anything at all! He would *simply* disappear. I said, 'All right,

baba, you go away—most probably, you want to see a picture—' so that you don't *dig* at him. That's how I used to
keep him in good humor."

"He never told you anything?"

"He *never!*" said Hussain. "My god, you mean to say
my wife would have tolerated my speaking to that man
something-something in secret? My god, she'll—she'll simply blow at me! So . . . we used to talk sitting *all* together."

"When they were employed," I asked, "they lived in
their own houses?"

"Oh yes," said Hussain. "They had separate apartments
for them. Nobody would encroach on their apartments.
And some of them played very intriguing parts in the history of the royal families. Now, for instance, if some
problem should develop between certain parties—they had
that *knack* of seeing that things could be brought to a certain pitch . . . People said, *hijra kum makth hai*. They were
looked *down* upon.

"They were looked down upon," I asked, "even when
they were in royal households?"

"Yes," said Hussain. "Because everybody thought:
something against nature. Something against nature is always looked down upon. After all, who would like to become one? And when the hijras felt that they were not able
to get boys voluntarily, they used to purchase them . . ."

"The hijras themselves?"

"The hijras themselves," said Hussain. "And there's a
particular sort of instrument that they used . . ."

"They make them sit on something . . ."

"And gradually," said Hussain, "they used to make
them used to it. With the result that, at a certain stage, they
would relish only that sort of an act, and not any other."

"Prostitution, you're saying, had to have been there for
a long time."

"Absolutely," said Hussain. "Where is the difficulty about it? Of course, there is no history, as far as Hyderabad is concerned, where they were patronized during the Kutb Shahi regimes. Mughul regime, they were patronized, in the sense that they were allowed to exist . . . See, that old system completely gave way after that institution of the kingship disappeared. Afterward, they were left on their own for their survival. That changed the power. Once the nobility shifted—that's the great change in their life . . ."

"What year would you say?"

"I would put it," said Hussain, "somewhere in the period when the Nizam was able to ascend the throne—that is about 1911 or so. That is the time when he was able to stand on his own. Then gradually, he was controlled by the Britishers. That is a separate story, in which lust, and his own greed, brought him down."

~

Claude Martin joined the army of the East India Company as a common soldier at the end of the eighteenth century. He rose to be a General in the army of the Navab of Avadh where his services were later transferred. In 1774 he served as military and political advisor to Shuja ud Daula in Faizabad, where he lived in grand style with four concubines and a large staff of eunuchs and servants. . . . He had amassed a large fortune by trade and by winning bets on cockfights . . . and left properties worth three laks to be spent equally for founding three schools for orphan children in his home town, Lyon, in Calcutta, and in Lucknow.

Abdul Halim Sharar
Lucknow: The Last Phase of an Oriental Culture

FIFTEEN

KIRAN WAS DRAWING WATER from the center of the courtyard. A small girl, in a red dress, loitered near the well. A boy, about eight, leaned against the wall. I wondered if the hijras would feel intimidated by the fact that I had used police intervention, but, if anything, they seemed more relaxed. I did not bring up their court case.

"Do they live here," asked Shivi, "all these children who are staring at us?"

"Our place," said Kamal Baksh, "is just littered with kittens. Three belong to one family, two belong to another. That girl, you know, with the string of pearls around her neck? She's the child of that tenant," referring to the woman who had asked for medicine the other day. "These kids, they blow glass behind the post office. Even my sister-in-law blows glass. Some children polish mirrors in the bicycle shop. One boy works in a photo shop."

"But blowing glass—doesn't it do anything to them?" asked Shivi.

"Yes," said Kamal Baksh. "It makes them blind."

"Can we see this compound?" I asked.

"Yes," said Kamal Baksh, "but you have to be clean. The area over there—is our elders' area."

"Are you menstruating?" asked Shivi. "Because menstruating women and children aren't allowed there."

I shook my head to indicate I was "clean."

Kamal Baksh rose slowly, and walked, bent at the knees, body pushed forward, toward a bolted door. This she unlocked with one of the large keys hanging from her petticoat, taken from the cluster at the hip. Sayeed Baksh got up to help.

"Generally, I don't go anywhere," said Kamal Baksh. "I can hardly move around—earlier, when I had to move around, I couldn't go to the toilet for four or five days. Even now, I have to sit on the floor. I can't do it."

I was drawn to the sudden yellow light, the spareness of the huge room. There were Persian writings—delicate, in black—painted on the walls—and a window.

"So clean, so hygienic," said Shivi, looking in.

"My 'mother' takes care of it all," said Kamal Baksh, indicating a hijra 'mother,' in this case, Sayeed Baksh. They called each other son, brother, mother, replicating the system of kinship in an extended family.

"If it's not kept hygienic," said Sayeed Baksh, "it doesn't look good. Everything that is nice and clean is good for the *insan*—for humanity."

"In this way, ma," said Kamal Baksh, "I give medicine for jaundice and everyone comes here for it."

Sayeed and Kamal Baksh often spoke on different levels. The guru, always literal, the mother-husband-wife, with irony or insight.

"It's the *nishani*," said Kamal Baksh. "Where the elders sat. The seat of power was here."

"Who?" asked Shivi.

"The big guru," said Kamal Baksh. "The first guru."

"The first," I asked, "who made this place—the original founder?"

"Yes," said Kamal Baksh.

"Who was the first guru?" asked Shivi.

"What's the point of the name?" said Kamal Baksh.

"Please," said Shivi.

"No, no," insisted Kamal Baksh, "we don't say their names. They are with us. We only call them 'guru.' "

I asked her what was written on the walls.

"It's from the Koran," said Kamal Baksh. "People before us have written this."

"It's Imam Hussin's room," explained Shivi, speaking of the martyred Shi'a prophet, "where they pay respect to him. So everyone who comes here is a Muslim?"

"Everyone who's Urdu speaking and Muslim says prayers here," said Kamal Baksh. "And now, look here, this is where the Hindus pray."

She moved slowly toward another bolted door, and opened it. It was filled with exuberant colors—orange, red, yellow: a framed image of the Mata, garlanded, and the scent of sandalwood, from the nearby, though unlit, incense burners.

"Muslims here," said Kamal Baksh. "Hindus there."

"The gurus are all Muslim?" asked Shivi.

"Yes," said Kamal Baksh. "The gurus are all Muslim."

"This is all of the old days," said Shivi.

"Yes," said Sayeed Baksh.

"Ma," said Kamal Baksh, sitting back down, "I don't know about our children's future—these buildings; now that our seven or eight gurus have died, what to do about this? You can take it as the truth, or you can take it as a lie: I have a debt of one and a half lakhs. Keeping all my hijras' troubles in mind, I think of my family later—now that's the truth, why should I lie, what is there to hide?"

One and a half lakhs was about $15,000, an exorbitant sum for the average Hyderabadi, who earned about $37 a month.

"Where did you get the money?" I asked.

"I got it from the hijras," said Kamal Baksh. "They don't charge interest. Some I got from Surat, and some from Delhi."

"When did you all meet," I asked, "to discuss these finances?"

"My clan's people," said Kamal Baksh, "they're in all of Hindustan, right? I went to Delhi. Those people also come here. So I said, 'Look, you know where you were sitting earlier? That was built by me, when I went to Surat and got 25,000 rupees.' Then whoever came from elsewhere said, 'It's not looking good'—some hijras from Delhi said that—so I said, 'Look, give me some money.' And they gave me a loan."

"Did you go to Delhi just for the money?" asked Shivi.

"No, no," said Kamal Baksh, "just for the money, but they had come here, no? That way we also go—among my people—if there's someone who's almost dead, like me—for a funeral, *all* hijras have to come. I only charge rent for the newly made areas, but I don't like to charge my own people."

In her oblique way, Kamal Baksh had described the manners within the community of hijras throughout India. Apparently, all were welcome to stay free of charge within households in every city—and visiting amongst them was common. But though she'd managed to build an annex to the original house from money she'd borrowed from the Surat hijras, the Delhiwallas—apparently quite an elite—did not like the extension. So she'd borrowed more money from them. This concern about the household and its maintenance ironically mirrored the nobility's. But there was also the pettiness here of the petit bourgeois—what will the relatives think of the new sofa, na?

I wanted to see the entire property, and asked if I could go upstairs. Kamal Baksh insisted on escorting me through the dark stairway that led to the roof. Sayeed took up the tail. Kamal Baksh unbolted the door at the top: a few finely woven pillows resting here and there. But the view was extraordinary: the High Court, a white princely building, completed in 1919, and surrounded by gardens in the distance; the Mughul latticed windows on one side of the roof, and a row of thatched huts between cement buildings just below.

Across the road, a few hijras peeked out of a doorway and looked up at us. In a garden, with a high cement wall concealing them at ground level, a young man stood close to a hijra in a yellow lungi, a bright hibiscus in her hair. These, presumably, were some of Kamal Baksh's tenants, and the land below us, hers.

"This *whole* area used to be a hijra area," Kamal Baksh said, indicating half a mile or so with her arms. "Everywhere, in the old days . . ."

But Kamal Baksh was quickly becoming embarrassed by the staring hijra, and his obvious male partner, and soon lost her concentration. "Well, they're sleeping, maybe they shouldn't be disturbed," she said, trying to lead us away. "Those houses are different," she said quickly, indicating the one where the hibiscus-in-hair hijra was now waving to us. "Our way of life they don't understand, their way, we don't understand . . . I've heard their husbands have prostitutes." But then she veered off, saying, "But you don't find it here in Hyderabad—only in Madras, more or less." And now her voice rose against her tenants. "For men like that," she said, "to educate their women, to marry them in their quarters, and then keep"—she meant a hijra or transvestite mistress—"those people in Madras do that kind of thing! Among our people, it's not like this. . . . We don't mix up with their kind." And now she railed on against the younger generation: "All our boys used to live there, but now they've become *spoiled*. I couldn't even keep one of my nose rings or earrings—everything had to go—they just took it, all these hijras!"

Sayeed Baksh led us downstairs again and pointed to the peeling walls along the way. "This part," he said, "is very old," showing us a watermark above our heads.

"When the monsoon came," said Kamal Baksh, "the floods [1908] . . . So this is the mark left by the impact of the water—this is how high the water came—so I said, Allah [god, Muslim], Bhagwan [god, Hindu], it left a mark even on the wood, which all the termites later ate—it's all started falling down—god forbid it should fall on us! So I got rid of the rotten wood."

When we were seated again, I thought how strangely used to this we had all become, the rhythm of the hijras and our presence amongst them. We might have stayed and slept there, such was the sense of familiarity. And though Kamal Baksh was obviously telling a few white lies—they kept prostitutes only in Madras—they have transvestites only in Madras—she did not insist on them. This kind of lying, apparently, did not require consistency. She had also alluded to her own rough treatment at the hands of the "youth," and to disharmony within the community.

"Does the Nizam's trust give you anything?" Shivi asked.

"No, nothing," said Kamal Baksh.

"How will you manage?" asked Shivi.

"Now, listen to what I am saying," said Kamal Baksh. "Now these hijras are there, no? All of them different, all mixed together—their children come and go; but half of what the children earn comes to me, and half they keep; then I put this money into filling my stomach, into household affairs, into judging the good and the bad, and for when they fall ill. But how can I do this on ten rupees? I have the burden of this loan. If I die, whoever sits on my seat will have to carry on with it—that's what it is."

To me, listening to Kamal Baksh, the words "all of them different" meant that today, some of the hijras under her had chosen not to be castrated, against the pressure of the elders to conform. Kamal Baksh's voice had risen with that pressure of having to maintain the status quo against all odds, "traditions" which were right to be questioned. The central fact of their land set them apart from the destitute in India; and it was left to Kamal Baksh, a juridical head within the community of gurus, to safeguard "her children's"—those ingrates'—future.

"How much," asked Shivi, "do you usually get from weddings and births?"

Kamal Baksh undid the pouch around her neck and slowly counted out thirty-five rupees.

"Ten rupees from medicine," she said. "The rest the hijras brought this morning."

"All this with such integrity?" asked Shivi.

"Yes, they have integrity," said Kamal Baksh. "Now I say, Bhagwan, whatever you give me, that is a blessing. This was brought by four. They go in the morning until dark—sometimes into the night . . . When a child is born, then they give to them. For two to four days, there's a sign on the door—the mark we put remains for a few days. You go, and eventually they give to you."

"How many are in your group?" I asked.

"Sixteen to seventeen people," said Kamal Baksh. "Thirty-five rupees . . . I don't feed them, it's just for the house, tax, repairs, paint, water . . . But the rent also comes in, so it helps. Hijras give me their portion, so how can I take rent from them? My hijras come and stay here, but outsiders, no. In my house, the disciples—the chelas—stay. And their disciples, their children, can stay . . . So you

know my chela who was here the other day?" She was referring to Munni Baksh. "Some thugs tried to sell off our
land—not this land, but another piece—there's my building there for the elderly—the thugs said it was government
land—and with that excuse, they tried to sell it. Then I
showed all the papers, letters, and having claimed the land
back, and having gotten permission, I'm now building
there. Now it's become essential to charge rent, so I said,
'My son, you construct there, or all the other hijras will
construct there—the land around there is selling fast—so
all those other hijras will take it, and you'll lose out. So he
did . . . What will you have? Sugar cane juice? Tea? Coffee?"

"Maybe tea," said Shivi. "But you'll have to go and get
it, no?"

"No," said Kamal Baksh. "I'll call him. Kiran will
go . . . Will you have sherbet?"

"Tea," I said, giving into politeness.

"O Kiran," called Kamal Baksh. "Kiran!"

Kiran appeared from outside, in a pale chiffon sari, carrying wood in her arms.

"Two teas in a glass," said Kamal Baksh, "and two
tiffins. I also want to have, so three teas."

Shivi now asked Kamal Baksh whether she would perform for us. I added that we'd heard that they were excellent cooks.

"Yes," said Kamal Baksh. "We can cook. Come . . . I'll
do everything. I'll make the children sing . . . You tell us
what day is convenient for you."

"Give us a time tomorrow," said Shivi.

"What day is tomorrow?" asked Kamal Baksh.

"Tuesday," said Sayeed Baksh. "It would be better on
Wednesday."

"Come in the morning," said Kamal Baksh. "I eat at ten,
then again at two."

"Take it to mean eleven," said Sayeed. "Maybe we should invite outsiders, otherwise it might not be very good."

"No," said Kamal Baksh, "if we call outsiders, they'll probably expect at least two to five hundred rupees. But if it's just us, it will be our pleasure."

"Where are the others?" I asked.

"They've all gone to Nizamabad," said Kamal Baksh, "two hours away from here, for Holi, with other hijras. Remember the one who was here the day before yesterday? Rani Baksh? She has gone with them."

"Whatever she brings, she'll give you half?" Shivi asked.

"No," said Kamal Baksh. "They will only give me one share. If nine go, they will give me one-ninth. If eight go, they will give me one-eighth."

"So, who are the others?" I asked.

"The old ones who sing are from there," said Kamal Baksh. "The dancers are from our side—the younger ones."

I got up and walked around the place, examining the photographs on the wall. There were about fifteen, neatly framed, in a row. I moved toward one which was small, its frame inlaid with ivory: a dark-skinned hijra, dressed in Muslim clothes, a dupatta over her head, and long wavy locks; in semi-profile, as though a "bust," she seemed to be a truly beautiful "woman," if one might say so. I was reminded of the courtesan tradition, and perhaps it was another hint from history that the hijras lived only a few blocks away from where the courtesans once lived—now, the red light district.

"Is this Rahman?" I asked.

"No," said Kamal Baksh. "That is one of our gurus from before. From the 1920s."

"Rahman was here?" I asked.

"Yes," said Kamal Baksh. "Those photographs in the middle."

There, in the center, was a large "colorized" portrait of a wide-faced hijra, with one earring and a necklace, in a cream-colored sari and pink blouse. The hair was open. A round, dark, masculine face, and mocking eyes. Rahman: the Rahman who had spoken to Lynton and Reddy, and invited Shahpur Chenoy to an initiation ceremony. I examined the other two pictures: Rahman on bended knee, the arms held outward, the hair in stylized waves; and one in which he was more like a woman, modest, his hair in a braid.

"Rahman was a dancer," said Kamal Baksh.

I moved along the row to a group shot, taken in front of the Taj Mahal. About twenty people were assembled here, and it was difficult to tell if they were all hijras. Two small children, a boy and a girl, were in the shot, and perhaps, a few real women. They were well dressed; some carried shawls over their shoulders. The portrait was rather faded, showing spots of brown damage.

"Who are these?" I asked.

"They're from Delhi," said Sayeed Baksh. "They're from old times. Actually, the weather here is bad. All these pictures have been eaten by termites. That is one of my brothers," she said, pointing to a hijra in the center.

"Your real brother?" Shivi asked.

"My guru's disciple," said Sayeed Baksh.

"In front of the Taj?" I asked.

"No," said Sayeed Baksh, "not the Taj. It's a curtain of the Taj. They sat in front of it, and got photographed."

"Whose kids are these?" I asked, looking at an old photograph of what seemed to be a woman, with a boy and a girl in her lap.

"The girl is my guru's," said Kamal Baksh, explaining

that the "woman" was a hijra. "She adopted her when she was nine months old. The mother died, so she adopted her."

"Adopted." This was the word Kamal Baksh used. Hijras as surrogate parents.

"Is she married now?" Shivi asked, apparently oblivious to the strangeness of the idea, in her one-mother-in-law-to-another mode.

"I got her married," said Kamal Baksh. "Now she is the mother of children."

So, "no" was the answer to the question neither of us asked: Do they force these children into becoming hijras?

"Who is the boy?" I asked.

"Her sister-in-law's son," said Kamal Baksh. "They were staying here. When he was young, he was very attached to me."

Now Kiran came through the door with the tea and tiffins. These she set down at her feet. Then she disappeared inside a darkened room, and emerged with a brass tray. Before serving us, she proceeded to polish it with a duster.

"Lo ma," said Kamal Baksh. "Take tea and drink!"

We all took the tea. I kept moving, to the far side, and peered into the alcove leading to the open Muslim prayer room. There was a picture of a man with a tiger there, one of royal-seeming family, and a few others I couldn't quite see.

"No, no," said Kamal Baksh, "that is the god's area. We don't allow girls to go over there."

I stood respectfully at a distance. Had she forgotten that I was not "monthly"?

"Who is the person in the photograph?" I asked.

"Osman Ali Khan," said Kamal Baksh. "That is their whole family. If you are not monthly, you can go."

I took the liberty. There was a portrait of the sixth Nizam, Mahboob Ali Pasha, with a dead tiger; one of Guru

Nanak, the sixteenth-century religious leader of the Sikhs; and the king of Dhar, Kamal Baksh said.

"Why do you have Osman's portrait?" I asked.

"I will explain it to you," said Kamal Baksh. "What happened was, a son was born to the father, and to the son, at the same time. So when the hijras were in this Haveli, they went to the Nizam and said, 'Lord—Osman Khan has had a son, can we go there?' The Nizam said, 'While I am alive, what can he give you?' And then he sent the army over here. I was not born at the time, but my elders told us about it. On elephants they put us, on planks, and on that, dancing, they called us. The army was on both sides, and in between were the elephants and planks. They [the hijras] were kept there for four days. So they could not leave and go to Osman Khan's 'chhati.' So when they finally went to Osman Khan's, he told them, 'The way you came, go back. While I waited, you did not come. Why have you come now?' . . . That's all finished now."

The tale Chenoy had told. But I wondered at its allegory. Was Osman "offended" by this gesture of the hijras, or was he offended by something larger than that, by what they represented? Once the impotent eunuch had been the ironic symbol of the absolute power of the king; but by the late nineteenth century, the eunuch had come to mirror the tragic impotence of his patron. The king needed the eunuch now to preserve the image of his past. Thus one reason, perhaps, for the continuation of the eunuch tradition in India, lay in the nostalgia, or anticolonial pride—in public, we may be British, but in private we are Indian—of the kings. But when Osman Ali came to the throne in 1911, a new India, as Mustafah Hussain had suggested, and a new national consciousness, were being born. And perhaps Osman saw in the hijras, as in his father, a symptom of a lost age.

"At the time, you didn't get anything?" asked Shivi, referring to Osman.

"No, nothing," said Kamal Baksh. "At times, he helped. Later, he gave us shelter."

"Have you been to see the new Nizam?" asked Shivi.

"No, ma," said Kamal Baksh. "He's not interested. He doesn't even speak Urdu properly. Now he is learning a little bit . . . So what will they give? So if it's written in our fate, if one is blessed with a son, we will get. All these years, everybody gave, but from Osman's time, it stopped. So that's how things are."

"Where does Kiran stay?" asked Shivi.

"Where he got the tea—next to it," said Kamal Baksh.

"Do you call them all chelas?" I asked.

"I will explain," said Kamal Baksh. "If a child is born to you, he will be called 'son.' And if a son is born to him, he will be called 'grandson.' And if a son is born to him, he will be called 'great-grandson.' "

By 'born,' I assumed that Kamal Baksh meant a system of lineage that was appointed, the guru choosing the disciple, and down from there.

"And that tattoo?" I asked, pointing to Kamal Baksh's lower arm. Every hijra of the household had one.

"It's my brother's name," said Kamal Baksh. "My sister-in-law put it. It's from childhood."

"Is it in Hindi?" I asked.

"Telugu," said Kamal Baksh.

"Your real brother's?" asked Shivi.

"No," said Kamal Baksh. "My real mother's elder sister's son's name was put on my arm by her daughter-in-law. Earlier they used to do it—everybody, even ladies."

"Do you know how to read and write?" asked Shivi.

"No, ma, among us, nobody knows," said Kamal Baksh, softly shaking her head.

SIXTEEN

AT BARAKAT MANSIONS, a parody of kingship greeted me, offered me cakes, and lit my cigarettes too quickly, but disavowed any link between the hijras and the kings.

"Our kings were werry, werry Vestern," said the King's secretary. "They even had chandeliers!"

Did the sixth Nizam give land to the hijras, or renew the land grant of his forefathers?

"No, no, no," said the king's secretary. "Our king was influenced by French ideas, he was ahead of his time. Our king was werry, werry educated!"

Anything in the Nizams' papers on this subject? No—and he would know—he was the king's secretary. There were never ever any eunuchs in the king's court, he said, never in Hyderabad.

But there are references to kwaja saras everywhere in the Mughul histories, I said. Asaf Jah, the first Nizam, it is said, founded his kingdom with a group of loyal eunuchs. No, he'd not read this anywhere. Another cola?

A press release. But who, after all, was the Nizam today? Nothing but a myth to be preserved, a figurehead, an icon to be protected—all in the form of this long-haired, regal-looking, gold-vested secretary. Education, modernization, were at odds with this group of misfits.

Near Osmania Hospital, Ramzan pulled up and got out of the car. He asked a man selling chickpeas if he knew of the hijras' graveyard? No, he said. So Ramzan headed for a passerby. Yes, he said—it's right behind the hospital.

As we pulled in, several children approached the car, a timid formation of about seven, ranging in age from about six to fourteen. I'm not sure what I hoped to discover at the actual site: Land, grass, a few rough, cement tombstones.

Outside the car, Ramzan took over—I plying him, in broken Hindi, with questions to ask the children. They were all speaking at once, so Ramzan laughingly asked them to slow down—hands held up—a gesture of protection—since they were standing so close to us.

I pulled out a camera—and suddenly this group assembled itself in my view—a crooked, emboldened line of smiling children, ready to be snapped by the foreign memsa'ab.

"No, no," Ramzan was saying. "She wants to snap the graveyard." And they looked crestfallen, so I took one of them anyway.

"Okay," said Ramzan, making order from this chaos. "Who here has seen a hijra burial?"

A shaking of heads. Sweet children's voices. "Nobody sees! Nobody is allowed to see!" Shocked looks in the eyes.

"But everyone knows it's a hijra burial ground—how is that?" Ramzan was asking.

"They don't bring," a little boy was insisting. "They come after dark. Somebody else brings it—all covered." A twist of the hand. Omniscience.

"Then who brings it?"

"Maybe their friends," said the boy, with confidence.

"Men or women?"

"Men," all the children clamored.

"How do they bring it?" Ramzan asked.

"I told you," said the little boy. Clearly the leader, but we needed more authority.

"Then what happens?" Ramzan asked.

"We don't know. They don't allow us to see," another child said.

The eldest, so far, had said nothing, but he now stepped forward, a lanky adolescent in shorts.

"After that, they bury the body," he said. "At night, their people come."

"How long have they been coming here?" I asked.

"About . . . a hundred years," said the adolescent. Surely he was guessing.

"But there isn't enough space," I said.

"They bury them in the same place," said the adolescent. "Their man comes and opens up the graves."

"Two people in the same grave?" Ramzan said.

"Ha-aa," said the teenager. "You can use it for another sixty years. Some people don't make a cemented one. The ones which are not cement—these can be used over and over again . . . They also have another graveyard somewhere outside the city."

Achaa.

"When was the last hijra buried here?" Ramzan asked.

A round of vague mumblings—don't know, didn't see, can't remember. All the children shaking their heads.

"But it is over there," the eldest pointed, to an unmarked site of earth. "They come twice a year, and bring flowers."

And their ceremony?

None had seen it performed. It took place at night.

An English merchant, traveling with the entourage of a Maratha king, observed: *"Among the followers of the oriental camp . . . I must not omit the hermaphrodites; there were a great number of them in the different bazaars, and I believe all in the capacity of cooks. In mentioning these singular people, I am aware I tread on tender ground; I cannot resolve doubts and difficulties, nor shall I enter into particulars repecting [sic] them. There were a considerable number of human beings called hermaphrodites in the camp, who were compelled, by way of distinguishing them from other castes, to wear the habit of a female, and the turban of a man. I was called into a private tent, to a meeting between the surgeon-major and several medical gentlemen of the army, to examine some of these people: my visit was short, and the objects disgusting. Thevenot, an author of great veracity, writes thus: 'The first time I saw hermaphrodites was in Surat; it was easy to distinguish them; for seeing there is a great number in that town, I was informed beforehand, that for a mark to know them by, they were obliged, under pain of correction, to wear upon their heads a turban like men, though they may go in the habit of women.'"*

James Forbes
Oriental Memoirs, 1813
(This account from 1765 or earlier)

SEVENTEEN

At dhar prasad's again, I asked Reddy about castration. How was it done?

"Originally," said Reddy, "there was a crude system. The hair of the horse's tail is stronger than our hair; in pieces two-two they used to tie it around the organ, and then pull—tie it, and go on pulling—every day, tighter, and tighter—slowly—so it takes some time: and eventually it is cut, and falls off. And another method: These barbers used to cut—anesthesia was not there—there was a lot of bleeding, and several months of sickness. And there was the likelihood of—sometimes—death."

"Why did they cut the whole thing off," I asked, "and not just the testicles?"

"Potentiality," said Reddy, meaning erection, "can be maintained without testicles."

"Hermaphrodites," I asked, "also come to the hijra houses?"

"They come," said Reddy. "Because they are neglected in the other society."

"Tell her about the case," said Dhar Prasad.

"Ha-aa," said Reddy. "They 'marry', you know, the eunuchs. But they don't come to our homes. The man goes and visits his eunuch-wife. They maintain them . . . There was an exchange of knives in King Kothi because of this. The late Nizam VII's sons used to indulge in such offenses. Suppose I love a eunuch? If somebody takes him, then he is my enemy. So they used to fight. Such cases were reported. They used to send their cars and take the boys. The Nizam's sons."

"When was this?"

"Sometime in the year 1958," said Reddy. "There was an exchange of knives among the sahib zadas*—that is, the sons of the palace of the Nizam at King Kothi. The late Nizam—Osman Ali Khan.** He had his own palace police, and their security officer, and private employees. So the security officer, the chief of the palace's security forces, inquired into the charges, the cause of the exchange of knives—the stabbing—among the sahib zadas. And he found out that a particular sahib zada, who was in love with a eunuch, who was very handsome, was seen in the company of another brother. Thus there was a love-jealousy. And one or two times, he had pointed it out, tried to prevent his brother from taking that eunuch, but he did not oblige."

"Do you know the name of this eunuch?"

"His name was Rahman," said Reddy. "A young boy. Then the palace security officer—as he could not take cognizance of the crime—because stabbing is a crime—so the regular police—the government—had to take action."

"Who was stabbed?" I asked.

"Brothers," said Reddy. "Stabbed each other. So the palace security officer referred the case to the police. And by the by, he entrusted a confidential letter to the commis-

* sons of the Nizam's concubines, accepted as sons, and not his two legitimate heirs
** He was said to have over 200 children.

sioner of the city police to enquire into the allegations, and prevent such eunuchs from coming into contact with the males of the palace. Then that letter was entrusted to me. This was when the Nizam was not in power. He was already an exhausted king. So I worked on the subject, and found out, by my own methods, that after ten o'clock at night, the cars used to come from King Kothi. King Kothi did not have general license plate numbers. Since it was the royal palace, they could have K. K. on the numberplate—that honor was given to them. So such cars used to come to Chhoti Haveli, Bari Haveli, and, as somebody picks up prostitute girls in the houses, they used to pick up these boys and go. Then, at about four, four-thirty A.M., again the cars would come and drop them off."

"You were watching?"

"Naturally," said Reddy. "A continuous watch was there. Because I could not go to the palace and ask the names of the sons—it's also a big place—so through making friends with the drivers—right? We had to trap them . . . We would wait at their place. We know which car comes. No photos to cart around like you have—but eyes only, to create friendship with the drivers, by tipping them, and asking them, 'Which boy—which eunuch are you taking? Whom are you taking him to? What is the relationship? How do they do it? What house?' Then I entered Chhoti Haveli and Bari Haveli and came into contact with the gurus of the eunuchs—the heads of the eunuch palaces. Two gurus: 'Chhota' guru, 'Bara' guru. One for one house, one for the other. Then casually, after introducing myself as a police officer, I found out their history, their background, their genealogy, and finally, advised them not to mingle with palace affairs, as it is a serious matter involving criminal cases. So they were prevented. I was a detective in the Criminal Investigation Division, so the regular police—the uniformed police—were kept on guard. When the cars came, they would take the cars and the drivers, and then send up a report to the Nizam's palace—to the security officer—that such a particular car and a driver were found here in the city—roving and taking the eunuchs—and such driver was dismissed, and some action was taken; when matters of such drastic action came to the attention of the sahib zadas and khannazads,* they stopped a little bit. They might have been doing it secretly, but not openly. That's how I worked on the subject for about three years— as an academic interest, as an executive police officer; and I studied the law of eunuchs, under which they used to be prosecuted."

"What was the law?" I asked.

"The law says," said Reddy: "coming into homogeneal contact—offense; appearing in a female dress in the main roads and attracting young boys—offense; kidnapping male boys, converting them to be eunuchs—offense. According to the Indian Penal Code, Section 320, emasculation has been treated as 'grievous hurt.' In addition to the all-India laws, every state has its own local laws. In 1919, the Nizam's government framed rules and regulations against them known as *Kava-e-de-Mukhannisan*. The legal term for the eunuchs in Urdu is *Mukhannas*. Section 260 of the Asifiya penal code states that emasculation—*Mukhannas karna*—is a grievous hurt, punishable under the same code. According to these rules, the eunuchs had to register their names with the police, and the police had to check their movements, maintain a watch over them. An act was passed whereby they were punished if they contradicted the regulations. There were two kinds of eunuchs: eunuchs

---

* adopted sons of the Nizam, born or brought up in the house, who were part of the family circle

by birth, and those made by artificial means. This could
be done by force, or by willingness. Where there was willingness, there was no offense—but *even* if there was willingness, it could not be done openly. There was a famous
kidnapping case, during Osman's time—the eunuchs used
to kidnap boys, and make them eunuchs, and maintain
them as 'disciples.' Others volunteered, because they had a
female character and appearance . . . And I'll tell you another important thing: You're missing the entire subject.
The eunuchs have their own language. Unwritten language—you understand?"

"Not what they speak to us."

"No," said Reddy. "If they speak in Urdu, you understand, I understand. But they speak amongst themselves
against us, in their own language."

"What kind of language is it?"

"It's like a tribal language," said Reddy. "It's a dialect.
Urdu words you cannot find."

"Ah," I said. "That's how they protect themselves."

"Suppose, suddenly," said Reddy, "the police come in,
and they want to do something quickly. They'll speak in
their own language, and we'll stay like that! We will not
know what we are doing."

"It's a common language," I asked, "between all the hijras in India?"

"They all have it," said Reddy. "When they get together,
they all speak like that."

"Do any of them write?"

"Very few," said Reddy. "And you may ask: Muslims,
how do they offer prayers? Among Hindus, there is no particular way—going to a temple, or seeing the deities, and
saying 'namaskar.' But that is not sufficient for a Muslim.
He has to read particular verses of the Koran. So: they will
learn those verses by heart—they memorize them. See, al-

ways the uneducated will be cleverer than the educated. His brain is very good. You and I cannot copy a film song as fast as an uneducated recites."

"When you entered the house," I asked, "how did you get the histories? The younger eunuchs, do they know their own background?"

"The history," said Reddy, "of the eunuchs, generally, is an unwritten one. Unwritten history is handed down from generation to generation. It's the duty of the guru to tell them the stories, and the types of songs they sing sometimes relate some history."

"In Lucknow, they have a very advanced tradition?"

"Yes. Advanced. I've been there," said Reddy.

"Lucknow boys," interjected Dhar Prasad, "are more beautiful than you. You are nothing comparable! I'm really telling. The young boys, they die after them!"

"Lucknow people," laughed Reddy, "are known for their delicacy. Hyderabad eunuchs, they are a little bit rough. The Lucknow boys are more beautiful than the girls. Lucknow eunuchs—for delicacy, and neatness, also. This guru—Kamal Baksh—looks like a ruffian, doesn't he? But the same type of guru in Lucknow is like the maintainer of the courtesans of Bengal."

"They are keeping bad habits. Dirty habits," said Dhar Prasad.

"There are also some references," said Reddy, "in medical jurisprudence. You may ask: how is medical jurisprudence involved? These eunuchs are prosecuted for 'unnatural' offenses—for homogeneal offenses. So, before prosecuting them, or taking them to the court, we have to satisfy ourselves that he's in that habit. A medical test is required. The victim is sent to hospital, where he will be examined. His anus will be examined."

"Now," I asked, "are there any recent examples of kidnapping cases that you know of? In Hyderabad, like the one that was reported in Gujarat?"

"Not in the recent past," said Reddy. "Or even post-Independence. Because it was only in the pre-Independence era. That is, before 1948 . . . There is another legend they relate: when Ram, during the *Ramayana* period, was sent into exile . . ."

"He crosses the river," I said, "and says, 'All men and women go back . . .' "

"Ha-ha," said Reddy. "So that is only a joke. It's not a historical thing. 'So they are still sitting there . . . ' It's a joke they told in Parliament. We attribute so many jokes to eunuchs. Another thing I will tell you. You've read the words in English, 'Lal Ganderi Par'—that is Urdu."

"The 'instrument of torture'?"

"Ha-aa," said Reddy. "The maturity of the girl is known to all. The 'haram-piece'—the hymen—is there. Then how is a eunuch boy matured? So, they use a very crude method. They will dress that boy in a female dress, very nicely, and a ceremony will be performed. They celebrate in that locality, in that Allawah. And that boy will be made to sit on that rod and slowly, they push. So with that, the anus bursts. And a lot of bleeding will be there. They will be kept for about fifteen days, by applying all types of grease and ointments . . . So they prepare the boy, from the beginning, that way . . . for homogeneal purposes."

"So," I asked, "the castration ceremony is a different one?"

"The castration ceremony is a different one," said Reddy. "See, castration makes the boy more beautiful. If the organ is cut off, the skin softens. Hair falls. Features also change. So, that way, they make them more beautiful. More feminine. That's how they do it. When the organ is cut—not big, but small breasts come."

"What age do they do this?" I asked.

"This is about fifteen, sixteen," said Reddy.

"So people don't come to them before that age?"

"They don't," said Reddy.

"So," I said, "this whole business of six-year-old boys being kidnapped is unlikely."

"Ha-aa," agreed Reddy. "They don't do that business. Not in Hyderabad. They keep the boy fit for that purpose. And for that purpose, on a grand scale, they celebrate! Drinking, dancing. And among these dirty males, they challenge: 'Who will be the first user?' Some nasty bastards, they also participate: 'I'll give one hundred rupees for first use.' Among the prostitutes, in the brothels, the first girl will also have a big market. Like that, this boy will have a big market. So the men feel proud—'I am a man.' That is the ceremony they call among the girls, 'Nathu-thurna.' And marriages, also, they will perform. Grand scale. Biryani biryani, all this. Nicely."

"You've seen these?"

"I've seen it," said Reddy. "I'm telling you. I participated. I attended. Because I am not *new* to *them*." Reddy laughed. "Because we were officers, they respect us. And at times of any difficulty, we help them."

"Like now, they have a court case?"

"It's already excused," said Reddy. "Dismissed. And we warned them."

"Was it homosexuality?"

"Homosexuality," said Reddy.

"Prostitution?"

"Prostitution," said Reddy. "Some 'misunderstanding,' they say. Due to that, the policeman was 'mistaken,' and all those things . . . They blame like that . . . who will admit it?"

"How does a eunuch get ostracized?" I asked.

"From the guru's house?" said Reddy. "He also out-casts."

"The outcast of the outcaste?" I said.

"The outcast of the outcaste," said Reddy. "That is for disobedience of the guru. They do have their own jealousies."

"Why do they have to have the castrations now?" I asked.

"Now, it's not so common," said Reddy. "See, there's a lot of radiation between the old people's approach and the younger generations. In olden days—the feudals—they used to enjoy such things. But now there is no time for such things. We are living a mechanical life. And these are the devilish works of the feudalists."

~

The eunuchs are very much in demand with the aristoc-racy. They are generally very loyal and very attached to the interests of their employers. They are the favorite confidantes of their masters and mistresses and rarely abuse their confidence. They are admitted at all hours of the day and night in the zenanas, and often become rich, thanks to the generosity of their masters. Many eunuchs at Oudh have acquired an elevated social position and have had many honours and distinctions bestowed upon them.

Mrs. Hassan 'Ali Meer, Englishwoman
Observations on the Mussulmans of India
1832

EIGHTEEN

Aттɪᴀ ʜᴏsᴇɪɴ ʜᴀᴅ ɢʀᴏᴡɴ ᴜᴘ in Lucknow, half in and half out of women's seclusion. She had rebelled against that "feudal background," and had married a man she loved, against her mother's wishes. She was the author of two books, a collection of short stories, *Phoenix Fled*, and a novel, *Sunlight on a Broken Column*.

"I'll tell you what I remember," said Hosein. "Whenever there was any occasion for celebration—marriage, or circumcision, or when the name was given to the baby—though we had the whole Westernized way of life as well—"

"What year is this?"

"I was born in 1913," said Hosein, "so that it's very early on . . . There was an area where the men sat; and the women sat behind curtains, or those very fine bamboo chicks . . . There used to be a big space. A shamiana, a tent, was put up, and everyone sat on the floor; nobody sat on chairs, everything was cleared, and you put the white sheets down, and then the carpets. My memory is of those who used to sing, who were colloquially called 'rundi'— which is 'prostitute'—but they weren't exactly prostitutes. They were courtesans. They were amongst the best singers of classical music."

"These were the hijras?"

"No, these were the women," said Hosein. "Now, there would be the celebration with the women singing first, and then, the memory of the hijras is with me: because I'd sit there—I was small enough to be allowed to sit inside and watch them—and this band of men would come in as if they were saying, 'Ye ghoray hai!' 'The horses are coming!' They'd come along as if they were riding the horses, you know, miming it, and then they'd describe these horses that were coming. They came in miming: that is why it stuck in my head as a child, but as I grew up, I knew that these were called the 'bhands.' They would sing and dance, but mainly, their role was to entertain with all kinds of songs, jokes, and allusions to people you couldn't normally talk about in that disrespectful way. They would have satire about everyone."

"In the room, and in the society?" I asked.

"Yes," said Hosein. "This was entertainment. This is why, later, when I grew up, I thought of the fool in Shakespeare. In his greatest plays, there's always the character that can say the things that no one else can . . . to the king. And they used to do that: they'd tear to shreds the most important of people. Amongst the bhands, there were some who were not hijras, but there were others . . . because hijras were part of the entertainment of the time. They were not looked down upon; nobody said anything against them in a way of abuse; they were *the hijras* who came."

"They wore women's clothes?" I asked.

"These bhands did not," said Hosein. "They wore men's clothes—turbans, pajama, kurta . . ."

"It was only by the way they moved?"

"But there were hijras amongst them," said Hosein. "Because people used to say, 'hijra hai,' 'he's a hijra.' Though the hijras who were like women, or dressed like women, were at a wedding I went to in Rampur. My husband's sister-in-law was from Rampur."

"The palace?"

"And her half-sister," said Hosein, "was the Begum [queen] of Rampur. I was a spectator. And you must remember that I was also rather rebellious, as I grew up, against all the things that were happening in feudal society. I was mostly with the very left-wing people, though I came from a feudal background, and lived, in my mother's house, after my father died—I was ten—a very circumscribed life. But my mind wasn't in any way confined to that."

"So you would go to the palace?" I asked.

"So I went to my *friends*," said Hosein. "You know, this was like a trade union of feudal people—one went around amongst each other's homes, and there was no distinction between who was Hindu, or who was a Muslim—they were all 'uncle,' or 'aunt . . .' "

"But to your family," I said, "they were the more decadent?"

"No," said Hosein. "I didn't think of them as decadent at all. I was politically angry in the 1930s, with the British, principally—this imperial power—and then, the whole system of feudalism, because of the fact that one thought that this is the time it changes. The ones who were decadent amongst the class of feudal people were those who had not moved with the times, mentally. But I never thought of it as a term of disrespectfully addressing someone—'Oh, who wants to talk to that decadent person?' I thought, that's the middle-class term for all feudal people, just happily calling them 'decadent,' though some of the middle class, to my mind, were much worse."

"So—" I laughed.

"So," continued Hosein, "it isn't a question of decadence. It's a question of a culture that existed for—always, it had existed. After all, historically, you go right back to when the Ottoman Turks had all their eunuchs around, and when everybody had, in the old empires. That was not a part of decadence, but a part of the fact that—once you kept women safely away from marauding men, who was to guard them? The best people would be tough physically—male—but castrated, so they wouldn't be a problem."

"This was a practice you knew of?" I asked.

"I knew that this happened," said Hosein. "And I knew that there were people in these places—in these states; the only state that I was close to was the Rampur state, because of friendships with the family. But, as a young person, when I went for the wedding, this was new to me, because we didn't have eunuchs in our homes: not in a single *taluq-dari* [wealthy landowner's] home did I know of a eunuch existing within the household. It's only in the Rampur family that I saw them; they were moving around, dressed as women, as far as I remember, but some of them were still dressed like men. They moved between the men's side of the palace, to the inner side of the palace. As long as they were castrated, it was all right."

"They could wear saris," I asked, "and they could wear turbans?"

"They could," said Hosein. "There was no distinction. As long as they were hijras, who looked after the women, who were watching over them, entertaining people. Their function *then*, at the wedding, was that they sang songs, and they went in between the two places, finding out when the food would come, what would happen—they were *part* of the household. They sang rather lewd songs, which was part of the custom when the bridegroom's people arrived, and they did it without all this doing it for money or deliberately: that was part of the way of doing things. The 'samdhi,' as they were called, who arrived from the bridegroom's family, would be made a target for all kinds of songs and jokes."

"So," I asked, "the hijras dressed as women were entertainers, but there were also hijras dressed as men who were moving about the space—from mardana to zenana?"

"And they could wear anything they liked," said Hosein, "these men—these non-men. Because the whole purpose of their being made into what they were made into was: that they were safe, to be where they could be, amongst the women, and could look after everything. They'd be major-domos, practically, of the household . . . And sometimes you'd see them—bands of them—these were not the ones looking after the zenana, in the palace—they would be on the streets, all dressed in saris and walking around, and everybody would say, 'Achaa, hijray ja rahay hain.' 'The hijras are passing.' But the whole point that always struck me was: it wasn't as if one turned against them, or turned on them."

"They had a place," I said.

"They had a *place*," said Hosein. "They were part of life. And life could take any number of forms."

~

In 1845, when an Englishman, Sir Charles Napier, conquered and annexed a part of India which was known as the Sindh, now mostly in Pakistan, he was disturbed to learn that his troops were being corrupted by brothels of an unusual nature. Wrote Sir Richard Burton: *"It was reported to him that Karachi, a townlet of some two thousand souls and distant not more than a mile from camp, supported no less than three lupanars or bordels, in which not women but boys and eunuchs, the former demanding nearly double the price, lay for hire. Being then the only British officer who could speak Sindi, I was asked indirectly to make enquiries and to report upon the subject; and I undertook the task on express condition that my report should not be forwarded to the Bombay Government, from whom supporters of the Conqueror's policy could expect scant favour, mercy or justice. Accompanied by a Munshi, Mizra Mohammed Hosayn of Shiraz, and habited as a merchant, Mizrah Abdullah the Bushiri passed many an evening in the townlet, visited all the porneia and obtained the fullest details, which were duly despatched to Government House. But the 'Devil's Brother' [Napier] presently quitted Sind leaving in his office my unfortunate official: this found its way with sundry other reports to Bombay and produced the expected result. A friend in the*

Secretariat informed me that my summary dismissal from the service had been formally proposed by one of Sir Charles Napier's successors, whose decease compels me parcere sepulto. But this excess of outraged modesty was not allowed."

Napier apparently destroyed the brothels *"by putting down the infamous beasts who, dressed as women, plied their trade in the Meers time openly."* He noted that among the chief clients of the brothels were the ruling Ameers or chieftains of Afghanistan, *"whose financial records revealed their deep involvement."*

The report Burton filed with Napier was not published by the British, and upon his death, the original was probably destroyed by Burton's widow. To this day, a copy has not been found. His travels amongst the brothels cost Burton his reputation in England, as no Englishman had ever written with such candour about sexuality.

Some of what Burton had observed in India he wrote about in the "Terminal Essay" of 1855, at the end of his translation of the *Alf Laylah Wa Laylah: The Book of A Thousand Nights and A Night*, in which he traced the history of pederasty in the East, calling it "Le Vice." Burton suggested that it initially moved from Greece to Rome: *"Roman civilization carried pederasty also to Northern Africa, where it took firm root, while the negro and negroid races to the south ignore the erotic perversion, except where imported by foreigners into such kingdoms as Bornu and Haussa. In old Mauritania, now Marocco, the proper are notable sodomites; Moslems, even of saintly houses, are permitted to keep catamites . . . Yet pederasty is forbidden by the Koran . . . the punishment being some hurt or damage by public reproach . . . But here, as in adultery, the law . . . will not convict unless four credible witnesses swear to have seen rem in re . . . As in Marocco, Le Vice prevails throughout the old regencies of Algiers, Tunis and Tripoli and all the cities of the South Mediterranean seaboard, whilst it is unknown to the Nubians, the Berbers and the wilder tribes dwelling inland. Proceeding Eastward we reach Egypt, that classical region of all abominations which, marvellous to relate, flourished in close contact with men leading the purest of lives, models of moderation and morality, of religion and virtue . . .*

"Syria and Palestine, another ancient focus of abominations, borrowed from Egypt and exaggerated the worship of androgynous and hermaphroditic deities . . . Plutarch notes that the old Nilotes held the moon to be of 'male-female sex' . . . Isis also was a hermaphrodite, the idea being that Aether or Air (the lower heavens) was the menstruum of generative nature . . . Julius Firmicus relates that 'the Assyrians and part of the Africans' . . . hold air to be the chief element and adore its fanciful figure . . . consecrated under the name of Juno or the Virgin Venus. Their companies of priests cannot duly serve her unless they effeminate their faces, smooth their skins and disgrace their masculine sex by feminine ornaments. You may see men in their very temples amid general moans enduring miserable dalliance and becoming passives like women . . . and they expose, with boasting and ostentation, the pollution of the impure and immodest body.

"Here we find the religious significance of eunuchry. It was practised as a religious rite by the Tympanotribas or Gallus, the castrated votary of Rhea or Bona Mater, in Phrygia called Cybele, self-mutilated but not in memory of Attis; and by a host of other creeds: even Christianity . . . could not altogether cast out the old possession . . .

"Resuming our journey Eastward we find the Sikhs and the Moslems of the Punjab much addicted to Le Vice, although the Himalayan tribes to the north and those lying

south, the Rajputs and Marathas, ignore it. The same may be said of Kashmiris . . . : the proverb says, 'Though of men there may be famine yet shun these three—Afghan, Sindi and rascally Kashmiri.' M. Louis Daville describes the infamies of Lahore and Lakhnau where he found men dressed as women, with flowing locks under crowns of flowers, imitating the feminine walk and gestures, voice and fashion of speech, and ogling their admirers with all the coquetry of bayaderes . . . Yet the Hindus, I repeat, hold pederasty in abhorrence and are much scandalized by being called Gand-mara (anus beater) or Gangu (anuser) as Englishmen would be."

NINETEEN

At the Secunderabad Club, I had drinks with an uncle thrice removed, who happened to be a doctor. Two frail, warm people in their sixties, Roop Karan and his wife were intrigued by my project.

"So. You want the medical point of view?" asked Dr. Karan. "It's for lust."

"That does not sound medical," I said.

"Lust for money," said Dr. Karan.

"And what about desire?" I asked.

"They're ready any time," laughed Dr. Karan. "Women, as compared to men—there is no limit. One of my friends, when asked how long a woman can take this treatment, took some sand in his hand, and said, 'As long as this is existing.'"

I looked at Mrs. Karan; she merely grinned.

"How exactly does this relate to the hijras?" I asked.

"I'm speaking about prostitution," said Dr. Karan. "Their patience is infinite."

"The kings, and nobility, were involved with all this . . ."

"They had a lot of wives," said Dr. Karan, "but people used to take pleasure in behaving with their subordinates. So this tradition must have started like that."

"You've treated them?"

"Yes," said Dr. Karan. "And they get all sorts of sexual diseases. After they're cured, they come right back. And I'm telling you—every single one is sexually active, even the very oldest."

"They can afford you?"

"Yes," said Dr. Karan.

"How do they urinate?"

"During that procedure," said Dr. Karan, "they put rolled gauze there, and every day, they clean that area, and replace the cotton. And little by little—each day—the urine comes out. They have to keep it open."

"They don't come to you for the operation?"

"No. They don't come to regular doctors."

"Isn't the operation dangerous?"

"It can be," said Dr. Karan. "But nowadays, they have antibiotics."

"At what age?"

"Mostly after puberty," said Dr. Karan, "from what I have seen. Because they do have some male characteristics that normally develop after that . . ."

~

In a footnote about the eunuchs in his translation of the *Arabian Nights*, Burton wrote: *"The parts are swept off by a single cut of the razor, a tube (tin or wooden) is set in the urethra, the wound is cauterized with boiling water, and the patient planted in a fresh dunghill. His diet is milk; and if under puberty, he often survives."*

It is probable, stated Burton's biographer, Fawn Brodie, that this description owed its precision to the observations Burton made while he dwelled in the brothels of Karachi.

TWENTY

ON THE DAY THAT Kamal Baksh was supposed to
sing, there was a perturbance about the place. Munni
moved quickly in and out, caught up in her own thinking.
Rani and Kiran were nowhere to be seen. Kamal Baksh sat
where she usually did, but her shadow, Sayeed, was missing.

Upon seeing Mr. Reddy, Kamal Baksh quickly greeted
him, covering her head with her scarf. Normally, he might
have required a chair, but he humbly took a place, cross-
legged, on the mat.

"I came to this house earlier," he explained, "when I was
an inspector of the Criminal Investigation Division for the
Police Commission."

"Why did you come here?" asked Kamal Baksh.

"To meet you all, and to make inquiries," said Reddy.

"No," said Kamal Baksh, "somebody else came. You
were not amongst them."

"I'll tell you when," continued Reddy. "When there was
a stabbing amongst the sahib zadas. It was some time ago.
Rahman, I believe, was his name. The Kotwali car used to
call us, and for some time, there was enmity and fighting."

"They were brothers," said Kamal Baksh.

"From King Kothi," said Reddy.

Kamal Baksh shook her head. "You must have gone to

another house," she said. "Maybe it was Chhoti Haveli [Small Palace]. You must have found out about *them*. They were 'on hire.' "

"I came because of a letter in the Police Commission."

"Among the six sons,"* said Kamal Baksh, "only one is any good. All the others are bad. They took them 'on hire.' The whole night they used to run around! But they didn't come to *my* house."

Reddy gently insisted. Now Kamal Baksh named the visitors she remembered over the years who had come to her house: Harriet Lynton, and the Reddy family, who had shown the hijras great largesse.

"Is anyone at home across the street?" I asked. I wanted to visit the shanties.

"There are people there," said Kamal Baksh, "but four of them are sick. Humayun is there. He's got some urinary infection."

"They looked quite well from the roof," I told Reddy, in English.

"There are certain trade secrets," said Reddy, in English, "they will not reveal. He, being the head"—indicating Kamal Baksh—"takes care of them all. The newcomer will be allotted a room in the back—outside. Each room will have three or four persons. There will be common cooking. Sometimes 'sick' is a euphemism **. . . They don't say it."

"Do those houses have the same guru? You?" I asked Kamal Baksh.

"No," said Kamal Baksh. "Each house has a different guru. One died. One has gone to Ajmer. There are four or five."

"Where is everybody today?" Shivi asked.

---

* It's not clear who Kamal Baksh is talking about among the sahib zadas'
** for the 'operation'

"Some have gone to do work," said Kamal Baksh, "and others have gone in the night . . . So tell me, what is to be done? There are two or three who promised to come by this time—the ones who dance. They should have come by now."

"Where is Sayeed?" I asked.

"They've all gone for work?" said Reddy.

"There was some fighting," explained Kamal Baksh, "between two groups of us. They said it was their town, and we said it was ours. They had gone to Nagpur to work—for Holi. There is strife between us . . . Last night, there was a telegram, so all of the hijras have gone there . . . Where does Berar fall? Does it fall under Mughlai, or another state?"

"Mughlai's neighbor," said Reddy.

"So, does it fall under Nagpur?" insisted Kamal Baksh.

"Yes," said Reddy.

"Where was Nagpur earlier? Was it in Mughlai territory?"

"No," said Reddy.

"Do you know," asked Kamal Baksh, "where Nagpur fell during Nizam Ali Khan's time? Around three hundred years ago?"

Kamal Baksh was evidently speaking of the territorial divisions among the eunuchs according to different states, but her frame of reference was taking her far back into history. The disputed land was apparently the city of Nagpur, in the state of Berar. But did Nagpur technically belong to Mughul territory, Kamal Baksh was asking? Was her group right, or was theirs?

"Nagpur . . . Ellichpur . . . Chanda . . . ," said Kamal Baksh, "they were in Bewan Berar."

"Yes," said Reddy. "Later on, the Nizam went to the other side . . ."

"Okay," said Kamal Baksh. "But after that, all these areas were in the state. I have a map, but I need someone to read it. It is in English and Urdu."

"Bring it," said Reddy.

So Kamal Baksh called aloud for Kiran. "Oh, son! Come here," she said.

Now Kiran appeared, through the alley door, followed by a child, and a young man, who hovered in the entrance. Kamal Baksh handed Kiran the keys, and she opened the door to a room. Kiran dragged out a trunk, and pushed it in front of Kamal Baksh.

"Why do you rent out this place?" Reddy asked.

"It's good to have a man in the house," said Kamal Baksh, contradicting herself. "Do you know Urdu?"

Kamal Baksh leaned into the trunk, and pulled out cylinders, one by one, until she found the one she wanted. She unrolled a large, old map of Hyderabad and Madras, which she put on the floor between us—a map of the railway lines in 1924.

"See, please, where Nagpur is," implored Kamal Baksh.

"Nagpur falls in the Chanda district," said Reddy, looking over the map.

"Does Chanda fall under Berar?" asked Kamal Baksh. "See, the Nizam won this district from Raja Gondwana, then he returned it, but he kept this area of Berar," she said, drawing an outline with her finger.

"Nagpur is here," said Reddy. "Berar finishes there."

Reddy was implying that Nagpur did not fall in the right district. Kamal Baksh's group may have been at fault. But Chanda was clearly, in Kamal Baksh's memory, part of their territory, and Nagpur should have fallen within it. Seeing no resolution in the map, she opened another cylinder, and pulled out a large piece of paper—frail, crinkled, Scotch-taped, and yellow with age.

"This was given as *inam*," said Kamal Baksh, "a gift . . .

You know Persian a little bit? Doesn't it have the name 'Chanda'?"

Reddy said that his Persian was not good, though he could read it. He studied the document.

"It's from Nizam Ali Khan's time," said Reddy.

"Yes," she said. "He gave us this land. The paper says 2259 jirat. But I don't understand the word 'jirat'."*

"Jirat is ration," said Reddy. He read aloud: "Nine . . . thousand . . . nine . . . hundred . . ."

"No," said Kamal Baksh, not looking at the paper. "Not nine thousand. Two thousand, two hundred and fifty nine." She either knew these numbers by heart, or had memorized part of the document!

The penmanship was very faint. I asked Reddy to read the date. He turned to the back.

"1 . . . 1 . . . 2 . . . hej . . . ," Reddy struggled with the Persian.

"1204 Hejira," Kamal Baksh interjected, again, without looking.

"It's their land contract?" I asked.

"Gift," said Reddy. "From the Nizam."

"The Nizam himself?" I asked.

"No," said Reddy, "somebody else would have signed it. This is the Nizam's government stamp." He read the Persian aloud: " 'Shah Alam . . . Asaf Jah, Nizam ul-Mulk, Mir Ali Nizam Khan.' That is the second Nizam." These dates put us between 1763 and 1803.

"Look how nicely she's kept it," said Shivi.

But Kamal Baksh was less interested in this museum piece, and our marveling. She wanted to know about Chanda. Again, Reddy said that he couldn't tell what the document said.

* may mean "zirat"—land

"Okay," said Kamal Baksh. She had another piece of paper. Perhaps it was written there . . . And from that cylinder, she pulled out another document, smaller in size, very old, and also faint. She handed it to Reddy.

"This one is in Urdu," said Reddy. "It's about all the houses—a number of houses." He bent over the document, reading it aloud, with difficulty.

"After they gave us this land," said Kamal Baksh, "people said, 'we want to have a locality—a colony.' "

"What's the date?" I asked.

"It's not in Persian," said Reddy. "It's Urdu. 1298 Fasli. It's a different kind of year. It's later than the other document."

But Reddy did not know how to correlate Fasli, or Mughul revenue years, to our years, or perhaps he wasn't sure what he was reading.

"The whole road," said Kamal Baksh, "used to be ours."

"Yes," agreed Reddy. "Later on, more land was given, where the Dispensary is, and City College. Mulayam Jung gave you the land—where the graveyard is."

"When we were having a court case," said Kamal Baksh, "with the other Haveli people—Chhoti Haveli—I presented these papers to the authorities, and they were all so startled."

Reddy continued to try to decipher the wording. He read it aloud, then changed his mind about the date. He said, "This is 1298 Hejira, not Fasli. See, this was an old locality. The houses are . . . 152 . . . 3 . . . 4 . . . 5 . . . 6 . . . 7 . . . 9, 162, 4626, 4627, 4628. These houses are not here now. There have been many changes. Now, this is a new locality."

"What's the number of your house?" I asked Kamal Baksh.

"21.1.557."

And to verify this, Kamal Baksh unrolled yet another set of papers—receipts of municipality taxes the hijras had paid.

Reddy began reading one of the tax documents.

"In whose name was this house?" I asked.

"Chotam," said Reddy.

"That must be Chotam Baksh," said Kamal Baksh.

"So Baksh is the guru's name?" I asked.

"See," said Kamal Baksh, "before Chotam Baksh was Inam Baksh. Before Inam Baksh was Saeedar Baksh. Before Saeedar Baksh was Murad Baksh."

The line of succession amongst the gurus: what Kamal Baksh had refused to enunciate, until the intervention of the police. They were all male names.

"This document," said Reddy, glancing up, "when Chotam Baksh was guru—is 1388 Fasli." He now tried to calculate. "It means 1938."

He took hold of another: "This is 1446. It means 1946."

"And this?" I said.

"1343," said Reddy. "Sometime at the turn of the century." He couldn't be more specific.

Yet another document revealed that Kamal Baksh had been purposely burned in childhood. Her hands had been swollen, she said. She showed us the scars.

"It's an old practice," said Reddy. "When hysteria comes . . . Many boys and girls have these scars."

Kamal Baksh asked us what we would drink, but when I offered to go out, she insisted that Kiran would do it. She called her, but to no avail. I offered again. She feared a scene—public tension—if I were to be seen bringing soft drinks into the hijra household, she told Shivi.

When Kiran arrived, Kamal Baksh said, "Go, son. Get three Limcas . . . Nobody has come . . . Otherwise we'd have danced and sung. You must be in a hurry, but what can I do? I'm also in a hurry."

"They may still show up," Shivi said.

"No," said Kamal Baksh. "They won't come. It's almost one o'clock."

Munni appeared in the doorway, and told Kamal Baksh that the food was ready.

"We already ate," said Kamal Baksh to Reddy. "But we prepared food for them. Will you also have?"

"No," said Reddy. "I take only one meal."

Munni brought out metal *thalis*, and served the food. Lamb, and a sour dal, she said, which was the specialty of the hijras of Hyderabad. We sat in a semicircle on the floor, including Kiran. The chef chose to watch us. Rice and bread were in abundance. The lamb, with cardamom, was of excellent quality, though I wondered about the expense. And the dal, in which there was also spinach, was spectacular. Conversation became light—was I eating hotel food? Good to have a home-cooked meal? Did I speak Urdu in America? Cook at home? My parents?

"This person has no arrogance," said Kamal Baksh, turning to Reddy. "She wears simple clothes. She's without pretense. And she's interested in knowledge."

"Thank you," I said.

"God bless you," translated Reddy.

I had grown to like Kamal Baksh. She had taken my questions without offense. The veils, the alleyways, the oblique routes she sometimes used were also part of their truth. But, in this journey, I had deferred to their way, hadn't persisted with the more intrusive questions—say, about their castrations and sex lives; when that time came, the hijras would show a different face.

~

According to the scholar Laurence W. Preston, a British merchant, James Forbes, was the first foreigner to mention the presence of hijras in India, in the camp of the Maratha king Rahunathrav, where Forbes was employed; these he described as in abundance as cooks for the travelling entourage of the king, marked by their peculiar dress in saris; on their heads they were evidently required to wear turbans, as a distinguishing sign. However, Preston wrote that Forbes was most likely "mistaken" in his observation of the hijras' attire, "a medley of male and female clothing," and also doubted that they could have been cooks for a Brahmin, or highest-caste, king.

The presence of man-made eunuchs in India horrified the East India Company, wrote Preston in "The Right to Exist: Eunuchs and the State in Nineteenth-Century India," and led to an unusual correspondence about them amongst the British regents: this was necessary because the hijras claimed that they had a right to beg, and in some cases, a right to land or cash grants that had been held in perpetuity, given to them by Indian kings. The British, having assumed the rule of state from the Indian kings, did not wish to appear to be supporting the institution of eunuchs.

A man known as the "subcollector of Pune" (the city of Poona today, just outside Bombay), whose name was R. D.

Luard, wrote to the collector of Poona, a Mr. R. Mills, in 1836, having compiled seven histories of hijras, ranging in age from thirty to seventy-five. He recorded that the *"operation is performed by one cut* [,] *the whole of the membra are taken off and a straw put into the urethra to keep it open, no means are taken for stopping the haemorrage; no opium or other narcotics given before the operation* . . . No *initiate"* was subjected to *"any force . . . by those already degraded."* A qualifying factor was sterility and impotence, and the subject was made to test the permanence of this state by lying beside a prostitute before he could undergo the operation, which was performed by a senior member of the community, known as a *dai*, or "midwife." Some, Luard added, had castrated themselves on their own; and most sexual misfits found a home in the community of "hijeras."

"It is lamentable to think," Mr. Luard wrote, that *"we are living amongst people who look upon infanticide*[,] *suttees (wife burning)*[;] *tuggee* [ritual murders] *and hijeras without apparently a feeling of horror; but we also know by experience that they resign these ancient practices with apathy."*

All seven hijras, added Preston, came from rural India; most were of Hindu "cultivating" castes, three were shepherds, and one was a Muslim. All assumed fanciful Hindu names afterward, followed by common names, like surnames, given as a sort of family name, to distinguish them from other hijra groups, and possibly revealing the line of succession from guru to disciple.

At the same time, wrote Preston, an Englishman named Goldsmid of Indapur, another district of Poona, recorded that although the hijras came from many castes, they *"upon emasculation take the names of Mussalmani women, and as such, live and are buried."* Other British district officers stated that Muslim and Hindu hijras were alike in all respects except that they did not dine together. Preston added that the British, in their zeal to organize social categories, compounded the problems of a hijra history with false distinctions; in reality, he wrote, the hijras *"seem to have borrowed rather freely from the cumulative social backgrounds of those who joined the community."*

The cult of the hijras, wrote the nineteenth-century ethnographers, was "Shivaite"; those of western India worshiped the goddess "Bhavani," fourteen rupees paid to her whenever a new hijra was initiated. *"In the nineteenth century,"* wrote Preston, *"the hijras are often identified with males born with some (always obscure) congenital malformation. A common assertion, never verified, was that they perpetuated their kind by recruiting hermaphrodites. But at the same time it was generally known that the hijras were in fact created eunuchs."*

R. V. Russell, in *Tribes and Castes of the Central Provinces of India*, described two classes of eunuchs: those naturally so, called "khasua," and those created, called "hijdas." (In fact, the word "khasi" was an Arabic word for created eunuchs, so that the identification here is either confused or, for some unknown reason, reversed.)

But, Preston argued, religious sanction was not the only force behind the perpetuation of the institution of hijras: their claims were more "potent," and came in the form of ancient "sanads," "vatans," or "rights," to beg, as well as "inams," tax-free gifts of land or cash allowances.

In Poona, the eunuchs were located in a part of the city known as "Hijera Peth," or Hijra Quarter, where *"the practices of some of the younger members of the community,"* wrote Goldsmid, *"are of a nature too revolting to be mentioned."* By this he meant that they were prostitutes. Goldsmid reported that *"the nakakin* [today, "naik"], *or*

*elderly mistress denied all knowledge of the passive abom-
ination"* and said that they *"only beg with decency and
character."*

"In each subdistrict," wrote Preston, *"there was a
'vatandar hijra,' or holder of the hereditary right ('vatan')
to collect a 'hak' (prerequisite), from the villagers."* They
claimed four paisas from *"cultivator households"* and
"food from fellow vatanholders." Goldsmid wrote that the
village householder gave the begging hijra alms because of
dread; *"refusal to render prompt payment was apparently
followed by the whole of the wretches lifting up their
soogras [petticoats] and outraging the feelings of the females of his family, by the most shameless and abominable
exposure of person . . . For the Hijera is supposed not only
by the common people, but even by intelligent Brahmins,
to have powers of detecting impotency. This belief affords
a ready means of extorting money from the married and
childless, who, aware of the contempt and derision which
a charge of impotency, coming from such a quarter would
subject them to, are glad to purchase secrecy at any price."*

Goldsmid's report led to an edict against public exposure, issued by the British India Company: *"Be it known to
all,"* wrote Goldsmid, *"that in the course of enquiries in
the Indapoor Purganna, it came to light that oppression
has been exercised on shopkeepers and Ryots in the following instances . . . The Hijera on visiting the villages lifts
up its soogra, for the purpose of collecting its haks and ex-
torts money from the impotent by the threat of punishing
their want of sterility . . ."* In other words, the hijras were
hereby forbidden to extort alms by public exposure.

"This edict," wrote Preston, *"was apparently directed
against a single offending vatandav Hijda. Being a native
of the Nizam of Hyderabad's territory, this unfortunate*

was expelled from the British districts on failure to furnish a cash security to refrain from the prohibited extortions."

This intelligence and edict on hijras made its way to the highest level of British government in Bombay (from sub-collector to collector to Revenue Commissioner to "Government"), and met with unanimous approval.

The question now arose in the Bombay Presidency as to how to prevent men from joining the community. Goldsmid wrote: *"I can suggest no means of at once checking a system so revolting; all that we can do is to prevent Hijeras exacting money by exposure of person and abominable practices but I am not aware of any regulation by which we can prevent others becoming Hijeras, and to punish those already initiated would, I think, be inadvisable for many reasons, if practicable."* He added that because hijras existed *"in thousands"* all over the Bombay Presidency and throughout India, any measure *"against them would have to be instituted in all jurisdictions."* Goldsmid was sure, too, that those who performed the operation could be prosecuted.

The collector of Poona, Mr. Mills, concurred, and argued that punishing those who perform the operation, prohibiting exposure, and punishment, under due course, would eventually reduce any *"inducement to become Hijeras."*

The opinion of the chief criminal court of the Bombay Presidency was sought; it responded with a sort of laissez-faire attitude, arguing that the police's prosecution of "public acts of indecency" under the existing law was probably enough to reduce the menace; there was no need for further legislation; and *"the rest will soon be mitigated . . . under the advantages of education."*

But Goldsmid of Poona disagreed: the villagers, he felt,

believed that the state now received a portion of the hijras'
profits, as it did under the previous peshwa government of
Maratha (because the British now assumed the rule of state
as colonizers), and the tradition continued to require permission from the Indian revenue officer, the "mamlatdar,"
for every new initiate. Their right to beg was even said
to have been sanctioned by legitimate documentation or
sanads. Many villages did indeed hold these rights to collect revenues, so that this perception by the Indian citizenry
was therefore not implausible.

Indeed, such was the case; the kings of yore had not only
issued the rights of hijras to beg, but had also protected the
hijras' territories from encroachment by other hijra groups.
In the case of two hijras who petitioned the king Sahu of
Satara in Maratha state (he ruled from 1708 to 1749), a
written "sanad" did exist. The two claimed their right to
beg had been issued by the king Shivaji (a major king, who
fought the Mughuls during the emperor Aurangzeb's time),
but these documents had burned; thus they wanted King
Sahu to reissue their "right." They were doing so in the
name of their *dai*, or midwife. The king responded on the
merits of the case. *"The swami considered the matter,"*
wrote Goldsmid, *"and the alms for the dai were continued
without molestation."* Wrote King Sahu: " 'Having made
and given these promises to you, this order was issued.
So, now and henceforth the enjoyment of the alms in the
subdistrict will be continued to you, Kondan Hijda and
Sankvar Hijda. Therefore do not expect a new sanad each
year for the continuance of alms; make copies of the document; return this original document concerning the enjoyment [13 April 1740, Wednesday—sent to the hereditary
district officers throughout the subdistricts].' "

In 1842, the then-collector of Poona had actually tried
to break this cycle of history: he had attached forty-one

acres of hijra land, their inam, and had withdrawn their claims of revenue *"pending a thorough investigation."* But he then learned that this land grant had *"descended through six generations of hijras, from master to disciple,"* and its legitimacy was borne out by a document of 1730–31, issued by King Sahu, in which he had *"continued the land to the disciple of the first grantee"* from two other hijras—Radhi Hijda to Ansi Hijda. Thus this inam, and its succession, was legalized by the state of Maratha.

The Revenue Commissioner had argued against upholding the inam: *"No encouragement should be shown to persons of this class, the claim to the privilege of succession through the lineage of disciples ought not . . . to be acknowledged."*

According to Preston, the Bombay Presidency assumed that the hijras did indeed have a right to their inam; but *"as they did not want to acknowledge succession through disciples,"* the government converted the generational inam into a *"life-holding of the then current incumbent."*

When Ansi Hijda died, in 1849, the next "master" petitioned the government to rescind the ruling. *"Saguni Hijda by name"* is said to have argued that *"it is the sad lot of her race not to bear children they being eunuchs. That their race is continued by taking chelas or disciples and therefore their property is inherited by their disciples."* She then presented three copies of royal sanads bearing out the claim.

The Bombay Presidency decided not only to reaffirm its previous ruling, but wrote new legislation—Act XI of 1852—establishing the "Bombay Inam Commission" to oversee claims of this kind: a general exclusion *"disallowed any grant . . . which could not be held without breach of the laws of the land, or the rules of public decency."*

In 1853, the sanad of Satara came up for review, and afforded the Bombay Presidency a chance to rid itself of this

nuisance once and for all. Attendants of the hijras petitioned the Satara commissioner to uphold the right of the
former government to accompany the hijras on their
rounds, claiming a sanad *"empowering us to . . . beg 4
piece from each shop and 2 or 4 piece from each house"*;
these "attendants" were needed because the hijras themselves were apparently not able physically to collect alms,
as they were considered "vile and polluting" sights. The
commissioner of Satara declared that while he could not issue a right to beg, he could protect them from being accosted: *"No persons should be allowed to molest, so long
as they conduct themselves properly."*

But the Bombay Presidency ignored the sanads and declared unilaterally that *"measures should be taken for pre-
venting these wretches from extorting alms . . . The right
of begging or extorting alms, whether authorized by former government or not, has been discontinued."*

The British thereby rejected precedent, regarding both
sanads and inams, which posed serious moral problems for
the British; the hijras clearly had both such rights, and yet
the idea of the British paying the hijras was to them pre-
posterous; further, in the case of the land grants, because
the hijras did not farm their land, and instead rented it
out, the British were in effect *"encouraging Hijda land-
lordism."*

But the then-collector of Satara was not happy with this
ruling: he argued that the hijras' holding of an inam did
not, in itself, constitute a *"breach of public decency,"* and
though he did not condone their *"abominable"* practices,
since they were now prohibited from begging, and since the
grants were of *"insignificant amount,"* they should at least
be continued for the life of the incumbents.

The Inam Commission did not want to set a precedent
by making an exception for the collector of Satara; instead,

it referred to the exception already made in 1842, and converted all hijras' claims of land to life grants, *"with the view that as . . . the discontinuance of their haks would not have any effect in raising them from their degraded position . . . Knowledge that their haks are to cease with their lives would be sufficient to deter others from following their example."*

If the goal was to rid India of her *"debased oriental practices,"* Preston concluded, the *"Bombay's Hijda 'policy' never quite realized these bland hopes. Castrations perhaps ceased, though we may wonder if even this achievement was permanent . . . At best, the halting steps gradually stopping the objectionable revenues and rights may have forced the hijdas from the countryside into towns and cities. Here they became confirmed beggars, perhaps prostitutes, and they joined the large urban underworld which the British most often ignored."*

TWENTY-ONE

"She seems to have caught a cold," said Kamal Baksh to Shivi. "Tell her to boil an egg in the night, peel it, and put it in a pitcher. Keep it there for three hours, then eat it. All the cold will disappear."

"Indian chicken," said Sayeed Baksh. "Not the English one."

All the hijras were present. Rani was done up in a bold flowered sari, and wore anklebells. Kiran looked a bit like a capon to me, in her yellow sari, with all this talk of eggs, but that was part of it all—their happy-sad natures. Sayeed, I was told, was going to sing. Munni held the dhol loosely in her lap—yes, the day had finally come when she deigned to sit with us.

We were waiting for "Reddy Sa'ab," as Kamal Baksh put it, so I took the opportunity to write down their proper names, ages, and any personal information they would part with. Surprisingly, Kamal Baksh wanted me to write to her from abroad. When I asked for her address, she lifted the side of the red mat we were sitting on—about ten by fourteen feet wide; below were hundreds, perhaps thousands, of blue aerograms. Kamal Baksh handed me one, from which to copy the address, written in English.

"What are all those?" I asked.

"Letters from my brothers," said Kamal Baksh.

"From where?" I asked.

"All over," said Kamal Baksh. "India, Pakistan, Mecca, Medina . . ."

"What is the meaning of Baksh?" I asked.

"The meaning of the Baksh," she said, "is that God has blessed or forgiven us."

With Shivi's help, I asked Rani how she had come to the hijra household, how old she was then, her age now. When she seemed hesitant, Kamal Baksh gently nodded, allowing her to speak. He came at the age of twenty, she said, referring to herself as masculine. He was now twenty-five. He was from the village of Heeryagunda. His mother died after he joined; his father before. They used to mistreat him. His father, his brother, were verbally critical of his character. "Every day they used to abuse me. So my heart wasn't there," said Rani. This house was a very popular place, and known to everybody. "So I came among the hijras." When he came, he was very "lean." Now he was "happy," meaning, "plump." Had he dressed like a girl before? No, only after he joined the community. His parents had been Muslim.

Reddy pulled the curtain aside, and quietly entered the circle on the mat. Kiran Baksh was speaking; she felt "herself" to be a hijra at the age of ten; she joined when she was twenty. Her parents belonged to the Lambari community—she was from a farmer's family. They were Hindus. When she came to the household, she did the cooking, washing, and fetching of water. She learned to sing and dance by accompanying her elders—as a silent observer. In her village, she had come upon the hijras, and that's how she'd learned of this house.

I asked Reddy to ask Kiran about the initiation ceremony, but he conspired with the hijras to avoid a direct wording of my question. The concept of "initiation"—

which I used as a euphemism for castration, more or less—
he calmly called the "festival" within the house. When was
the festival in the house, na? Obliquely, Kiran Baksh said
that she'd learned of this from her "elders," but did not
give a date for her own.

Munni came from Kagaz Mandi, the "Paper Bazaar"
area of Hyderabad. Her parents were servants in a company—a business. She joined when she was "sixteen, seventeen." Why had she come? "What can you do when your
parents abuse you? When your brother and sisters get angry at you?"

Now, as before, every story had begun to sound the
same; and when Sayeed's turn came, all he said was that he
was seventy years old, and that he didn't want to speak.
Why? It is the same, he said. You've heard it from the others. And, in that wry way, he was also suggesting that my
skepticism was not unfounded.

That proud, ancient face, reminding me of the eunuchs
of the past; that doubleness, in which a word, a gesture,
could become its opposite. It was there in Sayeed Baksh—
his supreme irony. As though all along he knew I would
stumble on the truth, bits and pieces of fiction, like a jig-
saw, and he would simply watch me. Watch as I tried, in
this labyrinth of silence, half-lies and mundane reality, with
my code, and theirs, to assemble a picture which might
resemble a constellation of facts. Who are you, Sayeed
Baksh, I wanted to ask; but the asked turned his face from
the question. Kidnapped? Handed over? A choice? You
will never say. It will be left to a thousand inferences. Many
will speak contradictory things, but these you will not resolve. A word, here and there, to throw one on course, that
is all I can ever hope for. Because in you is a renunciation
of power, and that is your power.

And it makes one think: that kinship here is so many

rules, so much an order around the idea of a family. And where is the place for the man in India who cannot procreate? It is a desperate choice, can hardly be called a choice— this archaeology of the eunuch. Repression, not freedom, to be what you are, is what is offered. Though I had been absent from judgment so far, it could only be an ambivalent narrator that moved closer to the hijras.

I gazed at the slingshot and the key above Kamal Baksh's head. They hung together on a nail, and their imagery was haunting: a slingshot—to keep outsiders at bay—and for those who had suffered outrageous misfortune; and a key—to what? To a new gender, perhaps, and to a past they would not reveal.

Rani stood in the center of their circle. She had a pillow stuffed under her sari. Munni had started a rhythm on the drum. Kamal Baksh was beating out a tiny pulse on the cymbals. The others were all clapping; a few voices there clearly could not carry a tune. Sayeed led the singing, and it was his voice that returned as a soloist, giving direction to the others. But just as we began, two men opened the side door and entered.

"No! No!" yelled Kamal Baksh. "Hey, out!"

And out they went.

Now Rani's eyes darted back and forth to flirt with us— as she prepared to act out every month of pregnancy. The first song was in Purabiya, the old-fashioned Hindi of the poet Tulsidas, from the state of Uttar Pradesh:

> In the first month, I didn't know what to do,
> In the second, I felt ignorant of everything,
> In the third, I felt giddy, my chest hurt, my head hurt,
> In the fourth, I liked eating lemon,
> In the fifth, I couldn't move around,
> In the sixth, I felt like going to my mother's place,
> In the seventh, I became breathless,

In the eighth, I became dark,
In the ninth, I expressed all my wishes of getting a car!

At the end of each phrase, the hijras shouted "Ha-ji"—
"yes!" as Munni paused, waiting with the silence of her
drum. Rani jumped and twisted, and twirled her sari palla;
she ached and mimed and tumbled backward; she groaned
and clutched her belly. But these were the songs of beggars,
a patchwork of necessity and sad histories, in the most
ironic theme of all: begetting, where they begot not; in liberal speech, where they moved nothing.

Oh ma: we will never be able to have children
So we've come to bless your child
And wish him happiness.

I couldn't watch Rani. Instead I focused on that still point,
Sayeed Baksh. His voice had an energized weariness which
bore all the traces of its history. Somehow that voice, even
in its nasal unpleasantness, seemed true. In Urdu, he sang,

Lord of the universe,
Because of you, Ram is born.

And the hijras sang,

Because of you,
Ram is born.
The instruments are playing in Avadhpur.*

Lord of the Universe
Because of you,

* Interestingly, they named Ram's birthplace as a town in the Muslim state
of Avadh (now part of Uttar Pradesh), not Ayodhya, the Hindu city.

All the money is being thrown around,
And the one who steals is stealing it.

Lord of the Universe,
Because of you,
Ram is born,
The instruments are playing in Avadhpur.

Lord of the Universe
Because of you,
Ram is born.

Why is Ram born?
Ram is born
Because Ram is to die.

"Could you sing a solo?" I asked Sayeed.
After some mock protest, but not vanity, he sang,

This is a time of spring, with flowers blooming all over.*
But I am afraid that the gardener will fall asleep.

I am going to the bar, where there is no sadness. The one
who wants to see heaven should come with me.

For how long should my heart be deceived on your
promises? You do any such thing so that my hopes are
shattered.

The dignity of my wounded heart will one come to know
only if somebody tries to test me.

Oh barman, the tale is not funny. It has established and
destroyed so many houses.

Sometimes from Qaba, and sometimes from the bar, I am
calling you from every area.

* from the film *Nikaah*

Look at the disappointment of such disheartened souls.
They themselves have darkened the source of the light in
the evening.

So many springs have passed before eyes, that now the
heart shakes or sinks at the name of spring.

He / she is completely oblivious of my name. The one to
whom the world calls by my name.

There was deceiving in the heart,
Sweetness on the lips,
And love in the eyes,
that Shawmin fell so convincingly on those.

My heart's desires were left in my heart
And I was left alone.
In spite of my loyalty,
It is me who is left alone.
And my wishes of heart
Flew out as tears,
And I was left alone . . .

Afterwards, with much struggle, Kamal Baksh would
accept 101 rupees for this performance, and no more, because, she said, we were her guests.

~

In 1871, the British government in India passed a law against the hijras, which extended to all of its local governments, excluding the princely states. "Act No. XXVII . . . for the Registration of Criminal Tribes and Eunuchs," thus states:

24. *The Local Government shall cause the following registers to be made and kept up by such officer as, from time to time, it appoints in this behalf:—*

(a) a register of the names and residences of all eunuchs residing in any town or place to which the Local Government specially extends this Part of this Act, who are reasonably suspected of kidnapping or castrating children, or of committing offences under section 377 of the Indian Penal Code, or of abetting the commission of any of the said offences; and

(b) a register of the property of such of the said eunuchs as, under the provisions hereinafter contained, are required to furnish information as to their property.

The term 'eunuch' shall, for the purposes of this Act, be deemed to include all persons of the male sex who admit themselves, or on medical inspection clearly appear, to be impotent.

25. *Any person deeming himself aggrieved by any entry made or proposed to be made in such register, either when*

the register is first made or subsequently, may complain to the said officer, who shall enter such person's name, or erase it, or retain it as he sees fit.

Every order for erasure of such person's name shall state the grounds on which such person's name is erased.

The Commissioner shall have power to review any order passed by such officer on such complaint, either on appeal by the complainant or otherwise.

26. Any eunuch so registered who appears, dressed or ornamented like a woman, in a public street or place, or in any other place, with the intention of being seen from a public street or place,

or who dances or plays music, or takes part in any public exhibition, in a public street or place or for hire in a private house,

may be arrested without warrant, and shall be punished with imprisonment of either description for a term which may extend to two years, or with fine, or with both.

27. Any eunuch so registered who has in his charges, or keeps in the house in which he resides, or under his control, any boy who has not completed the age of sixteen years, shall be punished with imprisonment for a term which may extend to two years, or with fine, or with both.

28. The Magistrate may direct that any such boy shall be returned to his parents or guardians, if they can be discovered. If they cannot be discovered, the Magistrate may make such arrangements as he thinks necessary for the maintenance and education of such boy, and may direct that the whole or any part of a fine inflicted under section twenty-seven may be employed in defraying the cost of such arrangements.

The Local Government may direct out of what local or municipal fund so much of the cost of such arrangements as is not met by the fine imposed, shall be defrayed.

29. *No eunuch so registered shall be capable—*
    (a) of being or acting as guardian to any minor,
    (b) of making a gift,
    (c) of making a will, or
    (d) of adopting a son.

30. *Any officer authorized by the Local Government in this behalf may, from time to time, require any eunuch so registered to furnish information as to all property, whether movable or immovable, or of to which he is possessed or entitled, or which is held in trust for him.*

Any such eunuch intentionally omitting to furnish such information, or furnishing, as true, information on the subject which he knows, or has reason to believe, to be false, shall be deemed to have committed an offence under section one hundred and seventy-six or one hundred and seventy-seven of the Indian Penal Code, as the case may be.

31. *The Local Government may, with the previous sanction of the Governor General in Council, make rules for the making and keeping up and charge of registers made under this Part of the Act.*

A Collection of the Acts,
Passed by the Governor General of
India in Council in the Year 1871

TWENTY-TWO

"THE LAST TIME I WAS IN DELHI, in 1981," said Shehbaz Safrani, a painter and curator, "there were several murders—something like eighteen people killed overnight. One was a hijra. But it was a political thing—a feud between two politicians. And this is the nefariousness of Indian politics; instead of having it out, they pitted Hindus and Muslims, of absolute innocence. It was not anything against the hijras, but because, you know, the hijras live together, like on a kibbutz; in that sense, there is that unity with the land, in this microcosm of India, where the two— Muslims and Hindus—live together . . ."

Safrani lived in New York, but his family was from Hyderabad. He had volunteered to translate some of the songs of the hijras, because he himself was interested in the cultural life of the city, and was writing a book about it. As it happened, he was also a consummate storyteller. We sat in his library; his two-year-old son had fallen asleep in his arms.

"What they did," said Safrani, "was to arrive at a home. And they had a network, an electronic circuit, whereby they knew that the daughter-in-law of Lord So-and-so will give birth to a child in six months . . . three months . . . depending on the frequency and importance of households, and their own contact. In some households, they were simply given money or asked to leave; in others, they were asked to entertain. And this became quite a social setup— at times associated with the decadent sectors of Hyderabad rather than the more progressive ones, but nonetheless, the hijras made their rounds, just like a municipal officer would.

"And I'll tell you a story about an illustrious member of Hyderabadi society, who's still financially very affluent, and makes a living through investments. His name was Mohammad Ali. And usually, depending on the household, the greater the importance of the hijra that goes. For instance, a person who has a better voice, an individual who plays the dhol, or the better dancer. So every Tom, Dick, and Harry among the hijras doesn't go to a noble's house . . .

"This was at the height of the summer in Hyderabad in May, when it is so hot that not even flies fly off the sweetmeats that they sit on, and the snakes in the grass just sit there. The lawn was sprinkled, the water fell like pearls on it—beautiful, the whole thing—and the hijras arrived. Incidentally, among all Indians, they're the most punctual. You give them a time, they'll be there fifteen or twenty minutes before, if not half an hour before. So when the hijras came, the 'dulhan' hijra came. You see, *dulhan* means 'bride.' But how can there be such a person? She would be the matriarch, and she was always well revered, well liked . . . There were all sorts of kebabs, and wonderful aromas were coming from the kitchen. The dulhan hijra went into the kitchen and said, 'What is your name?' The chef was a huge, well-built man, a bulky, Herculean character. Some of the chefs, at one time, at least, had a demeanor, with gaucho mustaches—and he was in an undershirt, because he was cooking. So he said, 'Jaffar Ali.' The hijra said, 'Umf. Please, give me a break, your name's

Jaffar Ali.' 'My name is Jaffar Ali! Look at my tabeez.' He showed his *tabeez*, usually a sacred thread of sorts, attached to a locket, with a ritual written inside it—Koranic or mystical—that conservatives, at one time, wore.

"The hijras then went and sat below a tree. The dogs were leashed, incidentally—because for some reason, in Hyderabad, they will always attack the hijras, maybe because they're trained to do so, or there's a certain scent—whatever. At six o'clock everyone gathered, and this little shriveled-up kid was born after twelve years of marriage. This is the more important aspect of the narration; that he was born after years; and all Mohammad Ali's male friends, the macho Hyderabadis, had cautioned him, saying, 'Don't invite the hijras. You'll be brutally insulted!' He said, 'How can I be brutally insulted when I'm paying them?' They said, 'If that's what you wish—you're a sultan.'

"And everyone who was anyone, and a select pairing of the elite, arrived. The sun had set; it was getting to be a bit cool; and hors d'oeuvres and sherbets were being served. They're Muslims, of course, they would drink later on, but for the sake of ceremony, and the mullas, and all these fundamentalists, they just decided to have the sherbets. And they said, let's have the thing, and the hijras came.

"There was one dhol that I had been hearing about, and I have seen it; this was the dhol that was used for the elite of elites. It was cut-glass, blown, manufactured in Czechoslovakia. A *dhol* is a cylindrical drum, with skin on both sides, and it's hung around the neck with a contraption, so that the individual can play. It's usually used by mendicants, or bear entertainers, which is now almost a dead thing . . . And the dulhan hijra was also dressed in white, and she came and sang, 'A-a-a-a'—the tune, there's nothing, really, there's no *Carmen*, there's no Giuseppe de

Stefano, or anything of the sort—she sang, 'Aaaaaa' . . .
Though the father's name is Mohammad Ali, the child, as
he was born, called out 'Jaffar Ali!' " Safrani paused before
he said the name, and clapped in the manner of a hijra.

"The son is the chef's?" I asked.

"That's right!" said Safrani. "So he is insulted at his own
party! The man, who after twelve years, has a child, has
been insulted by this hijra, who has said that the child is not
his, in the song! And the whole party was over. And it became the talk of the town—the hijras said the son is not
Mohammad Ali's, but Jaffar Ali's—imagine that! And so
the song went, and so the hijras clapped. Because that is
their poetic license—the kind of parody or satire they use,
in order to cut."

The other story Safrani remembered involved an uncle
of his, whose name was Kuchu.

"Hyderabad fell in 1948," said Safrani. "It fell to the
government of India. A 'police action,' it was called—but
it was a boy-scout thing. At that time, my uncle was a
printer, and had created the first printing press, and he arrived at the Royal Headquarters because he needed paper:
1947–1948, a very critical time—a shortage of paper. And
there, in front of the office of Colonel El-Edroos, a very famous military officer—always, whenever there was any
trouble, El-Edroos was the man in command—my uncle
had to go past protocol, and the last fellow who held the
door to El-Edroos' office was a tall fellow, whose name was
Sandal Baig. Now, imagine the word *sandal*—sandal is per-
fume; it's like calling him Mr. Musk or Mr. Yardley. He had
a big nameplate, which said 'Sandal Musk,' and the thing
was slightly tilted. So while this was a military situation,
there was something about this fellow that was not there.
He was six foot four, incidentally, so he was an absolute

Afghan. When he got the call, Colonel El-Edroos said, 'Come in,' so Sandal Baig said, 'Sa'ab, come in . . . ' "

Safrani now paused to imitate the gruff, macho voice of El-Edroos, and the whiny voice of Sandal Baig.

"And he had all his weapons," continued Safrani, "so he saluted him, like this"—here Safrani paused to indicate the boots being snapped together, and the wobbly hand that made its way up to the head—"and this my uncle remembered. Because, though he was a very macho man, he saw this particular gait, and he just made a mental note of this fellow. He went in and saw Colonel El-Edroos, and got what he wanted . . .

"Years later, he was walking on the main thoroughfare of Hyderabad—Abid Road—a very gallant character, impeccably attired, going to his bookshop—the Hyderabad Book Depot—which was frequented by individuals like Nehru, so it was a very serious place. He had to walk, and he loved to walk, about a mile and a half to get to his place, although there was no need for it. This was during the rush hour—between eight and nine—and whom does he see but a hijra following him . . .

" 'Sarkar . . . my lord . . . don't you recognize me?' " Safrani imitated the peculiar drone of the hijra voice.

"And my uncle, you know, his mustache proverbially turning redder, became its absolute reddest! He said, 'You idiot! Nincompoop!' All sorts of epithets, you know, 'Rascal, irascible, incorrigible!' They were pretty harsh words, and the hijras, of course, consider themselves to be very delicate, almost like peonies or hyacinths that cannot be exposed to the sudden change of temperature, and these words were offending him, so he was saying, 'No, my lord, no!' as if my uncle had shot a volley at him. To the hijra, my uncle said, 'Hut! Get out!'

" 'Oh my lord, don't break my heart!'

"And the moment my uncle paced up, this fellow, of course, also paced up; and he kept up and up. And there's a small corruption that goes on in Hyderabad, as elsewhere. There was a policeman—the 'theen patti jhavan'—he's always regarded as the highest-ranking officer on duty. And usually, in the morning, they saluted with full force to get money for their tea. So my uncle said, 'Amin Khan . . .' 'Yes, my lord?' 'Get rid of the dirt that's following me.' So Amin Khan said, 'Are you out of your mind, following his lordship?' So the hijra said, 'Arre, what will the lord give you . . . ? If he gives you a quarter, I'll give you a dollar . . . What are you saluting him for? Let this be a dialogue between my lord and me . . .'

"So Amin Khan was completely checkmated! You see, the hijra is very perceptive: Amin Khan is saluting my uncle, and the hijra *knows* why he is saluting the master. He's saluting him to get the quarter for the tea. So the hijra is saying, 'Get out of my way, I'll give you four times as much as he will; I want to talk to him . . .' So the hijra is now using his *wealth*, which is an undisclosed element—they can be very poor—but their wealth has *never been known*, and some say they're very affluent, because where does all this money go? Into organization, into building another home elsewhere . . . in Bloomfield, New Jersey, so that more hijras can be active there, and so on . . .

"So, because Amin Khan had started barking, she said, 'Why are you simpering like a dog . . . Take this.' And she actually handed him four times what my uncle was going to pay. At this point, Amin Khan, not wanting to lose business at both ends, saluted the hijra also! He said, 'Forgive me, my lord . . . Long live, my lord . . . You too have a soul, you too have a heart . . . Of course I recognize, I am terribly sorry . . .' And, at this point, he had to address my uncle, Kuchu—'Please talk to him . . .' he said; so my uncle just *had* to deal with him. So he turned around and said: 'You crazy fellow!' But he came on so strong that the hijra said, 'My lord, why are you acting like a canine?' So my uncle said, 'What do you want?'

" 'Arre, my lord,' said the hijra, 'all I want to hear is your voice, in a very melodious way, so that it falls on my ears like honey on beeswax . . .'

"*Shehtoot,* the word she used, is a mulberry, and it's very delicate; it's the plant that is eaten by silkworms. 'Let that voice, which is as soft as the mulberry, fall on my eardrum like a curtain'—this is what the hijra is saying; and my uncle is acting very Germanic in the morning, and the traffic is going *voo-voo,* and Amin Khan is waiting to get his annas, and a few people have gathered around—you know, a typical scene.

"The hijra said, 'My lord, don't you recognize me?'

" 'No, I don't recognize you!'

" 'Arre, my lord, barking again? Remember the war?'

" 'I remember!'

" 'Remember Colonel El-Edroos? 'My lord, you were in need of paper . . . You got the paper . . . Before you entered Colonel El-Edroos' office, who was standing at the door?'

" 'Huhhh . . . ! O hoo hoo hoo . . . Sandal Begh!'

"So, for the *first* time, my uncle looked up, and then he recognized this six-foot-four character, emaciated, and dressed in a sari, of course. Before, he at least had his badge going one way, his medals falling another—and here he was on the street, dressed in a sari—whimsical whispy character, wishy-washy, to say the least, and early in the morning, you know, slightly dishevelled . . . I mean, they get going after noon—and he said, '*What happened to you?*'

"The hijra said, 'At that time, I was a crack force in the

Afghan division . . . but *this*' "—Safrani paused to clap in
the manner of a hijra—" 'is what I am.' You see, it's all in
the action, because there's no word! He said, 'What I was
I may have been, but THIS,' Safrani clapped, 'is what I am.'
And at that point, my uncle took out money, and gave it
to the hijra, but the hijra refused. Because he only wished
to be recognized, one human being to another. He said,
'Give it to him,' pointing to Amin Khan, this beer-bellied
policeman, who takes money under the counter—'Don't
give it to me!' —in a proud way—very proud.

"And usually," said Safrani, "the hijras depended on
being extremely well-informed, and having almost like an
underground system, whereby they kept a tab on the
maternity wards, and they were tipped off by the *dais*, or
'midwives'—'Oh, we've got fifteen women admitted to the
hospital, three will be in labor tonight, three on another
night, and so on.' *How* they did it without making their
presence felt, or going into the hospitals—you'll never find
a hijra in the hospitals—and yet they get that information
mainly from the hospitals, no matter how sophisticated the
clinics are. For instance, the clinic I was born in was run by
a German woman, and she said, 'Baba, I have never seen a
hijra in my clinic, and I don't know how, the *moment*
my patients went home, they found the hijras waiting for
them . . .'

"The basic purpose," said Safrani, "that the hijras
served, long before all this business of playing up for the
children and the newborn came into being, was their role
in the harems. While the women sat idle, so to speak, or
grooming themselves, their minds wandered. To guard
them, and to have their faith, the hijras, purportedly,
played a very crucial role. Because they were there, obsten-
sibly, to guard them—not *physically*—but to *inform*, as to
what went on. And there again, they became mitigating

factors to playing on *both* sides, like double agents. So this system—which was here in Hyderabad during the Kutb Shahi times—may account for the early foundation of their being very astute entrepreneurs—of knowing how to negotiate information, and how to leak it out. So, by letting a young concubine go and have a good time with someone else, while she is meant to serve the monarch or the prince, is in the hearsay of this man—this hijra—but he will not report it if he is given a certain number of gold coins, or five pounds of wheat, or whatever. Their dependence on the hijras became quite a paramount feature of the courts . . . What I'm implying is that those individuals who lived at court—at Golconda Fort—lived with barely two or three changes of dress, and, once in a while, visited their homes, and then came back swiftly, because they were in constant attendance. Where was all this money for the hijras, especially, coming from, if the person was there to serve as a guard? So you see, this was the means: they *bartered*, rather than took it all in gold and money, and that was how it kept the system going. So if a person said, 'Look, I've got ten horses, what do you want me to do?' So give a colt. The colt, then, would be latched on to a carriage that took three hijras out another ten miles, instead of their being limited to the city perimeter alone. So they have a tremendous sense of organization, is what I'm trying to say. This is something I had heard from my grandmother—that they were so well organized and highly disciplined, that they didn't always take everything in cash, and then be caught with a pot of gold. The reason why I know this is because my father died at a very young age, and I was very close to my grandmother . . . The original families of Hyderabad were a basic oligarchy."

"Did she have hijras," I asked, "in her home, when she was growing up?"

"No, no," said Safrani.

"So where did she learn of the hijras?" I asked.

"She learned of the hijras," said Safrani, "because, when she was a young girl, her mother, and her grandmother, were probably in close touch. I mean, she didn't tell me that much about them, but among the people she asked me to stay away from were mendicants, mystics, and hijras. And she was quite specific."

~

"*In modern India,*" wrote Norman Penzer, in an appendix called "Indian Eunuchs," attached to his translation of *The Ocean of Story,* published in the 1920s, "*although in dwindling numbers, there still exist classes of eunuchs forming separate communities. The most widely known name under which they go is Hijra or Hijda, but numerous other names are found in different parts of India.*" These he categorized as "mukhannas," for the northwest provinces; "Pavayas" or "Fatadas," in the Bombay Presidency; "Khasua" in the Central Provinces; and "Khoja" in Madras. In some states, there were two different names for eunuchs, one implying "natural born," the other, "artificially created," but Penzer did not put much stock in these categories. For example, he wrote, in Saugor, artificially created eunuchs went by the name of hijra, while in Madras, natural eunuchs carried the same name.

The eunuchs of Gujarat, he wrote, were said to be "*the castrated votaries of the goddess Bahuchara . . . a sister of Devi.*" Bahuchara earned her status as a martyr when, legend had it, she and her sisters were plundered by neighboring Kolis; Bahuchara took a sword from one of the attacking boys and cut off her breasts; she died, and her two sisters killed themselves. Thus they became "Devis," objects of worship. Her deification was a result of self-

mutilation; her worshipers emulated this by emasculation, and by copying Bahuchara in dress, manners, and
sexuality, to *"make themselves as near as they can to
their goddess."*

Penzer cited Ethoren's *Tribes and Castes of Bombay,*
1922, culled mainly from the *Bombay Gazetteer,* for this
description of the hijras of Ahmadabad, Panch Mahals,
Kathiawar, Kutch, and Khandesh, who were known as
"Pavayas": these eunuchs worshiped Bahuchara; they were
both Hindu and Muslim (though they did not dine together) and were similar in appearance. They traced their
origin to the king of Chipaner, who had prayed to Bahuchara to give him a son. Bahuchara answered with a son,
named Jeto, who was born impotent: the king donated him
to her service. Bahuchara appeared in a dream to the impotent Jeto and asked him to cut off his genitals and dress
as a woman. Jeto did, and this *"practice has been followed
by all who join the caste."*

Impotence was mandatory to gain entry into this
"caste." When an impotent man wished to join, he applied
to one of the Pavayas; the hijra breathed into his right ear,
pierced both his ears, and made him vow never to steal or
to *"act as a procurer to any woman . . . He eats coarse
sugar, puts on women's clothes, receives a new name, generally ending in 'de' such as Dhanade, Thinide, Ladude
and Khimde."* For the next six to twelve months, the man
was on probation, and his impotence tested. Only afterward did he undergo emasculation.

"For this purpose," wrote Penzer, *"the novice bathes,
dresses himself in clean clothes and worships the image of
the goddess. He prays to her to grant a propitious day for
the operation. It is believed that if the operation is performed on a day approved by the goddess the result is sel-
dom fatal. Behind a screen set up for the purpose, the*

cutting is performed with a razor by the person himself, without any assistance. This is held to correspond to a birth ceremony, which makes the patient a member of the caste. After the operation, the patient lies for three days on a cot on his back without moving. During that time, thirty pounds of sesame oil is continuously poured on the parts affected. For ten days more, or till the wound is healed, it is washed with a decoction of the bor (Zizyphus jujuba) and babul (Acacia arabica) bark. On the sixth day after the operation coarse flour mixed with molasses and clarified butter is distributed among the caste people. The patient remains screened for forty days, during which he eats light food. Clarified butter is his chief nourishment, and he is forbidden the use of red pepper, oil and asafoetida."

The Gaikwar of Baroda forbade castration in his state in 1880. It *"saddened the Pavayas,"* because they believed that without sacrificing *"their useless member,"* they were doomed to remain impotent through seven incarnations.

"The Pavayas keep images of Bahuchara in their homes," wrote Penzer, *"worship them daily,"* and visit her shrines in Chunval. *"They keep Hindu and Musalman holidays."* They buried, not cremated, their dead. *"After death,"* he wrote, *"the body is washed and laid on a cot covered with a sheet and perfumed. The body is shrouded in a clean coverlet for burial. As they are neither males nor females, they do not touch the coffin, which is carried, and the burying performed by Musalmans, the companions of the dead standing by mourning. On the dasa or tenth day and on the chalisa or fortieth day after the death the dearest companion of the deceased is bound, on pain of expulsion, to free the caste-people and the Musalman bier-bearers. A tomb is raised over the dead."*

The Pavayas, he wrote, made their living through begging, and if met with stinginess, *"stripped naked"* and hurled abuses—*"believed to bring dire calamity . . . They beg in bands on different beats and receive fixed yearly dues in kind or cash from shopkeepers, carpenters, tailors, shoemakers, goldsmiths, lohars, etc."* The Pavayas were also summoned to dance before the house of a woman who had a male child after barrenness, or who had no male child; fixed sums were given to them by *"every Kunbi"* on the birth of a son.

From the *Bombay Gazetteer* of 1899, presumably after castration was declared illegal by the king of Baroda, Penzer received another account of the initiation ceremony. The ritual was said to have taken place in the temple of the goddess Bahuchara, about sixty miles northeast of Ahmadabad, in the village of Sankhalpur, *"where the neophyte repairs under the guardianship or adoption of some older member of the brotherhood. The lad is called the daughter of the old Hijda, his guardian. The emasculation takes place under the direction of the chief Hijda priest of Behuchra. The rites are secret. It is said that the operation and initiation are held in a house with closed doors, where all the Hijdas meet in holiday dress. The fireplace is cleaned and the fire is lighted to cook a special dish of fried pastry called talan. While the oil in which the pastry to be fried is boiling, some of the fraternity, after having bathed the neophyte, dress him in red female attire, deck him with flower garlands, and seating him on a stool in the middle of the room, sing to the accompaniment of a dhol or small drum and small copper cymbals. Others prepare the operating room. In the center of this room soft ashes are spread on the floor and piled in a heap. The operator approaches chewing betel-leaf. The hands and legs of the neophyte are firmly held by someone of the fraternity, and the operator, carelessly standing near with an unconcerned air, when he finds the attention of his patient otherwise occupied, with great dexterity and with one stroke completely cuts off the entire genital organs. He spits betel nut and leaf juice on the wound and stanches the bleeding with a handful of babul (Acacia arabica) ashes. The operation is dangerous and not uncommonly fatal."*

In 1922, Penzer noted a group of north Gujarati hijras who worshiped Bahuchara but did not dress as women or undergo emasculation. *"They affect only the wincing talk and manners of lewd women."* They married and had children. They were known, he said, to perform plays at the birth of sons among poor Muslims. *"Hijdas of the play-acting class are to be found in and about Ahmadabad. As a class,"* he added, *"Gujarat Hijdas enjoy independent means of livelihood and have not to engage in sodomy to any active extent. As votaries of Behuchra [sic] they hold fields and lands, and rights on lands awarded to them from of old by native chiefs, village communities and private persons. They have rights on communities also, receiving yearly payments from them. Woe betide the wight who opposes the demands of a Hijda! The whole rank and file of the local fraternity besiege his house with indecent clamor and gesture."*

"In southern India," wrote Penzer, *"the eunuch caste is practically non-existent, and even in 1870 the numbers were only small."* He quoted J. Shartt's article of 1873, published in the *Journal of the Anthropological Institute*, which said: *"The true Kojahs, or eunuchs, are chiefly seen in the houses of wealthy Mussulman nobles, by whom they are placed at the head of their zenanas or harems. Sometimes they hold important charges with a considerable amount of general control. The ladies of the harem look upon them as their confidential advisors in all matters relating to their personal concerns, whilst to them is left the entire management, arrangement, supplies, etc., of the*

interior. In fact, all that concerns the female apartment is confided to their care."

The initiation rites amongst south Indian hijras, Penzer wrote, were similar to those practiced in Gujarat, but *"we get fresh details of their clothing and behavior: The hair of the head is put up like women, well oiled, combed, and thrown back tied into a knot, and shelved to the left side, sometimes plaited, ornamented, and allowed to hang down the back; the whiskers, mustache and beard closely shaven. They wear the cholee or shortjacket, the saree or petticoat, with an apron or scarf which they wrap around the shoulders and waist, and put on an abundance of nose, ear, finger, and toe rings. They cultivate singing, play the dhole, a country drum of an oblong shape, and attitudinize. They go about the bazaars in groups of a half-a-dozen or more, singing songs with the hope of receiving a trifle. They are not only persistent but impudent beggars, rude and vulgar in the extreme, singing filthy, obscene and abusive songs to convince the bazaarmen to give them something. Should they not succeed they would create a fire and throw in a lot of chilies, the suffocating and initial smoke producing violent coughing, etc., so that the bazaarmen are compelled to yield to their importunity and give them a trifle to get rid of their annoyance . . . as they are not only unable to retain their seats in the bazaars, but customers are prevented from coming to them in consequence. With the douceur they get they will move off to the next bazaar to resume the trick. While such were the pursuits in the day, at nightfall they resorted to debauchery and practices by hiring themselves out to a dissipated set of Moslems, who are in the habit of resorting to these people for the purpose, while they intoxicate themselves with a preparation termed majoon, being a confection of opium and a kind of drink termed boja, a species of country beer manufactured from raji, which also contains bang; in addition to this they smoke bang. The Higras are met with in most of the towns of Southern India, more especially where a large proportion of Mussulmans is found."*

In 1890–92, *"numbers of . . . basivis,"* dedicated to the goddess Huligamma, who also dressed as women, could be seen *"at the goddess' temple on the left bank of the Tungabahdra River, Raichur, in the Nizam's territory."* Men who believed they were temporarily or permanently impotent, wrote Penzer, also donned women's clothes in the name of this goddess, in the hope of becoming potent.

The hijras of India, concluded Penzer, resembled *"the Galli, the eunuch priests of Artemis of Ephesus [Greece] and the Syrian Astarte of Hierapolis . . . who made themselves as much like their goddess as possible."*

TWENTY-THREE

SHIVI AND RAJESH FOUND an Urdu teacher who knew Persian and taught at one of Hyderabad's colleges. Her name was Mani. Tall and elegant, her bearing bespoke her class. Though she recoiled slightly when I mentioned where we were going, an inner sense of duty propelled her nonetheless.

At the Hijron ka Allawah, there was a change of mood. The hijras were clearly beginning to feel harassed. And when Mani betrayed an instant of hesitation sitting on the floor beside Kamal Baksh, Munni's expression went from wary to suspicious. She glared in our direction. Mani's voice was soon shaking with fear. The hijras, ever the mirror of those around them, had become intimidated, and therefore, intimidating. I instantly regretted bringing Mani—sensing her discomfort too—but hoped that focusing on the documents might appease everyone.

Kamal Baksh had the deeds brought out, and Mani took up the oldest and largest one.

"What is the date, ma?" asked Kamal Baksh.

"1204 Hejira," said Mani. "It is more than a hundred years ago."

"No," said Kamal Baksh, "it's two hundred or three hundred years ago."

"No," said Mani.

"See," said Kamal Baksh, "our house is three hundred years old. Since the great flood, it has been seventy years. Our house was built many, many years before that. It should be written there."

Mani slowly read the document aloud. Where she stumbled, Kamal Baksh provided the words.

"But you remember," said Mani, "why don't you say?"

"No," said Kamal Baksh. "I don't know how to read. Those old people who knew Persian—when they read it, I overheard them . . . It's something I know by heart . . . In fact, the people in the tax office were also very astonished, looking at this. And the lawyers."

"This is the seal of Nizam ul-Mulk Asaf Jah," said Mani. "It says: 'Location: Hyderabad 2259 mauvazi [villages]. Recab Bazaar. Nizam ul-Mulk, King. Administration of Nizam Ali Khan. 19 Safar. 1204 Hejira. I, the authority, give to you the aforementioned land . . . as a reward to you—the *khannazad**—and it should now be put into effect. Keep the land whole, for your graciousness, for your understanding . . . I've written the last . . .' According to my calculations, it is 1826 . . . According to Kamal Baksh, it is still older . . ."

"The second Nizam didn't live then," I said. I pulled out a conversion chart. "According to this, 1204 is 1793 or 1794."

Kamal Baksh handed Mani one of the smaller documents.

"This is for the houses," said Kamal Baksh. "For people to build . . ."

Mani looked it over.

"They gave land to others, also," said Mani, "to build houses, so here are the numbers . . . It was a big plot, so it was subdivided."

* those who have been in the service of the family for generations

"It is of earlier times," said Kamal Baksh. "There is a stamp . . . what is written there?"

"It is written," said Mani, "Muhammad Ali Khan, but it could be anyone, really—it's a very popular name. The date is 1249 Hejira. According to my reckoning, it is 1871 . . ."

"According to this chart," I said, "it is 1830."

Kamal Baksh handed Mani a third document.

"This, according to me," said Mani, "is 1920—1298 Hejira . . . So in a matter of fifty years, they built these houses . . . The land was already there."

"It is before the flood," said Kamal Baksh. "Do you see this road? All this road—the high court and the dispensary and City College and government land—used to be ours."

"The chart says 1298 Hejira is 1880," I said. "That would correspond to Mahboob's time."

"Did they always live outside the palaces?" I asked Mani to ask Kamal Baksh.

"There were never any hijras in the palace," said Kamal Baksh. "We were patronized till Osman Ali's time. Then it stopped."

"Before Mahboob's time," asked Mani, "did you live here or elsewhere?"

"Only here," said Kamal Baksh. "Even before his father's time."

"See," said Mani, "wherever there was a harem, hijras were there."

"Never," said Kamal Baksh.

"Not even for the noblemen?" asked Mani.

"No," said Kamal Baksh.

"Put a question mark there," said Mani to me.

"We hijras do not do any job," Kamal Baksh said. "Perhaps you're speaking of the zenanas, I don't know. Our main function was to celebrate the birth of a child."

"Since when has this tradition started?" I asked.

"If you ask about the tradition," said Kamal Baksh, "it is since the time of Ram. In the *Ramayana*, and even before, in Ram's father's time—the hijras went to make merry and celebrate the birth of a child. We go wherever there is happiness, not sorrow."

"Why, then," I asked, "if you were not employed by the kings and noblemen, would they have given you this land?"

"They gave it as a blessing," said Kamal Baksh.

Mani was not satisfied with this answer; it was very vague, she said. But in her efficiency and desire to get the job over with, she was moving too fast. It unnerved the listening Munni.

"How do you get new members?" I asked.

"If they come, we keep them," Kamal Baksh said.

"Do you have any young ones?"

"No, no," said Kamal Baksh. "They don't come when they are small."

"What age?"

"Fifteen, twenty," said Kamal Baksh, "twenty-five, thirty years of age . . . They come of their own accord. They come according to the wishes of god."

"Have you ever had impostors?" I asked.

"We have ways," said Kamal Baksh, "of finding out if he is genuine. By looking."

"Do many come these days?" I asked.

"Earlier," said Kamal Baksh, "there were many. But now, there are few . . . What does it matter? If the person is decent, and not the ones who eat of others . . ."

"How many years ago was the last one?"

"Fifteen years ago," said Kamal Baksh.

Kamal Baksh's sense of time tended to be vague, in any case, but Chenoy had witnessed an initiation ceremony only ten years ago: Rani Baksh was twenty-five.

"Now, if nobody comes," said Mani, "will the tradition end?"

"What can I do if the tradition ends?" said Kamal Baksh. "That is up to Him. If He wants us to flourish, we will survive. If He finishes us, it is His choice. It's all in His hands."

"But if from childhood," I said, "one comes to know that one is a certain way . . ."

"See," said Kamal Baksh, "if their parents give them away happily, or pleasantly, it's fine. They go through the papers. But nowadays, nobody is giving, nor are we taking."

"Go through the papers?" I asked.

"If the parents give them away," said Kamal Baksh, "they write it on a paper. But nowadays, nobody gives."

In the old days, said Mani, men and women were separated, but now that the genders were mixing, and wearing each other's clothes, the whole tradition was giving way.

"Nowadays," agreed Kamal Baksh, "there are lots of 'rathiya' [bisexuals, "two-sided"]. They fight with us. They go to our shops, and ask for money; they take away our share and they take away our signs; they say we are their gurus, they are our daughters; thus, by cheating, they take our money."

"There is factionalism between them," said Mani.

"What was their original profession?" I asked.

"They painted their faces," said Kamal Baksh, "and asked for money, but now they have learned the traits of the hijras. They have families, and wives, and mothers. They wear underwear, and put saris on, so nobody can tell that they are males."

The crime of these rathiya, then, was that, unlike the hijras, they could procreate.

"Are there lots?" I asked.

"Lots," said Kamal Baksh.

"Are your numbers more?" I asked.

"They are more," said Kamal Baksh, "and they are more spread out."

"What does hijra mean, exactly?" I asked.

"Hijra means neither male nor female," said Kamal Baksh. "If you want, you can even see."

Oddly, Kamal Baksh was offering to "prove" herself to me, to show that she was "the real thing." Even more oddly, I had no interest in seeing the proof of this physical mutilation. And one might wonder: I had spent months in pursuit of this subject, but when the moment came, I was repelled. Though I knew the hijras often threatened to lift up their garments, I had felt protected from this crude, indifferent gesture, in the private world of Kamal Baksh. Was not this offer on the part of the guru, to some degree, an affront to me, and to my translator? Was Kamal Baksh actually so threatened by Mani, and our questions, that she felt the need to repel? Was this a feature of the hijras' doubleness, or ambivalence? Or: as banal a fact as Kamal Baksh, now, in her matter-of-fact way—was suggesting.

In any case, I kept saying no. I had avoided just this moment, content to have it described, a fact that made me less than an objective journalist. Then a reverse motion overtook me.

"Can I take a photograph?" I asked.

Now Kamal Baksh was offended.

"No, now we will not give," she said. "We have given *enough*. If you want to see us, we will stand here nude, but we will not give any more."

Mani said, "Perhaps just one or two?"

No, Kamal Baksh was adamant. I had already taken some photographs, she said, why was I forcing them?

"When you were born," said Kamal Baksh, raising her voice, "were you like a boy? Because we were impotent, we became like this. See, nowadays, many get into the house of a different sort [prostitutes, zenanas]. But if we do, it brings a bad name to the hijras. This way, we can go into to the places where women are. People know we do not have male powers, so they let us in."

"When do you go to where only women are?" I asked.

"When the child is born," said Kamal Baksh.

This required some analysis: today, in India, *purdah* or female seclusion was practiced only by deeply conservative Muslims, and would involve only a small minority of the population, though even as late as the 1940s, it was imitated by wealthy Hindus. Thus Kamal Baksh's reasoning lost some of its power. But she was suggesting that this alone—to have access to secluded women, and, therefore, to newborns—was the historical reason for castration.

"Was she castrated during an initiation ceremony?" I asked Kamal Baksh via Mani. And perhaps this was an error of judgment on my part, but since she herself had brought up the subject, I was going to run with it. Mani had no trouble with the direct approach.

"Now I am seventy," said Kamal Baksh. "Then, I must have been thirty . . . I had gone to Molla ka Moharrum for a ceremony. In the night I did it. Everyone said, 'You're not a hijra,' and I couldn't prove it, so I was ashamed. Nobody saw what I was doing. I was in an outlying village. An old lady was with me; she looked after me. 'What kind of hijra are you?' they were saying. So I did it myself."

"She said she did it with her own hands," said Mani. "This I don't believe," she muttered in English.

"How did you do it?" Mani asked.

"We do it ourselves, with a knife," said Kamal Baksh. "We cut it and throw it."

"Everybody does it on their own?" asked Mani.

"Yes," said Kamal Baksh.

"But why would it be important," I asked Mani, "to prove oneself as a hijra?"

"At that time," said Mani, "there was purdah—women's seclusion—no?"

I wanted details. Again Kamal Baksh said, raising her voice, and repeating the Lynton allegory almost word for word: "I had gone to ask for money, and they started laughing at me. So I decided to do it. On the way back, I did it. There used to be an old lady with me; she stayed with me and cooked. Suppose there is a birth in your house? How could I enter? Especially the men would ask, who are you? So we have to prove ourselves."

"Afterward," I asked, "was there any change, physically or emotionally?"

"No," said Kamal Baksh, flatly.

"Do you have desires like men?"

"No," said Kamal Baksh.

"Like women?"

"No," came the reply.

"Is there any change in bodily hair?"

"No."

"You are asking in one language," said Mani, "and she is answering in another."

Now Munni moved closer to us, and I heard a low hiss coming from her direction. The hair rose on my skin. We were the outsiders suddenly, on this voyage into the lives of the hijras. I had gone too far; Sayeed Baksh stared at me disapprovingly. I could feel Mani's agitation—she was ready to leave. It was all coming undone, because of the directness of my question about castration.

Inwardly, though, I was sure of Kamal Baksh, sure that if I could disarm this moment, and find a more oblique way, we could pass through to the other side, to our relationship of mutual respect, to the stability of their world,

with its Singer sewing machine draped over to protect it
from dust; to the slingshot hung every day in its usual place
beside the key; to the routine of the water, drawn at particular times, and no other. But before I had the chance, Kamal Baksh shook her head at Munni.

"See, the other day," said Kamal Baksh, "Mr. Reddy
was also asking certain things! Why is this child so interested in the hijras? Children shouldn't ask so much!"

"Because nothing has been written," said Mani.

"But there are hijras in America!" bellowed Kamal
Baksh.

"It's not the same," said Mani.

"Yes," yelled Kamal Baksh. "That custom is there too.
But the difference is, there they live with men. We don't
have that kind of custom. We don't keep men."

"Yes," said Mani. "Homosexuality is not here."

Mani was now so frightened, she was agreeing with anything Kamal Baksh said.

"Everywhere," said Kamal Baksh, "all over India, in villages, cities, there are hijras! There is no place where you
wouldn't find them. Pakistan. Mecca. Medina. Do you understand? There they enter the mosque, they work, they
sweep—so they are allowed inside Mecca, and Medina too.
But within this whole locality, we don't have anybody who
does bad work. The tenants of ours, they run a bicycle shop."

"Do you accept anyone," I asked, "who wants to join as
a disciple?"

"Only the one who comes with dignity," said Kamal
Baksh. "We have a probation period of four to six months.
After that, we decide."

But Kamal Baksh was irritated; and though she had
backed away, Munni held on in the doorway, throwing ma-
lign glances.

"See, she has been coming for so many days," Kamal

Baksh told Mani. "She has seen everything. She has seen how we live at home. How we go outside to perform."

As a gesture of peace, and because Shivi had asked me to, I suggested that Kamal Baksh come and dance at Shivi's.

"No, now we don't want to go," said Kamal Baksh. "You came before and saw. You gave us bakshish. We were happy."

I said I wanted to pay them.

"Will you accept money," Mani asked Kamal Baksh, "for all your time—for talking?"

"If you stay," said Kamal Baksh, "I will give you tea or lemonade, or anything you like."

"But she'd like to give you something," said Mani.

"The day before, she gave," said Kamal Baksh.

"That was for dancing," I said.

"No," said Mani. "Not for dancing. For speaking."

"See," said Kamal Baksh, "she has come, leaving her own country, so why should we take? No, no, she gave to us the day before yesterday. You have left your own country; you have come so far," she said to me.

Munni, sensing a peace, yet independently resisting it, left the doorway, leaving the hovering half-shadow of herself as an impression I will never forget.

"But she is happy to give," said Mani, "why don't you accept?"

"If she wants to give happily," said Kamal Baksh, "tell her, whenever she comes next, she can give—not now. She is a child. And I will not take."

"You are young—a traveler," said Mani to me, "so she will not take any more."

"For talking?" I insisted, in English.

Kamal Baksh laughed. Sayeed looked at me with half a smile.

"For talking," said Kamal Baksh, "there is no fee."

Mutilation of the penis and even castration are occasionally self inflicted by lunatics or by individuals who want to be eunuchs or wish to dedicate their lives to the goddess, Bahucharaji, in the Gujarat State.

On September 17, 1932, Modi saw one Hijra, called Ilaichi, aged 28 years, who had cut off his penis and scrotum with the testicles by one sweep of a knife, causing an incised wound, 4″ × 4″, below the pubes and directed from above. When he was brought to the hospital, the wound was covered with mud and a piece of a dirty rag. He was discharged cured after ten days.

Dr. Jaising P. Modi
Medical Jurisprudence

TWENTY-FOUR

Cнноti haveli, the "small" palace of eunuchs, was tucked behind a few buildings, in a crowded bazaar in Char Minar, about a quarter of a mile away from Kamal Baksh's place. Detective Reddy was to meet me there.

Ramzan gestured that I should wait inside the car; he would go and inquire. Soon Ramzan reappeared, followed by one of the most beautiful people I had ever seen: a six-foot half-man, half-woman apparition, in a lungi and kurta, with long flowing locks to the waist. I was drawn as though gazing at an ancient myth. The hijra was bunning her hair, as she came toward the window. Her face was almost Roman, and her clumsiness contrasted with her innate beauty and youth.

The hijra excitedly took us inside. Ramzan also wanted to come. Yes, I said. In the car, we had discussed the possibility of my making a film about the hijras. And you could be the production coordinator, I had said, optimistically. Somehow, we both knew it wouldn't happen, and were trying not to dream too much. This was India. And though we were the same age, and he had a mind like mine by nature, whatever was between us would remain unsaid.

There in a circle on the *taqat* sat a motley assembly of three old hijras, toothless, in ragged saris, with Mr. Reddy in the middle. The Chhoti Haveli was not nearly as regal as

Kamal Baksh's house, its walls peeling and yellow with age. Yet there was an ease about the place. And the reason for that ease, and the young hijra's spiritedness, became clear when the fifth hijra emerged from a back room.

Shameem Baksh was perhaps in her mid-forties, of fair complexion, and had a handsome face of Kashmiri or Lucknowi origin. She wore her patterned silk sari in the manner of an airline stewardess, neatly tucked in at the waist. In deportment and manners, she recalled an upper-class memsa'ab, the kind of "bride" described by Safrani, the courtesan praised by Dhar Prasad. She was intelligent and commanding, and by the general air of wittiness, I knew I had come upon the more "liberal" faction amongst the hijras.

Shameem Baksh took a place beside us on the floor. Her eyes followed every nuance; it was clear that she was the leader here. I was curious, I said, about the hijra who had led us inside. With a nod, Shameem Baksh permitted her to speak.

Her name was Anita Baksh, she said. She was twenty-five years old. She was a native Hyderabadi. Throughout, though, her eyes kept seeking Shameem's.

"How long have you been here?"

No answer.

"From childhood," said Shameem Baksh, "she has been here, in this house."

"How old was she when she came?" asked Reddy.

"She was four," said Shameem Baksh.

"How did you get here?" I asked.

"I don't remember," said Anita.

"She doesn't know how she came?" I asked.

"My parents gave me away themselves," said Anita. "I don't know."

So Shameem Baksh explained: Anita, she said, was a true hermaphrodite, born with visibly intersexed characteristics, and therefore, like a deity amongst them. She was their star dancer. Her parents had "dropped her off" at the hijra household. Shameem Baksh had "adopted" her. Anita couldn't remember her parents, or anything about that time.

"I only know what the others have told me," said Anita. "She is like my mother," she said, indicating Shameem Baksh.

"You are the guru?" I asked Shameem Baksh.

"I am her guru," said Shameem Baksh, "but my chowdhry has gone to Lakshmangarh—to Rajasthan—for a conference. I am his chela."

I asked Reddy whether or not they had had "the operation."

"No, no," said Shameem Baksh, in English. "And what is your name?"

When I answered the question, Shameem Baksh, again in English, deflected it: "And what is your interest in the hijras?" Her charm was disarming, and her knowledge of English quite good.

Reddy explained that I was tracing their history from the "Turk's" time.

"So you are asking," said Shameem Baksh, "in Delhi and here—how many of us—and what kinds of work we do? Those who have professional jobs are called 'zenanas.' The hijras also work, but differently. In Bombay, the zenanas do not sit with us, and we do not sit with them. We go for only happy occasions, and nowhere else."

"What exactly is the difference?" I asked.

"We are bound by codes," Shameem Baksh said. "We have chowdhries."

"What is a chowdhry?" I asked.

"A head," said Shameem Baksh. "Like mine is Yusuf Naik."

"Naik, then," I asked, "is the same as a chowdhry, and above the guru?"

"Yes," said Shameem Baksh, "like Kamal Baksh. Yes, that is her title."

"So what is a zenana?"

"A zenana does male prostitution," said Reddy.

Shameem Baksh disagreed. "From childhood," she said, "they behave like girls, but they stay with their parents or have families. We don't do any other job. They cook; some who have studied work in big offices; some do trading. They are free; we are not. We have a society—we are attached to it. We have laws."

"Are these all chelas?" I asked.

"It is a happy occasion," said Shameem Baksh, "to be called 'chela.' " (The word once meant 'slave.')

"Who chooses whom?" I asked.

"The moment they enter this house," said Shameem Baksh, "they become 'chela.' The guru chooses the chela."

"How do they come to the house?" I asked.

"Some people's parents bring them," said Shameem Baksh. "Sometimes they come on their own. Then we make them bring the parents to the *panchayat* [judicial meeting], so the one who has come can decide whom he wants to be the chela to. He can choose his own guru."

"For what reasons," I asked, "would parents drop their children off here?"

"When they see that he is not one among them," replied Shameem Baksh.

"How?" I asked. "How do they realize that he is a hijra at the age of four, for example?"

"From childhood," said Shameem Baksh, "you can

tell what the child's bent is . . . If he is a boy, he acts like one. But if he has a feminine bent, he will play among the girls. Parents feel the pulse of the boy through his character . . . Isn't it like that in America?"

"Well," I said, "there are transvestites, but that's no equivalent. There, there's no 'operation,' as you have here; they can surgically be turned into women—the equivalent is a transsexual."

"It's one and the same thing," said Shameem Baksh. "Over there, they also become like us."

"They don't wear saris," I said, absurdly.

"They must be wearing gowns," countered Shameem Baksh. "Yes, it is the same thing over there. After the operation, they turn them into females. So basically, and internally, if the soul is feminine, they become that."

"At what age," I asked, "do you have the operation?"

"No," said Shameem Baksh. "We don't have an operation. What I am explaining is: if the child's soul is feminine, then whether there is an operation or not doesn't make any difference."

"It is their decision?" I asked.

"It is according to their own sweet will," said Reddy.

"Is there any particular time," I insisted, "they think is good for the operation?"

"No, no," said Shameem Baksh. "No time. You can write in the book, whose soul is there, he will do it."

"How many chelas are here?" I asked.

"Our guru has gone," said Shameem Baksh. "So there are three. In total, four. I have one, and another has come from a village."

This explained the five people in the house. Whenever they went to a wedding or birth, said Shameem Baksh, they teamed up with Kamal Baksh's house. If there were two functions on the same day, they split up, she said. I asked her: did she know when the tradition of the hijras had begun in Hyderabad?

"We can't say," said Shameem Baksh. "Some say our house is four hundred years old. Others say it is three hundred years old."

"You see," said Reddy, "it started in Turkistan. Turkistan's kings had many wives—so, for looking after them, this tradition started."

"Absolutely correct," said Shameem Baksh.

"What about the tradition," I asked, "of blessing the child—or going to weddings?"

"It's from earlier times," said Shameem Baksh.

"What is the meaning?" I asked.

"See," said Shameem Baksh, "in the Hindu religion, it is like this: 'any good occasion.' Now, how to tell you the story of the whole religion? We are called *Mangala Mukhi*—'auspicious face.' Suppose there is a happy occasion in your house: out of respect, the youngest of the household will not dance or sing before their elders, so they call us. So *Mangala Mukhi*s' work is to go on happy occasions, and sing and dance and bless."

"Why is it a good omen?" I asked. "It's interesting that someone who is neither man nor woman is a good omen, as an idea—at a marriage or childbirth—something so sexual."

"That a mythologist or philosopher can tell you," said Shameem Baksh.

"Why 'auspicious'?" I asked.

"This is from earlier times," said Shameem Baksh. "The Sikhandi avatar, in the Hindu religion . . . It has come from the 'Mohini' avatar . . ."

So Reddy explained the legend of Holi, the spring festival: Bhishma was a man-eater. Lord Shiva owed him a blessing, and Bhishma had asked to be immortal. But he abused this privilege, and started killing everyone. The secret was in his hand, which turned anyone he encountered to ash. So the apsuras approached Lord Shiva and asked for help. Lord Shiva said, "I can't take back my blessing"; but he thought of another way out. A boy, named Manmatha, was born; he became a great dancer. In the guise of a woman, Manmatha approached the immortal Bhishma, and danced before him. Bhishma wanted to make love to Manmatha and Manmatha replied that he would, only if Bhishma would dance with him. Bhishma was asked to copy Manmatha's dance movements: Manmatha put his hand over his head, and Bhishma imitated the gesture, turning himself to ash.

"So," said Shameem Baksh, "this is from God's time. Even God took on an avatar—the incarnation of the dancer—to kill the devil. Since then, a lot of avatars have come, and we start our work with their names."

"Which Hindu gods do you worship?" I asked.

"Hindu, Muslim—all mixed," said Shameem. "We don't make a distinction."

"Which of the Hindus?"

"Shiva, Krishna—and his incarnations," said Shameem Baksh.

"You see," said Reddy, "Shiva was a good dancer."

Shiva was also known for his male and female counterparts, a symbol of transsexuality; Shameem Baksh was linking herself to the tradition.

I asked Shameem Baksh if she was educated, because of her ability to follow so much of our conversation in English, and her tendency to complete our sentences.

"While sitting at home," said Shameem Baksh, "we try to read Hindi and English."

But it occurred to me then that she may have been intimate with someone who spoke English.

"Can you tell us," I asked, "a few words of your private language?"

"What language?" said Shameem Baksh.

"Amongst yourselves," I said.

Shameem Baksh looked quickly at the other hijras.

"Well," she said, "if you're angry, and have to speak to the children, we'll say it . . . in few words."

"Like what?" I said.

"Say one or two words," said Reddy.

"Like *Ej*," said Shameem Baksh. " 'Keep quiet.' If before elders, I want to scold the child."

There may actually have been a double meaning in her words. Perhaps she was warning the others. Clearly, she was uncomfortable.

"In front of us," said Reddy, "they would not like to talk."

"If I want to drink water," said Shameem Baksh, "and you are all sitting here, I'll say 'bring the wheel.' "

"That's their language," said Reddy. "They will not tell."

"There are a few other words for water," said Shameem Baksh, closing the conversation.

"Say that they are keeping bad habits," said Reddy.

"They are keeping bad habits," mocked Shameem Baksh.

"What does that mean?" I asked.

"How can I explain it to you?" said Shameem Baksh. "You're a child."

"She wants to speak openly about all that," said Reddy.

"Openly?" said Shameem Baksh. "It's not a good thing—not the done thing. Prostitution in the night, and in the day, they sing."

"Who does?"

"All," said Reddy. "Though some people have gone old and ugly, so nobody comes for them."

"No," said Shameem Baksh. "Not only the young, even the old boys do. Those who have lust do male prostitution—they have men, and they are kept like mistresses."

"Then, where are the men?" I asked.

"They come and go," said Shameem Baksh.

"At night?" I asked.

"Day or night," said Shameem Baksh. "They come and go; you wouldn't be able to tell . . . You see all those gentleman in Kamal Baksh's house? The so-called tenants?"

So even the man who came in with his wife for medicine was probably shared by a hijra mistress—Kiran Baksh?

I thanked Shameem Baksh for her candor.

"Yes," she said, "you will never be able to find such clear information . . . You will never get that . . ."

Reddy suggested that I give them thirty rupees for their time.

"That's why they are known as Baksh," said Reddy.

"Yes," agreed Shameem Baksh. "We live on bakshish."

Reddy laughed—the joke being prostitution.

"Did you see *Heat and Dust*?" asked Shameem.

"Yes," I said.

"Anita was in it," she said. "I couldn't be, because I was invited to Raj Kapoor's birthday party in Bombay. Are you going to Bombay?"

"No," said Reddy. "She's going back to America."

"What a pity," she said. "Come to India again."

As I was taking notes, she added, in English: "My name is Shameem Baksh . . . Forget-me-naat."

The High Risk Groups at risk in the community to suffer AIDS are thus: (i) Homosexuals / Bisexuals, (ii) Prostitutes both male and female, (iii) Eunuchs, (iv) Drug addicts specially, (v) Drug abusers and (vi) Groups who may have sexual interaction with foreign travellers.

Dr. Jaising P. Modi
Medical Jurisprudence
1993

*Sayeed, the oldest "chela," or disciple, of the guru,
Kamal Baksh, at the best-known hijra household of Hyderabad,
the Hijron ka Allawah. A female child belonging to one
of their tenants loiters nearby.*

ABOVE: *Kiran, one of Kamal Baksh's younger disciples, cleaning rice; at left, their well. The central courtyard, giving on to many rooms, is typical of houses built in the nineteenth century.* BELOW: *View of the High Court from the roof of the Allawah. Osman Ali Khan, the seventh and last king of Hyderabad, allegedly forced the hijras to sell off this plot of land in order to construct government buildings there in 1914.*

ABOVE: *Three hijras peek out from the shanties below the Allawah.*
BELOW: *Kamal Baksh, the "guru," or head, of the household, carefully removes a scroll from a trunk. It was an "inam" (gift), or land deed; though she could not read or write, she had memorized its Persian.*

Rani, the star dancer of Kamal Baksh's group, celebrating the birth of a child. The hijras are said to check a boy's genitals to see if they are malformed, then threaten to return when he reaches puberty to induct him into their society.

LEFT: *Senior wives with an elderly eunuch playing chaupar in the court harem. Mughal, Lucknow, ca. 1790.* Courtesy of James Ivory

FROM LEFT TO RIGHT: *Kamal Baksh, Sayeed, Munni, Kiran, and Rani, giving a performance at their house. Rani's hands are extended in the characteristic "hijra" way. Kamal does not allow her disciples to wear much make-up, and men, allegedly, are not allowed in the house.*

Detective Reddy investigated the activities of the hijras of Hyderabad in 1958, when he received a confidential letter from the palace security officer regarding a stabbing between two of the seventh Nizam's sons over the love of a eunuch named Rahman (below, three top photos). "Because we are police officers," said Reddy of the hijras, "they respect us. In times of trouble, we help them."

ABOVE: *Among the carefully kept photographs of the hijras at the Allawah (center), a beautiful male dancer, perhaps a courtesan, in Muslim clothes, from the 1920s.*

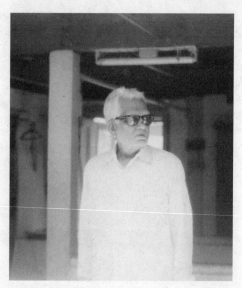

Detective Dherni Dhar Prasad, at home.
He was a street cop, then a detective,
in the locality in which the hijras lived.

Rani, washing her feet. Though people think of the hijras as
"unclean," members of this household were fastidious and maintained
their home with great care.

RIGHT: *Self-defense and secrecy: the slingshot and the key on the wall in Kamal Baksh's house seem fitting symbols for the hijras' lives.*

BELOW: *Kiran and Munni Baksh in the courtyard of their home.*

Anita Baksh (left), a "true" hermaphrodite, dances in
Merchant Ivory's 1983 film, Heat and Dust. Photo by
Christopher Cormack.

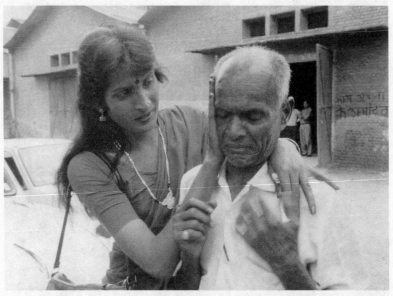

In 1994 Jagmohai Dhyani, 25, filed charges against his castrators in Delhi. At 15, he had "voluntary contact" with the hijra community, he said, but was later drugged and emasculated against his will. He is shown reunited with his father, who says that he "accepts his son" as he is. Photo by Pramod Pushkarna/*India Today.*

Kamal Baksh's own guru, with her "adopted" daughter (left). The hijras used to be cooks and nannies in the homes of kings and nobility, though they do not consider this their main function. Kamal Baksh personally arranged a marriage for her guru's child.

Munni Baksh in the doorway of the Hijron ka Allawah.

All photographs by Zia Jaffrey and Catherine Caplan, unless otherwise noted.

EPILOGUE

I HAD WORRIED THAT THE BOOK on hijras in the Hyderabad Police Commission Office might disappear if the authorities were alerted to the fact that a foreigner was writing a history of them. At the time, Pavitran had been banned from his office, and had not been able to get it for me. In 1994, I went back to India to find it. After all, this was a taboo subject, and might embarrass what I had labeled "the Indian government" in my mind—as though such a coherent entity existed. And there was sure to be a new police regime in power, one which might not be compatible with Mr. Pavitran's.

It was with great sadness that I learned that Mr. Pavitran had died. And my aunt in Delhi told me that she believed that Mr. Shahpur Chenoy, "if he's the one who was married to a widow," had also passed away. I use this euphemism now because I remember hearing her words about a man she hadn't known—in her vibrant, casual way—and they had caused in me a deep grief. I wanted immediately to contact Chenoy's wife, Prem. My aunt believed she had moved to Hyderabad, although her name, she said, was not Prem. For some minutes we discussed the possibility that the Chenoy she was thinking of, and the one I had known, might not be the same person—but in the end, I resigned myself to the fact that it probably was.

The only other link I had to the officials of Hyderabad was Detective Reddy, but absurdly, I had never known his first name. And only once had he allowed my driver to take him home after endless hours of interviews: Daily he came and went by public transportation from some far point—and since he lived in a hut by choice, it would be impossible for me to trace the route we had taken. I hoped that Mr. Reddy would be known to the police community for his work in the neighborhood of hijras, even though he had retired.

For all of these reasons, I thought it best to go to Hyderabad myself, rather than ask someone there to look for the book Mr. Reddy had called *The Eunuchs*, by Sayyid Majidullah, former police commissioner of Hyderabad in 1938, who had retired as inspector general for the state of Maharashtra. The man, it was said, had had an illustrious career, and was regarded as a scholar.

The question became: how to make contact with the new regime of police officers in Hyderabad? In Delhi, people said that the police departments in India were corrupt—hotbeds of intrigue and collaboration in the recent series of bombings that had occurred in Bombay and Calcutta. As a last resort, my cousin handed me a piece of paper with a name written on it—Mehdi Arslan—a friend of a friend's who was involved in communalism and direct political action, and therefore had some contact with the new deputy commissioner of police in Hyderabad.

A journalist in Delhi, Tavleen Singh, had also had some dealings with the Hyderabad police over a child-bride case, and she suggested a strategy: play up the fact that you're a foreigner, she said, and they'll want to help. Go directly to the police commissioner's office and speak to him; because if you begin at a lower level, and you are denied, it causes a problem at the top. Just call up the new commissioner, and don't mention the name of the former one.

I was also able to learn the outcome of Vora's case. In an article published by *India Today* in April of 1994, it was reported that three other adolescents had come forward and filed complaints against their castrators. Officials stated there were fifteen thousand eunuchs in Delhi alone, of which one thousand had been castrated against their wills. But this last figure, of all things, was a quote from Lal Bhola; it seemed that he had now become an advocate for kidnapped adolescents.

Vora's torturers had been given a mere five years of imprisonment; the three hijras who had recently taken their cases to the highest juridical level had had difficulty getting their complaints filed at all in their local police precincts until the courts had intervened and ordered investigations. One case had been dropped for lack of evidence, and two others were still pending. Jagmohan Dhyani, twenty-five, was shown in a sari, reunited with his father after this gruesome fate which had started with admittedly "voluntary contact" with the hijra community and then forced prostitution.

The subject of kidnapping among the hijras was a controversial one, and part of the problem belonged to the hijras themselves; while it would be true to say that many hijras underwent the castration ritual by choice, the entire community was held back by its vow of silence. By not denouncing such practices and disavowing allegiance to these hijra groups, they created a credibility issue for themselves. This gray area was one reason why I found it difficult to merely endorse the idea of a transsexual equivalency in India among the community: the story, it seemed to me, had many strands and the river of narratives was peculiarly Indian. The transgender discourse was peculiarly Western;

not once did I hear the word uttered by a hijra; instead I had let those I had met speak for themselves.

I booked myself into the Banjara Hotel, because a night there cost $38 for an ordinary room and $43 for an executive suite. What was the difference between the two classes of rooms? Nobody at the desk could exactly say— free breakfast and access to the fax center, the receptionist thought, finally. Sensing that the "executive" label might imply quality of service, I opted for it; $5 was too little to argue about. When I ordered a car, I was given the choice of one with A/C and one without—code for "air-conditioning"—the former being twice the price. "A/C?" I said to the receptionist. "But isn't it winter in Hyderabad?" "Yes, ma'am," she said.

Only in Hyderabad did I realize my mistake. The air there was literally unbreathable—between chemical pollution and dust. The city had changed in ten years—too many hotels, insipid American food, yuppies or a new breed of Indian businessmen, and that bizarre fountain outside the Banjara, which resembled someone's idea of what Club Med might look like. Teams of marathon runners streaked the lobby, and the tipping of porters was no longer required—in fact, these young "management" professionals often refused. By the faces present in the lobby bar—and overheard bits of conversation—there seemed to be active business collaborations between the Indians and Australians, Swiss, and Japanese. The economy was alive: the prices of Indian fabrics and products, in general, were high, and often nonnegotiable; the quality was sometimes not as good, nor as varied, as before. On the other hand, Italianized, baroque-looking brocade saris hung in all the hotel shops—their prices somewhat daunting. "Ethnic" identification was in vogue, and the patterns one chose to wear signaled a political statement of sorts. A Hindu was a Hindu; a Sikh, a Sikh; a Kashmiri, a Kashmiri.

Perhaps "in vogue" is an unfair way of naming the political code of correctness I felt everywhere. After the Muslim-Hindu violence, the death of two Gandhis by first a Sikh, then a Hindu fundamentalist, and with Kashmiri violence daily front-page news, it was a nation in conflict—and class was at least on par with, if not second to, ethnicity and religion. One got into a taxi in Delhi, for example, and if the driver was a Sikh, one asked him politely if one could smoke, because it was against his ethics, rather than arrogantly assume class dictated these codes of behavior. In deference to the question, he usually did not refuse.

In a crafts shop in Hyderabad, as I was selecting a few terra-cotta images of Hindu gods—and this in darkness because of an electricity failure—a shopkeeper darted up and withdrew the gods from my hands, saying, "These are all the deities, madam, and you can't take a few, you have to buy the whole set"—yet there was something moral, and indignant, in his tone.

On the day I arrived in Hyderabad, I carried the name of a family friend who was said to have been out of town; I called to ask her servant when she might return, but the friend herself answered; she was leaving by train that night, could she pick me up after breakfast?

Uzra Bilgrami lived only five minutes away from the hotel—in a house she had designed like a reddish rock—to match the rocky terrain of Banjara Hills. Out of a sense of guilt, perhaps—almost all Indians feel obligated to provide for the guest (and this feeling exists even in me, though I was born and mostly raised in New York)—Uzra furnished me with a list of "in case" phone numbers, cracking the phone with her hand because the cradle was jammed, and one by one letting her friends know that I was in town, may need their assistance.

In the course of conversation, I asked her if she knew Mr. Chenoy, and when he had died, and she said, which Mr. Chenoy? "Shahpur," I said. "Shahpur senior—the fat one—died last year, but the thin one is very much alive," she laughed. The thin one? "The retired deputy police commissioner," I explained. "Yes, yes, I just saw him at the Nizam Club last week—oh, he's quite alive." The image of the man made her cheerful; and yet I couldn't quite believe it, so I questioned her till she convinced me. Funny how even people who know each other only remotely in every city in India know the details of each other's lives.

As it happened, the new police commissioner of Hyderabad, a Mr. Dora, made front-page news the day I arrived. There was a picture of him with a story that said that he and the Hyderabad police had cracked new clues to the Bombay bombings, and found that the gang responsible for these had originated in Hyderabad; Dora and his men had arrested the ringleader. Uzra did not know him personally, but handed me the telephone book. Dora's home number was listed.

"Mr. Dora," I explained, "I've come from New York, and am looking for a book that is in the commission office on hijras. I wonder if I could ask for your help."

"It's probably not there," Dora replied, "I doubt it, but call me tomorrow at the office, and I'll put my assistant on to it."

And that was that. Next I called any Chenoy I could find in the book, hoping that they might have Mr. Shahpur Chenoy's number, because he himself was not listed. A young woman said I had the wrong number, but after listening to my story, provided the correct one.

I called Mr. Chenoy that Sunday after leaving Uzra Bilgrami's. He himself answered, but I suppressed the urge to say, "Oh, thank god, you're alive!" I began tentatively— "Do you remember me? I came many years ago . . ." "Of course. Of course," he said. And his voice was as vital as I had remembered it. Perhaps by way of transference, I told him how sad it was to learn that Mr. Pavitran had died. Mr. Chenoy's voice grew quiet; he paused and said softly, "Yes, that was last year . . . he was a very dear friend of mine." "How?" I asked. "That bloody doctor . . . that bloody . . . you know, he died of tuberculosis—can you believe it? In this day and age! For two years it went undetected. All he needed was an X ray . . . If I could just catch hold of that doctor, I'd like to, I'd like to . . ."

"Kill him?" I asked.

"No," he said, "not kill . . . torture . . . I'd like to *torture* him!"

He should have tested him, Chenoy said, one simple little test—after all, "We all went out to the districts and were likely to be exposed." If they'd caught it earlier, if . . . Chenoy was beside himself.

Later he would tell me, when I explained how invaluable Pavitran had been in my research on hijras, that it was so like him, to take the time, and that, "I was there in the hospital with him in those last days . . . On Tuesday he said, 'Shahpur, this is a bloody bad business with Bhaskar*—they're trying to get him'—and now of course he's chief minister—Pavitran said, 'Just make a few phone calls and get him out of this mess . . .' And I did, right there in the room, and by Friday, Bhaskar was free, but Pavitran died on Thursday; his son was there—he died gasping for breath." Of Pavitran's own framing, he said, he lost the

* Vijaya Bhaskara K. Reddy

case and was "transferred" from his post as police commissioner and made the "housing" commissioner. "That's how they do it—it's all so corrupt in the ICS [Indian Civil Service]—a lateral move. They were trying to say that he had been bribed, but it wasn't true. He kept every slip of paper, every record of every transaction, just because he knew! And besides, he had no reason to, but he lost: the whole thing was concocted."

How was Prem? Fine, said Chenoy. She was out of town, visiting relatives. Would he meet me for lunch? "Well, of course, my dear, lunch with an attractive young woman— but do you realize that I'm a seventy-year-old man?" Seventy, I exclaimed: "Why, I thought you were about forty—ten years ago." "Well . . . no, no," Chenoy laughed. He'd help me in any way he could, he said. How about drinks at the Secunderabad Club? Fine. I asked him whether he knew the commissioner of police, or the deputy commissioner. "No, I don't know anyone these days—it's all the young ones . . ."

I was in Hyderabad, again—it takes only one person to make a city real. I then called Mehdi Arslan—even though Dora had said he'd "put his assistant on to it," I wasn't sure what this meant—and Mehdi agreed to take me over to the deputy commissioner's office the next day. "He's a very nice man, Mr. Sharma, and I've found him to be extremely helpful . . . I myself owe him a visit."

I did not call on Dora. Mehdi, his wife, Shahina, and I drove to the Secunderabad Police Station the next evening: Sharma had said that he might be in meetings all afternoon, because of the terrorist case, but Mehdi had said that we'd try our luck anyway. The station was a cream-colored gov-

ernment affair, dilapidated and rudimentary, and I had
trouble imagining both Pavitran and Chenoy in these bleak
cement offices. Chenoy later told me that Channa Reddy, a
former chief minister of Andhra Pradesh, who had appointed them to their higher posts, had once remarked,
"What are you two gentlemen doing in the police department?"

We were checked at the gate for weapons and then ushered on to Mr. Sharma's building. There we waited on
benches for over an hour—until finally Mehdi filled out a
slip of paper, handed to us by a guard—explaining that
we'd try again the following morning.

I was beginning to feel that we were not quite a priority,
but that was not true. The next morning, we were led into
the office, though a police officer explained that Mr.
Sharma was not well today, but expecting this visit, he
had asked me to call him from his office—at home. They
dialed the number—Mr. Sharma had a warm voice—and
made apologies for not being able to come in person. He'd
developed something like a cold, but his nose was inflamed—and he had a fever. Still, he asked, what could he
do for me? I explained that there was a book in the library
or record room, that I wanted him to check to see if there'd
been any criminal cases involving the hijras in the last ten
years, and that I needed a record of the 1958 case involving the hijras and the Nizam's palace. He said he'd look
into it, why didn't I come by in the morning around 10:30?
"But you know," he said, "we generally don't keep records
longer than ten years . . . these papers go to the chick-pea
sellers . . . And there is no library in the commissioner's
office." Sharma was referring to the fact that some vital
correspondence between Rajiv Gandhi and a chief minister
had recently been found, rolled into a cone, as a container
for roasted chick-peas, sold on the streets.

That evening, I headed for the Secunderabad Club. Mr. Chenoy, I was told, was in the recreation room: the tall man, bent over a book, now rising slowly with age, in a cardigan, was Mr. Chenoy. For an instant, I thought I was mistaken, because he had no hair. I shook his hand; he smiled, and after asking what I'd have to eat and drink, took the conversation right into business, as though we'd lost not a day of time between the urgency of the project ten years ago and now.

"What I've done is," said Chenoy, "I've called the librarian at the record room—he knows me very well, from way back—his name is Charan Das—and I've put him on to this book. And I know him—he'll drop everything, and he'll put others on to whatever he's working on—and he will find it if he can. Now, you know, the record room is a disaster, and where that book will be—maybe buried under piles and piles of paper. Because what we'd do is—whenever we were through with certain records, we'd send them there, and nobody ever really sorted through them. They'd just build up. But this Charan Das, he might be able to find it. Are you sure it exists?"

"Yes, I'm sure," I said. "I know about it because of a Detective Reddy—he himself read the book. Pavitran couldn't get it, because he was barred from his own office . . . Do you know Detective Reddy?"

"Which Detective Reddy?" asked Chenoy.

"I'm not sure of his first name," I said. "I just thought you might know him, because Pavitran did."

"Well, my dear," said Chenoy, "you know the old joke about the American lady who comes to Delhi, has a wonderful time, and raves about her trip when she goes back. And when she learns that another American is going to Delhi, she says, 'Oh then, you *must look up* Mr. Singh.' In this town . . . everybody's a bloody 'Reddy'."

I laughed. "Yes, I know. I don't know how to find him . . . Is Dhar Prasad still alive?"

"No," said Chenoy, "he died seven years ago."

"Oh god," I said.

"And did you call your Mr. Sharma?" asked Chenoy.

"Yes," I said. "He says there's no library in the police commissioner's office."

"What? No library? You tell that Mr . . . that bloody young one—that I myself created the library in 1968. You go and tell him! What rubbish—no library . . . You tell him Shahpur Chenoy said so."

So we sat there, thinking together. There must be a way.

"Who wrote it?" asked Chenoy.

"Majidullah," I said.

"Oh yes, a very learned man . . . Have you tried his family? What is the name of that car company that the older son runs . . . damn . . . I can't recall . . . you know, I'm not senile, I'm just forgetful . . . Well, that Banjara, they get their cars from him—you just ask that travel desk who leases them their cars . . . They'll be able to tell you."

Older now, and moving at a slower pace, he still commanded the air like an officer, rising to take me over to the phone, parked in the veranda of the club. I remembered the number, and recalled how difficult it was to get through to the Banjara Hotel: 22 22 22, which the operator pronounced, "double two double two double two"—the first time, she had said, "Double two triple two three—no sorry, triple two, triple two—," and I had wondered what was so wrong with my brain that it couldn't admit the error. The line was perpetually engaged, and I had no wish to spend hours on the phone trying to get through, but I sensed that Chenoy wanted to be helpful. Retirement seemed out of place in him, and there was the slight impatience at having to watch his body change, and with it, the structure of his world and habits.

Naturally, I could not get through, though I gave it a good five minutes. I then returned to where Chenoy was sitting. I said to him then, on our second scotch, that it had never occurred to me that Pavitran might die. "You and he were immortals to me." Chenoy smiled sadly, then laughed and put his hand gently on the side of my cheek—that gesture of tenderness from elder to younger. "If you need me to do some interviews with the hijras after you go, I can," he said absurdly, but in that moment, I realized that it had been curiosity that had made him join the Indian Civil Service—immense curiosity that bound him to Pavitran—a wonder at and in the world—a vitality that even today kept his face young and free of all lines but those of a gentle irony. It was not so absurd, after all, to imagine that cardigan-clad figure in the home of the hijras—there with a neutral mind.

"You know," said Chenoy, "we used to use them as informants—that is why they had a good relation with the police. I'm sure they still do . . . because, after all, they know everything—they hear it all—they are in every house—so, the first thing, there's a crime, you go to them."

"Yes," I said, "I want to make contact with the guru of the Hijron ka Allawah—the one whom I originally spoke to . . . When was there an Inspector for Eunuchs?"

"In the 1930s," said Chenoy. "Osman created the post. The nobility was against him . . ."

It was ten o'clock, and time to relieve the driver. Chenoy suggested that we meet the following day for lunch—by then he'd know whether Charan Das had found the book.

The next morning, I inquired by phone at the travel desk: "Who leases you your cars?"

"They're our own cars, sir," said the voice.

"You don't know the name of the company you buy them from?"

"No, sir."

It was an encounter with that absurd breed of English-rote memorization—terms of deference, without regard to content.

"Is there someone there who might know, and can you stop calling me 'sir'?"

"Sorry, madam."

But there was someone who might know: Meraj Pasha, the noble lady, who, in any case, I had meant to get in touch with. Meraj was home; yes, she said, she had known Majidullah very well, he was no longer alive—but rather than give me his son's number, she would call him and ask him to go through his father's papers. "But, you know, the family hasn't kept his things very well . . . The father was so scrupulous about all this . . . but not his sons." A few minutes later, she rang back to say that the son had looked through his index and found only three entries—a book on shooting, a book on birds, and an unfinished manuscript on the Mughul court.

"But it's an official police record," I said, "a bound tome of sorts—not a book for the public."

"He doesn't know anything about it—about its existence," she said.

"Might he be embarrassed by the subject, and concealing it?" I asked.

"No," said Meraj, "I think he just doesn't know."

She invited me over for tea, told me that Shivi and Rajesh were divorced, and said, as a last thought, "By the way—and I don't mean to be impudent . . . but these hijras . . . something homosexual about them . . . are you?"

"No," I said.

"Thank god," she said.

Not that it mattered, but her sudden boldness made me laugh. Indeed, something about the subject made people freer in their speech than they might ordinarily be.

Later that morning, I went with Shahina to the deputy police commissioner's office. Shahina had a visa problem to clear up at the compound and had taken the day off work. She also meant to act as my translator when we visited the hijras.

Outside the office, we gave a slip of paper with our names on it to the policeman on duty, and were quickly ushered in. Mr. Sharma sat at a large desk, surrounded by files, a man in his early thirties. And he had clearly come *only* to keep this appointment, since his nose was now so inflamed that it threatened to overwhelm his face. He seemed embarrassed by the boil on the left side and kept placing a hanky on it; and lowering his eyes, he explained that, after this meeting, he was going to the doctor again. He'd only been posted in Hyderabad for a year, he said, and although it had been his happiest time in the police force, he kept having unexplained illnesses and skin problems. He loved Hyderabad, he said, but he was being posted to Bangalore. A lateral move? I asked. No, he said, because his wife, also in the police department, had been transferred to Calcutta, and Indira Gandhi had made a rule about the Indian Civil Service having to accommodate the spouse in such cases; the only city with two such vacancies was Bangalore.

"I've run a check," said Sharma. "And there are no criminal cases involving the hijras in the last ten years." Also, he said, "There is no record of the 1958 case in the record room—probably because these papers have long been discarded—where can one keep them?" He gestured

at the piles around him which evidently required his signa-
ture, and said that they would most probably disappear
into obscurity in the record room.

"But what about the library?" I asked. "And, by the
way, Mr. Shahpur Chenoy, who once held your post, said
to tell you that he himself created the Police Commission
Library in 1968." Sharma raised his eyebrows and pressed
a buzzer beneath his desk. In Telugu he asked a policeman
to inquire into the matter.

"You speak Telugu," said Shahina.

"I had to learn it, since I was posted here," said Sharma.
"I'm actually from near Jaipur."

I told Sharma that it had been a Detective Reddy who
had known of the book on eunuchs. I had no way to find
him since I lacked a first name, though he was the friend of
an old detective, Dhar Prasad, of the hijra quarter, who had
died, though his daughter might know.

Again Sharma pressed the buzzer, and this time asked
a policeman in Urdu to look into it. And, he said, find me
the name and address of the oldest living detective from
the district in which the hijras live; get me the address of
the deceased detective, Dherni Dhar Prasad.

At the mere mention of the hijras, the policeman smiled.
He was going to like this job, and perhaps take a few lib-
erties with me?

The reports came back promptly: "Yes, sir, there *was* a
library in the police commissioner's office, but it was disbanded six months ago, and all the books were sent to the
Police Academy."

"You see," said Sharma, "nothing in India works
efficiently. We just go from crisis to crisis . . ."

"Yes, sir," reported the second, "the oldest living detective is a Mr. Rana—and we have an address." He, thought

Sharma, might know of the deceased Mr. Prasad, but the addresses of his relatives might be listed in the local Secunderabad police station, near the community of hijras.

"First," said Sharma, "try the police station. Second, try Mr. Rana, because he's an hour away from here. Do you want to go to the Police Academy? Unfortunately, it's two hours away."

On second thought, Sharma decided to call its director and inquire about the book himself. But he, like everyone else in India, was at the mercy of the phones. He had three lines, and used the one with a little red light on it. To the smiling policeman, he said, escort them to each place, and also, take them to the hijra community. The officer bore the name Ismail Jaffrey on a metal label.

Sharma kept having trouble with the phone; tried again; was holding on; finally got an operator and asked to be connected with the director of the Police Academy. Meanwhile, he called for buffalo tea, saying that the local cup would make me quite high. Sensing that Sharma had work to do, but felt obligated to chitchat, I suggested that we'd wait outside, till the return call came from the academy. He then suggested that we wait in his private room behind the office—one with a sofa and a bed.

And there it was: in about ten minutes, Mr. Sharma had organized me. It was all going to happen, and a police jeep awaited us outside.

After an hour, Sharma called me back outside.

"I'm afraid there's no record of the book," he said. "But that doesn't mean it's not there . . . It's just impossible to find."

My only hope was now Mr. Reddy, who might remember what the book looked like. There was also Charan Das in the record room. I shook Mr. Sharma's hand and wished him well.

"I don't know about you," said Shahina outside, "but I'm not going to the hijras in a police jeep." She suggested that the policeman assigned to us should follow our car, and keep his distance from the Hijron ka Allawah, so as not to frighten them.

But a police jeep it would have to be, at least for the time being, because our driver had disappeared. Could he have misunderstood? No, Shaheena and I agreed, climbing into the jeep. Along the way, however, we ran into the driver—madly rushing back—he'd had an engine problem and had gone to have it fixed. We got into our car in the middle of the road.

Jaffrey led us to the Secunderabad police station. There he disembarked and arrived shortly with a slip of paper with Prasad's family's address. We drove to a nearby set of apartments: Jaffrey inquired and was given another address, about a half an hour away. Prasad's daughter, Shashi, had died of cancer, we were told, but his son lived there.

Because we were in the locale of hijras, we stopped at the Allawah, leaving Jaffrey outside. There was the thin off-white curtain, the barrier to their house, which I pulled aside, as Shahina shouted "hullo? hullo?" to announce the intrusion. There was immediately a sense that something was wrong; the photographs had been removed from the walls, scattered cloves of garlic littered the raised platform on which two hijras sat—one, a poorly clothed fat eunuch, in a petticoat and blouse, who stared at us. Two other hijras came up from behind, and we were suddenly surrounded; the prevalent feeling was one of suspicion. I recognized only one—the oldest one—Sayeed Baksh; he, peeling garlic, looked up once at me vaguely, without smiling.

"Do you remember me?" I asked Sayeed Baksh.

"Of course I do," he said, ironically. "You came years ago, and nearly took our heads off."

"Where is Kamal Baksh?" I asked.

The fat one answered: She died three years ago of a heart attack.

As I took in the news, I was accosted by a truly ugly hijra who stood too close, made a fanglike expression with her mouth, and began to ridicule my bodily gestures. I felt the hair rise on my skin, and thought for a second about Ismail Jaffrey outside.

The fat seated one now seemed to soften her—she had known Kamal Baksh, she said; and then the hostile one, perhaps in her fifties, came and sat beside her.

"Where is Kiran Baksh?" I asked, in an effort to introduce the idea of a positive connection to the past; and because Kiran had had a smiling, gentle face, as I remembered her.

"She's gone . . ." said the fat one. "Just twenty-two days ago, she, and three of our kind, died of carbon monoxide poisoning."

I stood there, speechless.

"Yes," said the fat one. "They were in a village near Jaipur, and they slept with the doors and windows shut. The coal was burning. They never even woke up. They died in their sleep . . . That's why the house is like this."

"And Munni Baksh?"

"She also died in that house."

"And Rani?"

"She also."

"Do you know Shameem Baksh?" I asked.

"She isn't here," said the fat one. "She fell from a great height and broke her leg. They amputated it . . . Just now, she's gone to Bombay to get a false one."

The feeling was not a peaceful one, and the hijra who had imitated me was scrutinizing us throughout this conversation. She seemed displeased. I was rushing my words.

She kept shaking her head with disapproval, but the fat one again calmed her down. Sayeed Baksh was silent throughout.

"Who is the new guru?" I asked.

The fat one pointed at the scowling one.

"She is," she said. "It's all been so terrible . . . these deaths . . . and because we are in mourning, we cannot speak . . ."

There was a sense of chaos among the new order; I could see that the new leadership, under the new guru, would be a crude and defiant one. Gone was that gentle grace and politeness to outsiders who came with respect, embodied by Kamal Baksh. They barely said good-bye.

Shahina later observed that the hijras seemed defensive and fearful of the outside world—were afraid of us—but had quieted down only when they realized that I was not unfriendly to their "cause." They didn't give us the benefit of the doubt, though, I said. They took their mourning very seriously, said Shahina, that's why all the photos had been put away. Muslim mourning—no festivities, fasting, no joy—for forty days. She, too, had been frightened by two of the hijras, she said, but was glad that we hadn't brought in Ismail Jaffrey. It must be that their society is more threatened then when you came last, Shahina said.

We drove on toward Dhar Prasad's son's house; past the old Char Minar lanes with their shops of dazzling lamps, past the bazaars of silver and gold cloths. Soon we were moving along a spacious road which gave way to a government enclave—a compound of beige flats with a policeman at the entrance. Jaffrey jumped out of his jeep and made inquiries—we were directed to the flat number, and upon ringing, met by a woman who said that she was Dhar Prasad Jr.'s wife. Jaffrey's demeanor shifted, and though we were ushered into the living room, for some reason, he

chose to stand outside the house, though he might have
stayed in the foyer.

Mrs. Prasad explained that her husband was in *puja*—
prayers. I told her why we'd come—and gently she asked
me to describe the Mr. Reddy I had known. Upon listening,
her face grew quiet with recognition. I think I know who
you're speaking of, she said. I then played her a section of
tape which had Reddy's voice on it. Yes, she said, eyes
widening, his name is Tirpath—Tirpath Reddy; and if
you'll just wait, my husband will come and speak to you.

The man who finally emerged in a dhoti had a large mustache—the kind one sees painted—that drops down almost
like a horseshoe and curls outward. He greeted us traditionally—as Ismail Jaffrey darted in and suddenly saluted
him. Only then did I sense his rank: he was a high-level intelligence officer, a member of the Criminal Investigation
Division.

I played the tape for him and suddenly his face, daunting until now, showed an imperceptible emotion. His eyes
flooded ever so slightly. "Will you make a copy of these
tapes for us?" he asked. Yes, I said, but why? "Because my
father's voice is there," he said. "He told me about you,
and about the project, and we would like that—for remem-
brance." And yes, he had just gone to see Mr. Reddy—his
father's friend—last weekend. He's very knowledgeable, he
said. He might even have the book you're looking for, because his personal library is immense. The problem was
that he was out of town for a week, and as it was, he had
no phone. Even his address—I can only get there by sight,
he said. He asked me to write him a note, with my address
on it, and said he'd pass it along. His title? He had retired
as superintendent of police—district level.

Jaffrey, who stood hovering at the door, indicated that
he might be able to get Reddy's address. This he made his

mission, and for the rest of the day, absurdly felt he was reporting to me: Shall I call you later this afternoon? Will you be in? I'll go get the address. And so, later, at the hotel, he did call: he had not been able to trace it, but would try again.

We took leave of Mr. Prasad, and told Jaffrey that there would be no need to visit Mr. Rana, the old-timer, since we'd met with success. I was sorry not to be able to see Mr. Reddy—he was apparently in Warangal, tending to "some properties," and there was no phone there either.

At the Nizam Club, we met Mr. Chenoy for a lunch of proper Hyderabadi biryani—a dish of buttery meat and rice. Strangely, we ate in silence, though occasionally Chenoy asked us a few questions about how the day had gone. He listened quietly, without the usual exacting and exuberance. I kept saying that this biryani was the best food I'd had in Hyderabad. And we all commented on the poor choice of restaurants in the Banjara Hotel. Conversation wandered to small talk—what did Shahina do? Chenoy said, as though oppressed. I had no idea what to make of this—we suffered through dessert—and then Shahina took my car back. Only then did Chenoy relax. It was that Indian reserve, a reserve in front of strangers.

"In Warangal!" Chenoy exclaimed afterwards. "Then let's go! You know—the Naxalite area—two hours away from here . . ." He was a policeman again.

"Dangerous?" I asked.

"Political violence, kidnappings, yes . . . but do you have his address?"

"No," I said. I was amazed at his adventurousness, but I was leaving that night for Delhi. "I'll write to him from New York. Prasad said he'd get the address, and pass on the message—with my address. I also gave him your number."

"My number?" said Chenoy.

"Oh, sorry, did I do something wrong?" I asked. "I hope you don't mind."

"No, no," said Chenoy. There was something in his thoughts about two orders clashing—the world of Reddy and the world of Chenoy, possibly, Reddy's deferring to Chenoy's—and so my suggestion had reversed the hierarchy—but Chenoy went along with it.

"I can't call him?"

"No phone."

"Then, when he calls," said Chenoy, "I'll have him come over, and he can use my phone to call you."

"Too expensive," I said. "Maybe I'll call you at a pre-arranged time . . ."

"We'll do something," said Chenoy. "If he has the book, I can copy it, and mail it to you . . . By the way, Charan Das cannot find it."

"By the way," I said, "Sharma said to tell *you* that the library was disbanded six months ago."

Chenoy laughed.

"And about it he said, 'in India, we just go from crisis to crisis'—nothing has a logic."

By telephone, Dhar Prasad's son gave me Mr. Reddy's sister's number and address, and after several calls from New York, during which she kept trying to organize her brother's coming from his village to her flat, she succeeded.

"We have been waiting for you for two days," she said, "and, in an hour, he was about to take the bus back."

I was glad to hear Mr. Reddy's voice. He had not been well, he said. His eyes were weak, and he was having trouble with his leg. His sister had read aloud my letter to him.

The book, he said, was a collection of notes by Majidullah, and by the inspectors under him. He did not have it.

Nor could he imagine that it was ever sent to the Police Academy. It had probably been thrown out, he speculated, but he would write me a letter, clearing up my questions and doubts.

His frail, thirty-page, handwritten manuscript arrived a few weeks after our conversation. In it, he emphasized that legally and morally, castration was not to be witnessed by anyone other than a eunuch. He named the sources for his hijra jokes—Rahman himself, "who had been a great talker," and with whom he had been quite close. He included a few drawings in fountain pen of the anatomy of castration, apologizing for his bluntness and, to his mind, immodesty. He did not want to name the sons of the Nizam who had been involved in the stabbings. "It is my firm belief and hope," he concluded, "that you will be fair in dealing with the subject, so that it may not hurt the feelings of any caste or creed or person."

Outside the gate, the drivers lean on cars or gossip, crouching in small groups. Through the lanes of Old Delhi, the groom approaches on a white horse, clasped from behind by a small child. An endless wave follows, some on foot, others slowly driving the gray and white and black Ambassadors. Inside the gate, men in suits wait near where women huddle in silk saris, with gold borders.

Now the men dressed as women appear, past the drivers, through the other gate. They huddle in tattered saris, and belt out one dissonant note after another, one on tambourine, another on drum. They are old, as old as stones, and not pretty. They jeer at the men in suits, and flatter the floating women, screeching obscenities in husky voices, voices that have a cadence in them, an unmistakeable rhythm through repetition. Their hands mirror their obscene words: the hand becomes a swollen belly, over and over the contour of the baby, the contour of lust and of labor. Some laugh, others ignore. The outsider turns to the elegant men, sipping a scotch on the green.

Who are they?

With a turn of the hand, he says, Oh the hijras. They always come.

ACKNOWLEDGMENTS

I would like to thank my parents, Madhur Jaffrey and Sanford Allen, for their love and support; my sisters, Meera and Sakina Jaffrey; my brothers-in-law, Francis Wilkinson and Craig Bombardiere; and Cathy Caplan, with whom I traveled to India in 1984, intent on making a movie. Though we didn't, together we discovered the power of the human will.

My family in India: Krishen Bans and Maya Bahadur; Kamal and Hussain Tayebbhoy; and Yasmeen Tayebbhai; Mehreen and Rahul Khosla; Veena Bahadur; Siddharth Bahadur; Sanjay Bahadur; Abha and Ajai Kaul; Azhar Tyabji; and Yogesh and Naresh Dayal.

Those who became the book: Shahpur and Prem Chenoy; Mr. Pavitran, in memoriam; Mr. Reddy, and Mr. Prasad, in memoriam; Attia Hosein, Shehbaz Safrani, Meraj Pasha, Shivi and Rajesh (Rajeshwar), and Dilip Bobb; Kamal Baksh and her chelas, in memoriam; Sayeed Baksh; Shameem Baksh and her chelas; Mustapha Hussain, Roop Karan, and Mani; Ramzan; Shahina and Mehdi Arslan; and Mr. Sharma.

My friends, for their love, support, and editorial insight: Pau Atela, Jesse Browner, Margaret Cezair-Thompson, Judy Clain, Rufus Collins, Vania Del Borgo, Nazanin Ganjavi, Rodrigo Garcia, Peter Gargagliano, Eli

Gottlieb, Alon Gratch, Molly Hoagland, Maya Jaggi, Sandeep Junnarkar, Rebecca Karl, Tom Keenan, Ted Kim, Anthony Korner, Laura Kurgan, Heidi Lefer, Sean McCann, Ameena Meer, Julie Metz, Michele Millon, Stephen O'Shea, Jill Pearlman, Rosie Reiss, Michele Sacks, Vivian Selbo, Adam Shatz, Somini Sen Gupta, Gopal Sukhu, Giorgio Vigna, Grahame Weinbren, and JoAnn Wypijewski, who, in addition, helped me at a critical editorial moment.

Also: Aleene Allen, Esther and Kim Allen, Gini Alhadeff, Quang Bao, Anita Bassey, Gregory Beals, Jonathan Caplan, Charlotte Card, Doug Childers, Linda and Arthur Collins, Jaya Dayal, Robin Desser, Deborah Eisenberg, Kurt Eissler, Catherine Ettlinger, Ishrat Hussain, Cyrus Jhabvala, Fred and Dolores Karl, Robert Massie, Mira Nair, James Nares, Victor Navasky, Jonathan Nossiter, Susan Pelzer, Caryl Phillips, Lee Phillips, Michael Rips, Marc Robinson, Somi Roy, Vivek Sahni, Mark Schapiro, Jeff Seroy, Ben Sonnenberg, Wally Shawn, Claudia Swan, Veronique Vienne, and Art Winslow.

The scholars who generously assisted me in matters of language and theory: Muzaffar Alam, Iraj Anvar, Lawrence Cohen, Jill Claster-Midonick, John E. Cort, Wendy Doniger, Ainslie Embree, Robert Goldman, Jack Hawley, Stanley Insler, Ayesha Jalal, Robin Lewis, C. M. Naim, Serena Nanda, Veena Talwar Oldenburg, Geeta Patel, Frances Pritchett, Theodore Riccardi, K.S.S. Seshan, S.P. Shorey, Gayatri Spivak, Romila Thapar, Indu Vyas, and Leonard Zwilling.

Those who sent their papers, articles, or related material: Alyssa C. Ayres, William Elison, Shaffiq Essajee, Siddharth Gautam, in memoriam, Marcus Leatherdale, Sandeep Roy-Chowdhury, John Swan, and Sam Swope.

Also: Taraneh Bahrampour, Abhas Chandra, Mathew

Schmalz, Shashi Tiwari, Lalitha Reddy, A.K. Vajpay, Sandhya Kuruganti, Madhu Kalluri, Mr. Siddiqi, Charan Das, the Police Commission librarian, Zakiya and John Kurrien, Zehra and Hasan Tyabji, Uzra Bilgrami, Melissa Chung, Jaishri Abichandani, Thomas Levin, Haleh Nazeri, Arash Farahvashi, Tahir Raza, Lan Nguyen, Stephanie, the librarian at the Indian Consulate, and Vijay S. T. Shankardass.

For translation, Aurora Conti and Asma.

For typing, Ria Finazzo, Lisa Diamond, and Linda Ketelhut.

For their grants and fellowships: Ismail Merchant, Gil Donaldson, James Ivory, and Ruth Prawer Jhabvala, at the Merchant and Ivory Foundation; and Robert Towers, in memoriam, former chair of the Columbia University Graduate Writing Division.

At Wylie, Andrew Wylie and Bridget Love.

At Pantheon, Sonny Mehta, Chip Kidd, Kate Rowe, Susan Norton, Altie Karper, Kristen Bearse, Gia Kim, who helped me with legal and permissions issues, sometimes late into the night, and E. B. Friedlander.

And special love and thanks to my friend and agent, Deborah Karl; and to my editor, Shelley Wanger, who tirelessly read this manuscript in its many incarnations.

This book is for Louis Broman—for the love we shared, for half our lives. He died last year, at the age of thirty-eight.

SELECTED BIBLIOGRAPHY

Alikhan, Raza. *Hyderabad, 400 Years (1591–1991)*. Hyderabad: Zenith Services, 1990.

Allami, Abu' l-Fazl. *The A'in-i Akbari*. Translated by H. Blochmann. Delhi: Naresh C. Jain, 1965.

Alf Laylah wa Laylah: The Book of a Thousand Nights and a Night. Translated by Richard F. Burton. London: The Burton Club.

Ansari, Mohammad Azhar. *Social Life of the Mughul Emperors, 1526–1707*. Allahabad: Shanti Prakashan, 1974.

Artola, George T. "The Transvestite in Sanskrit Story and Drama." *Annals of Oriental Research*. Madras (1975), pp. 57–68.

Ayalon, David. *Outsiders in the Land of Islam: Mamluks, Mongols, and Eunuchs*. London: Varorium Reprints, 1988.

Ayres, Alyssa C. "Defining the Decent: Indian Hijras in the 19th and 20th Centuries. Undergraduate thesis, Cambridge: Harvard-Radcliffe College, 1992.

Babur, Zahiru'd-din Muhammad. *Babur, Emperor of Hindustan, 1483–1530*. Translated by Annette S. Beveridge. New Delhi: Oriental Books Reprint Corp., 1979.

Basham, A. L. *The Wonder That Was India*. New York: Grove Press, Inc., 1954.

Bawa, V. K. *The Last Nizam: The Life and Times of Mir Osman Ali Khan*. New Delhi: Penguin Books, 1991.

Bernier, François. *Travels in the Mogul Empire, A.D. 1656–*

1668. Translated by Irving Brock; revised by Archibald Constable. New Delhi: S. Chand and Co. (Pvt.) Ltd., 1972.

Bilgrami, S.A.A. *Landmarks of the Deccan: A Comprehensive Guide to the Archaeological Remains of the City and Suburbs of Hyderabad*. Hyderabad-Deccan: Government Central Press, 1927.

Bobb, Dilip, and C. J. Patel. "Fear Is Their Key." *India Today* (September 15, 1982).

Broder, Jonathan. "Eunuch's Lib: India's 'Third Sex' Vigorously Speaks Out for Equal Rights." *Chicago Tribune* (October 19, 1984).

Brodie, Fawn M. *The Devil Drives: A Life of Sir Richard Burton*. New York: W. W. Norton, 1967.

Buck, William, ed. and trans. *Ramayana, King Rama's Way*. New York: The New American Library, Inc., 1978.

Buitenen, J.A.B. van, ed. and trans. *The Mahabharata*. Vol. 3. Chicago: University of Chicago Press, 1973.

Burton, Richard F., Sir. *Sind Revisited: With Notices of the Anglo-Indian Army; Railroads; Past, Present, and Future*. London: R. Bentley and Son, 1877.

———. *Scinde, or the Unhappy Valley*. London: R. Bentley, 1951.

———. *Zanzibar; City, Island, and Coast*. New York: Johnson Reprint Corp., 1967.

———. *Sindh and the Races That Inhabit the Valley of the Indus*. Karachi: Oxford University Press, 1973.

———. *The Sotadic Zone*. Boston: Milford House, 1973.

———. *Personal Narrative of a Pilgrimage to al-Madinah & Meccah*. London: Darf Publishers, 1986.

Busquet, Gerard, and Carris Beaune. *Les Hermaphrodites*. Paris: Jean-Claude Simoen, 1978.

Campbell, J. M., ed. *Gazetteer of the Bombay Presidency*. Vol. 9. Bombay: Government Central Press, 1901.

Carstairs, G. Morris. *The Twice-Born: A Study of a Community of High-Caste Hindus*. Bloomington: Indiana University Press, 1958.

Claiborne, William. "India's Eunuchs Have Fallen in Esteem." *Washington Post* (April 7, 1983).

Coomaraswamy, Ananda K., and Sister Nivita. *Myths of the Hindus and Buddhists*. New York: Dover Publications, Inc., 1967.

Crooke, William, ed. *Hobson-Jobson: A Glossary of Anglo-Indian Words and Phrases*. Delhi: Munshiram Manoharlal, Oriental Publishers & Booksellers, 1903.

Dalrymple, William. *City of Djinns: A Year in Delhi*. London: HarperCollins, 1993.

Doniger, Wendy, ed. *The Laws of Manu*. Translated by Wendy Doniger with Brian K. Smith. New Delhi: Penguin Books, 1991.

Elison, William. "Communalism and the Safavid State: A Study of Sexual Orientation." Undergraduate thesis, Williamstown, Mass.: Williams College, 1989.

Elliot, F. A. H. *Gazetter of the Bombay Presidency. Vol. VII, Baroda*. Bombay, Government Central Press, 1883.

Forbes, James. *Oriental Memoirs: Selected and Abridged from a Series of Familiar Letters Written during Seventeen Years Residence in India*. London: White, Cochrane, and Co., 1813.

Franklin, C. A., ed. *Modi's Textbook of Medical Jurisprudence and Toxicology*. Bombay: N. M. Tripathi Private Limited, 1988.

Freeman, James M. *Untouchable: An Indian Life History*. Stanford: Stanford University Press, 1979.

Frowde, Henry, ed. *The Imperial Gazetteer of India*. Vols. 1–26. Oxford: Clarendon Press, 1909.

Gautam, Siddhartha. "Less than Gay." Delhi: AIDS Bhedbhav Virodi Andolan (ABVA), 1991.

Goldman, Robert P. "Transsexualism, Gender, and Anxiety in Traditional India." *Journal of the American Oriental Society* 113, no. 3 (July–Sept., 1993), pp. 374–401.

Governor General of India in Council. "Act No. XXVII of 1871: An Act for the Registration of Criminal Tribes and

Eunuchs" in *A Collection of Acts Passed by the Governor General of India in Council in the Year 1871*. Bombay Archives, Bombay Acts, Vol. 19196. Calcutta: Office of Superintendent of Government Printing, 1872. (Courtesy of Alyssa Ayres.)

Gulbadan, Begum. *Humayun'namah*. Translated by Annette S. Beveridge. Lahore: Sange-Meel Publications Distributors, Islamic Book Service, 1974.

Hastings, James, ed. *Encyclopaedia of Religion and Ethics*. Vol. 5. "Eunuch," by Louis H. Gray. Edinburgh: T. & T. Clark, 1914.

Hiltebeitel, Alf. "Siva, the Goddess, and the Disguises of the Pandavas and Draupati." *History of Religions* 20, nos. 1–2 (August–November, 1980), pp. 147–74.

Hussein, Mahdi, ed. and trans. *The Rehla of Ibn Battuta (India, Maldive Islands and Ceylon)*. 2d ed. Baroda: Oriental Institute, 1976.

Ibbetson, D.C.J., M. E. MacLegan, and H. A. Rose. *A Glossary of the Tribes and Castes of the Panjab and North-West Frontier Province*. Vol. 2. Lahore: Civil and Military Gazette Press, 1911.

Joardar, Biswanath. *Prostitution in Nineteenth- and Early Twentieth-Century Calcutta*. New Delhi: Inter-India Publications, 1985.

Joshi, Charu Lata. "Eunuchs Fight Back." *India Today* (May 15, 1994).

Karaka, D. F. *Fabulous Mogul: Nizam VII of Hyderabad*. Lahore: Progressive Books, 1975.

Kaul, H. K., ed. *Travellers' India: An Anthology*. Delhi: Oxford University Press, 1979.

Khan, Dargah Quli. *Muraqqa'-e-Delhi: The Mughul Capital in Muhammad Shah's Time*. Translated by C. Shekhar and S. Chenoy. Delhi: Deputy Publications, 1989.

Knighton, William. *The Private Life of an Eastern King*. London: 1856.

Lynton, Harriet Ronken, and Mohini Rajan. *The Days of the Beloved*. New Delhi: Orient Longman, 1974.

Mackenzie, Mrs. Colin. *Life in the Mission, the Camp and the Zenana; or Six Years in India*. Vols. 1–2. 2d ed. London: R. Bentley, 1854.

Manucci, Niccolo. *Storia do Mogor; or, Mogol India, 1653–1708*. Vols. 1–4. Translated by William Irvine. New Delhi: Oriental Reprint, 1981.

Meer, Mrs. Hassan 'Ali. *Observations on the Mussalmans of India*. Karachi: 1974.

Mitamura, Taisuke. *Chinese Eunuchs: The Structure of Intimate Politics*. Translated by Charles A. Pomeroy. Tokyo: Charles E. Tuttle Company, 1970.

Murray, Sir John. *A Handbook for Travellers in India, Pakistan, Burma & Ceylon*. 10th ed. London: John Murray, 1919.

Nanda, Serena. *Neither Man Nor Woman: The Hijras of India*. Belmont, Calif.: Wadsworth Publishing Company, 1990.

Nayeem, M. A. *The Splendour of Hyderabad: Last Phase of Oriental Culture, 1591–1948 A.D.* Bombay: Jaico Publishing House, 1987.

O'Flaherty, Wendy D. *Women, Androgynes, and Other Mythical Beasts*. Chicago: University of Chicago Press, 1980.

————, ed. and trans. *Hindu Myths*. New York: Penguin Books, 1975.

Opler, M. "The Hijara (hermaphrodites) of India and Indian National Character: A Rejoinder." *American Anthropologist* 62 (1960), pp. 505–11.

Patnaik, Naveen. *A Second Paradise, 1590–1947: Indian Courtly Life*. Garden City, N.Y.: Doubleday, 1985.

Penzer, Norman Mosley. *The Harem*. London: Spring Books, 1965.

————. *An Annotated Bibliography of Sir Richard Burton, K. C. M. G.* London: Dawsons of Pall Mall, 1967.

————, ed. *Selected Papers on Anthropology, Travel & Exploration, by Sir Richard Burton, K. C. M. G.* London: A. M. Philpot Ltd., 1924.

————, ed. *The Ocean of Story being C. H. Tawney's Transla-*

tion of Somadeva's Katha Sarit Sagara (or Ocean of Streams of Story). Delhi: Motilal Banarsidass, 1968.

Platts, John Thompson. *A Dictionary of Urdu, Classical Hindi, and English.* London: Oxford University Press, 1960.

Polo, Marco. *The Travels of Marco Polo.* Translated by Ronald Latham. London: Penguin Books, 1958.

Preston, Laurence W. "The Right to Exist: Eunuchs and the State in Nineteenth-Century India." *Modern Asian Studies* 21, no. 2 (1981), pp. 371–87.

Ranade, S. N., and Indu Vyas. "A Study of Eunuchs in Delhi." Report. Delhi: financed by Indian Ministry of Social Welfare and University of Delhi, 1981.

Rao, M. Ranga, and J. V. Raghavender Rao. *The Prostitutes of Hyderabad: A Study of the Socio-Cultural Conditions of the Prostitutes of Hyderabad.* Hyderabad: Association for Moral and Social Hygiene in India, Andhra Pradesh Branch, 1970.

Redpath, Henry A., ed. *The Holy Bible: The Oxford Self-Pronouncing Bible, S. S. Teacher's Edition.* Oxford: Oxford University Press, 1901.

Roy, Pratap Chandra, ed. and trans. *Mahabharata.* Calcutta: Oriental Pub. Co., 1962.

Sanghvi, Malavika. "Walking the Wild Side." *The Illustrated Weekly of India* (March 11, 1984).

Sarma, Abhyankar, et al., eds. *History of Hyderabad District, 1879–1950 A.D., Yugabda 4981–5052.* Vols. 1–2. Hyderabad: Bharatiya Itihasa Sankalana Samiti, 1987.

Schimmel, Annemarie. *Mystical Dimensions of Islam.* Chapel Hill: The University of North Carolina Press, 1975.

Seshan, K.S.S. *Hyderabad-400: Saga of a City.* Hyderabad: Association of British Council Scholars, Andhra Pradesh Chapter, 1993.

Sharar, Abdul Halim. *Lucknow: The Last Phase of an Oriental Culture.* Translated by E. S. Harcourt and Fakhir Hussain. London: Elek Books Limited, 1975.

Sharma, H. D., ed. *Indian Reference Sources: Generalia &*

Humanities. Vol 1. Varanasi: Indian Bibliographic Centre, 1988.

Sharma, Satish Kumar. *Hijras, the Labelled Deviants.* New Delhi: Gian Pub. House, 1989.

Spear, Percival. *A History of India.* Vol. 2. Middlesex: Penguin Books, 1966.

Sweet, Michael J., and Leonard Zwilling. "The First Medicalization: The Taxonomy and Etiology of Queerness in Classical Indian Medicine." *Journal of the History of Sexuality,* 3, no. 4 (1993), pp. 590–607.

Tavernier, Jean-Baptiste. *Travels in India.* Translated by V. Ball. Lahore: al-Biruni, 1976.

Thapar, Romila. *A History of India.* Vol. 1. Middlesex: Penguin Books, 1966.

Toledano, Ehud R. *The Ottoman Slave Trade and Its Suppression: 1840–1890.* Princeton: Princeton University Press, 1982.

Turner, R. L. *Comparative and Etymological Dictionary of the Nepali Language.* London: Routledge and Kegan Paul, 1965.

Upadhyaya, S. C., ed. and trans. *Kama Sutra of Vatsyayana.* Bombay: D. B. Taraporevala Sons and Co. Private Ltd., 1961.

Watson, Alan Hull, ed. *The Perfumed Garden of the Shaykh Nefwazi.* Translated by Sir Richard F. Burton. New York: Putnam, 1964.

Welch, Stuart Cary. *Imperial Mughul Painting.* New York: George Braziller, 1978.

Whitney, William Dwight, ed. and trans. *Atharva-Veda Samhita.* Vols. 1–2. Delhi: Motilal Banarsidass, 1962.

Zaki, Muhammad, ed. *Arab Accounts of India (during the fourteenth century).* Delhi: Idarah-i-Adabiyat-i-Delli, 1981.